CLIFFORD MATTHEWS

Managing
INTERNATIONAL
JOINT VENTURES

The route to globalizing your business

KOGAN
PAGE

First published 1999

Kogan Page Limited
120 Pentonville Road
London N1 9JN
UK

Kogan Page Limited
163 Central Avenue, Suite 4
Dover
NH 03820
USA

British Library Cataloguing in Publication Data

A CIP record for this book is available from the British Library.

ISBN 0 7494 27777 9

Typeset by JS Typesetting, Wellingborough, Northants
Printed and bound in Great Britain by Biddles Ltd, Guildford and King's Lynn

Contents

Acknowledgements

Over the past 20 years I have been privileged to meet many talented people in businesses around the world. My involvement with a broad spectrum of managers has had a significant impact on my thinking about the way that people of diverse experience and cultural background work together. Many companies in Europe, the United States and Japan have contributed to this book, either by providing case study information or simply by providing access to their managers, with their rich experience. Thanks are due to all these people and in particular: Kirit Vaidya of Aston University Business School for his insights on strategic management issues, Martin Reddington of Cable and Wireless for several years of assistance on the 'people issues' of management and Neil Haver; without his appreciation of cross-cultural human resource management issues this book would not have been possible. I am indebted to him also for his detailed guidance on IJVs in China and the Far East. Special thanks are due, once again, to Stephanie Evans for her excellent work in typing the manuscript for this book.

Clifford Matthews

Preface

Management, so we are told, is the craft of getting things done by working together. We know that people within an organization need to work together to achieve some common task or goal and that it is the role of 'management' both to encourage this to happen, and occasionally to join in themselves. All of this claims to be understood by almost everybody.

So how do books on management respond to this situation? They divide themselves into those that cover the skills of management superficially, or the ones that delve into it in focused theoretical depth; and then they break into disciplines, separating finance from strategy, quality from customer service, until the whole field resembles a patchwork of techniques, anxious to be fitted together. The weakness of this approach becomes clear when you try to apply it to a business which does not consist of a single company but is a joint venture between businesses – where it is necessary to work *together*. Things suddenly look more complicated and some of the management tools claimed to have general application (but in reality are tailored for use in a single-organization business) don't work.

This book is about the management of businesses that consciously choose to work with others in International Joint Ventures (IJVs). To manage within such a venture needs a high degree of competence because the job of getting things done by 'working together' is expanded across cultural and geographic boundaries – and becomes wider. This means you can't expect IJV management to be easy.

I have tried to make this a management book which is practical and readable so if you are a management jargon-hunter (or frequent user) it is, unashamedly, not for you. It is also a book which attempts to be *realistic*, in showing you the negative things that can happen in IJV management if you don't get it right. Try to see the positive messages in these examples because they also provide important pointers as to how you *can* get it right, building and managing IJVs which are stable and profitable.

Finally, remember that no management book can stand alone – each needs support from related books in its field. I have provided a short list of further references at the end of the book – each provides excellent coverage and adds to the overall picture of IJV management.

Clifford Matthews

Chapter 1

How to use this book

RETHINK WHAT DO YOU WANT FROM MANAGEMENT BOOKS?

Most 'management books' fall into one of three common categories, based on what it is that they have to offer. They promise to tell you about:

- *experiences* that other managers have had;
- *tools and techniques* of management;
- *instant trendy solutions* to management problems.

This information generally proves to be of varying degrees of use to practising managers. The experiences of others are interesting but may not be directly relevant to the situation or problems that you yourself face. Similarly, generic management tools and techniques are by now so well known that there is little purpose in reiterating them. Instant trendy solutions, whilst undoubtedly easy and trendy, are not real solutions because complex questions rarely have instant answers. Perhaps the biggest problem with most management books is that they don't tell you the hidden management ideology that lies behind their content – it is possible to read all the way through some without being told the underlying assumptions that support what the book is saying, or advising you to do. This limits the usefulness of what you read and can leave you with the impression that the book felt, somehow, as if it was written for 'someone else'.

THE FORMAT

This book contains a mixture of management tools and techniques supported by real-life management experiences. You will not find any trendy, instant solutions. The tools and techniques are drawn from the disciplines of systems thinking, organizational behaviour, financial management and personnel-orientated topics such as transactional analysis and the dynamics of groups. The common denominator is that they are introduced in the context of their use in the management of International Joint Ventures (IJVs) – and only in this context. This means that this book will not teach you all you need to know about, for example, the exhaustive techniques of financial or personnel management. This book is about IJVs.

The text is divided into 13 chapters, set out as a logical trek through the issues of IJV management. Chapter 2 examines the reasons for the existence and popularity of IJVs by looking at current business and economic trends. The cyclic pattern of independence and interdependence in business is seen as one of the driving forces behind the formation of the IJV format.

Chapter 3 looks at different models of business co-operation such as supply chain licensing, divisionalization and strategic alliance, that can lead to IJV formation. The IJV model is conceived as a form of group, working across cultural and geographic boundaries.

Chapter 4 introduces the basic idea of IJVs and their defining characteristics. They are seen to be a transient form of organization that have difficulty in maintaining stability. The basic IJV models of 'independent management', 'dominant parent' and 'shared management' are described. The IJV life cycle is explained, with its six main stages.

Chapter 5 investigates the business objectives behind the formation of IJVs, explaining what everyone is trying to achieve. These are referred to as the wider corporate and strategic objectives of business.

Chapter 6: Structure: this is intentionally the most generic chapter of the book. Its purpose is to provide you with a 'toolbox' of techniques to help you design the structure of a complex IJV organization. You are invited to rethink the structure of a business in systems-thinking terms. The chapter develops the idea of the 'viable IJV' using well-established systems principles. The objective is to build an IJV structure that will minimize internal conflict. Some of the concepts in this chapter may look esoteric, but all have practical application.

Chapter 7 looks at the problems of control in a joint organization, once it is built and working. There is emphasis on 'horizontal' control relationships between IJV partners as a replacement for traditional discussions on hierarchy and Chapter 8 is about money.

Chapter 9: People: this balances the systems content of earlier chapters by reminding you that people are the most important asset of any IJV. Practical advice is given on people-issues such as the global mindset (and the skillset that goes with it), cross-cultural integration and leadership actions. The chapter ends with a slightly controversial section on 'boardroom reform', which challenges the traditional idea of blocks of responsibility at senior management level.

Chapter 10 investigates the scope of formal agreements needed between IJV partners. It deals with ownership, financial matters, quality, staffing and the thorny issue of intra-IJV transfer pricing.

Chapter 11 is included because disputes are common features of IJV management. It explains why they happen and what they are about. There are some practical ideas on solving IJV disputes and (better still) how to prevent them happening in the first place.

Chapter 12: Regional experiences: this provides 'case study-type' information on the IJV situation in two specific countries: China and Turkey.

Chapter 13: Looking forward; anticipates the future of IJV management. It looks at current developments in business structure, levels of autonomy and cultural integration – all important players in the IJV field.

THE CASE STUDIES

There are two types of case study used in this book:

- *General case studies.* These are drawn from a wide selection of IJV businesses and included as practical applications of points made in the text. Each is intended to stand alone, on its merits.
- *The on-going case study – International Technology Partners IJV.* This follows progressively through the book (starting in Chapter 5), illustrating important aspects of IJV management and mismanagement. There is no concrete beginning, or finite end, to the story – its only purpose is to be informative.

Together the chapters form a series of steps towards the successful management of an IJV. I have tried to put these steps in the most logical order possible but they cannot pretend to represent strictly the chronological order in which real-world management issues are decided and implemented. The main message is to present an approach to IJV management which is structured, and which contains some kind of coherence. I have learned that these qualities are important in all business management situations, particularly in complex organizations like IJVs.

LEARNING FROM THE BOOK

No-one can learn all they need to know from a book – you need experience as well. This book in written for business people who have had some experience of the atmosphere and practical difficulties of IJV management. It is not necessary to have been (or have been called) 'an IJV manager' – many of the messages of the book should be recognizable by people who have been involved in the administration or operation side of joint venture activities, or perhaps seen the problems and challenges from a distance outside the IJV organizational boundary.

One of the main learning points is the pivotal role of the organizational design of IJVs. For every organization that has struggled owing to an overkill of structural design there are at least five that have failed because they had the wrong structure – one that developed by default, while everyone hoped that it would 'turn out all right' (but it didn't). Structure is important in IJVs so the book introduces some straightforward but proven techniques on 'systems thinking' to help you visualize the situation. The best results should be obtained by linking your own business views and experiences to the methodologies presented in the book. In this context the aim of the book is to help you put in place the mechanisms of good, positive management. It will show you how to design the structure and practices of an IJV, creating a robust business organization (or part of one) with a structure that does not fall apart or spend its life fighting with itself in a spiral of suspicion and unprofitability. Is there any point in creating any other type?

Chapter 2

Trends

The business world is full of so-called trends. Some are more imagined than real but there is undeniably a set of real ones in force at any time. Some trends, such as the existence of macroeconomic cycles, can be considered more or less permanent features; they are part of the landscape of business. Others are more temporary, dictated by circumstances and pressures; and some are absolute passing fads, the product of little more than fashion.

All these trends, real or imagined, act together to affect the business world of which they are part. There is little doubt that these trends do have cumulative effect, but their net impact is not always easy to predict and quantify, for example:

- The significant investment programmes of the late 1960s had the expected effect of stimulating general economic activity but overall growth was still constrained by other, less tangible economic factors.
- Few would disagree that the ethos of privatization and share ownership of the 1980s had an important influence on the social responsibilities of business – but did it produce other, perhaps less obvious, business trends? Some would argue, for instance, that it had an irreversible effect on the fabric of employee–employer relations, changing for ever the unwritten commitments of both parties.

There is a wide scope and variety of business trends. Many are complementary, helping each other along, even spawning families of related 'sub-trends'. Others have exactly the opposite effect, acting to counteract or contradict each other. Many economists view the business world like this – as an uneasy liaison between complementary and conflicting trends. It is indeed a complex picture. Thankfully, there is not much doubt about the two key points; that business trends do exist and that they combine to affect the values and practices of the business world in a largely predetermined (but rather unpredictable) way. Figure 2.1 lists nine current visible business trends. We will look at each briefly, with particular reference to the way in which each trend is likely to influence or encourage the conditions for co-operative or 'joint venture' working.

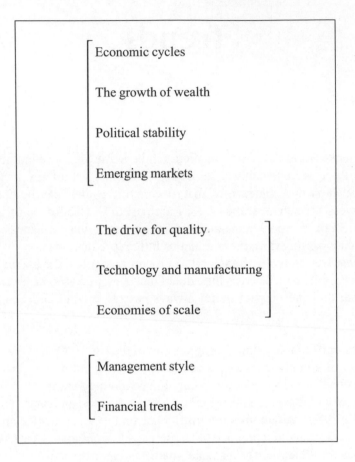

Economic cycles

The growth of wealth

Political stability

Emerging markets

The drive for quality

Technology and manufacturing

Economies of scale

Management style

Financial trends

Figure 2.1 Today's business trends

ECONOMIC CYCLES

It is one of the great paradoxes that business organizations are perceived as being stable. They are best thought of as being in a state of flux, reacting continually to their business environment. At the highest 'macro' level of this environment, nothing is static – there is always an underlying groundswell of change. It is generally accepted that the overall nature of these changes follows a cyclic pattern. The cyclic form manifests itself at all levels of analysis, so a study of economic trends by country, business sector or industry will show a similar pattern of results. The cyclic pattern is particularly well proven at the very highest level of economic analysis; just about everyone agrees about the existence of economic cycles.

The effect of this cyclic nature of the business environment means that organizations need an almost limitless range of behaviour if they are to be capable of responding rapidly and effectively to the resulting changes and challenges that present themselves. This causes uncertainty because organizations do not have limitless capability. The overall effect can perhaps be best summarized as follows: economic cycles affect:

- 'the *performance* of business;
- business *confidence* (in its most general sense);
- the *expectations* of organizations and people.

These are important common denominators. Organizations are driven by the expectations and confidence of their people – once these start to suffer, then the formal 'downstream' business activities of labour markets, capital markets, competitive strategy etc suffer from a lack of impetus.

The effect of economic cycles are, of course, never absolute. Some cycles have had surprisingly little effect on particular areas of business, and it can be argued that cycles may even act as a stimulus to certain types of economic activity. Whether economic cycles promote predominantly certainty or uncertainty, one trend is clear – these cycles are getting shorter. There is firm evidence for this in the records of many of the published economic indicators and more colloquial evidence in the overall 'feel' of the business world.

Shorter, steeper cycles mean more uncertainty, and the strategy of businesses has to react accordingly. Businesses (and governments) become more risk-averse, desiring quicker, less risky strategies for growth and expansion. At the other end of the strategy scale, the onus shifts towards risk *sharing* and diversification – both mechanisms intended to provide a measure of insulation from an increasingly cyclic environment. Fig 2.2 summarizes the situation.

An increasingly cyclic business environment

CREATES

- a more risk-averse approach to business;

- a tacit acceptance of uncertainty;

- diversification – as a defensive rather than offensive strategy.

Figure 2.2 Effects of a cyclic environment

CASE STUDY 2.1

The retail business: cycles of expectation

The retail business is one of the best examples of a cyclic environment. There is no logical reason why the consumer should want more, or fewer, retail goods this year than they did last year, apart from the influence on their decision-making of uncertainty about the future. Worries about future economic conditions such as interest rates and employment prospects affect sales of retail goods in advance of the conditions actually occurring. All sectors of the retail business, from manufacturing to distribution, sales and financing of the goods are therefore cyclic. This owes as much to the risk-averse nature of people as to the cold and impersonal rules of economics.

The net result of Figure 2.2 is a business environment with an increased trend towards *co-operative working*. Co-operation is seen as an efficient way in which risk can be shared, with even the most temporary and tenuous co-operation between organizations seen as being better than one organization shouldering all the risk itself.

THE GROWTH OF WEALTH

On balance, we are all getting richer. Does this promote an ethos of co-operation and sharing? No-one would deny individuals or businesses the objective of maximizing their own wealth. The problem with wealth is not the question of propriety, but the problem of measurement. There are numerous ways to measure wealth. At the upper level of analysis, key indicators such as Gross Domestic Product (GDP) are an attempt to quantify 'how rich' a country is. Businesses rely on traditional indicators such as Return on Investment (ROI) or capitalization value as their measure, while at the level of individuals it is net disposable income that really matters. These are all aberrations of sorts. Perhaps the least imperfect measure is that relevant to the individual – it is the individual who feels the economic need to work, and in doing so creates the need for businesses and organizations of all types.

Individuals world-wide are getting richer. In the developed countries of the world the personal wealth of the individual has increased steadily over most of this century with the 'survival' pressures of 50 or even 20 years ago being gradually reduced, to be replaced by more comfort-orientated pressures. Many of the richer societies of the world are becoming intensely consumerized with individuals striving for ownership of products that can truly be considered 'luxuries'. In such an environment, there is always the tendency for risk-aversion – it is understandable that relatively wealthy people do not want to lose what they already have. The result is that individuals themselves exhibit more risk-aversion which feeds forward into the strategy of the organizations on whose behalf they make strategic decisions – the trend of risk-aversion therefore compounds itself.

The situation is mirrored at higher corporate levels. The past 20 years have seen the rise of many genuinely global businesses for oil products, foodstuffs, motor vehicles, medicines and a vast range of consumer goods made by high volume mass production methods. These global corporations are highly profitable and successful – it is fair to assume that they *enjoy* their present position. Again, the result is a type of risk-aversion, with the avoidance of too much risk, taking precedence over the unfettered drive for profit.

POLITICAL STABILITY

There are three political occurrences that have caused major societal effects over recent years:

- the virtual end of the 'cold war' in Europe;
- the opening up of relations with China and the Far East;
- the downfall of communism.

These have spawned a series of more localized political trends within countries, as well as across traditional international boundaries. The consequence has been a more relaxed view of political differences. Ideological disagreements no doubt remain, but their effect as trade or business constraints has weakened, particularly in the past 10 years. While it is easy to dismiss this as merely a respite from old differences, soon to return, the fact remains that barriers to international business co-operation are far fewer than they were.

The result is a genuinely more international 'flavour' to business. Access is now possible to the manufacturing skills and lucrative markets of the world's developing countries. There is evidence that global co-operation is at last seen as being *possible*, if that is what businesses want. With the mechanics of co-operation has come the gradual realization of global interdependence – the understanding that companies in different continents have a mutual effect on the fortunes of each other.

EMERGING MARKETS

The emerging markets of the world have always provided a fertile source of business opportunity. Viewed globally, the overall industrial strategy of the world follows the broad pattern of Figure 2.3. New and developing countries start by developing a concentrated manufacturing base – initial impetus being towards those industries which are low-technology and labour-intensive. As the economy develops, industries start to shift away from primary manufacturing to lighter, more technology-based manufacture and assembly. This is accompanied by a rapidly developing technological base in which disciplines such as research and development and advanced design start to predominate. This stage is also characterized by an increasing amount of subcontracting of manufacture back to less well-developed countries. There is still plenty of room for wholesale shift of this type in the developing world. The next (and perhaps the final) stage is the move out of manufacturing-based industry altogether, into the field of pure service industries such as banking and financial services. Examples can be seen in countries such as Switzerland and the richer economies of Northern Europe which are already some way down this path.

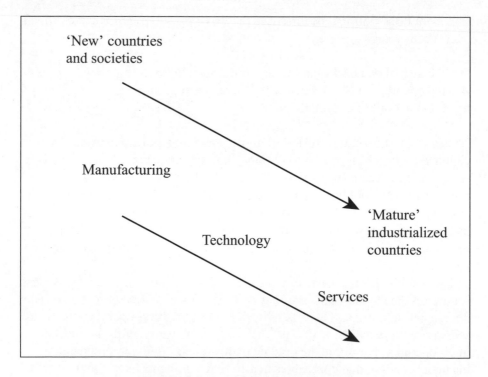

Figure 2.3 Today's business trends

The current developing countries of the Far East, Latin America and Eastern Europe are positioned at the 'manufacturing' stage, with Western Europe and the United States well into the technology-based stage. The relative positions vary with (among other things) economic cycles, but the overall trend remains. This shift of industrial structure between areas of the world is a provider of opportunity. It creates an environment in which new business concepts and ideas can take root – in short, it provides the space for businesses to grow, change, or develop their strategy in a way that they think fit. There is no single and concrete reason why the existence of emerging markets should *cause* the formation of alliances, joint ventures or other co-operative ways of working, but it provides the type of business environment in which these organizational forms can flourish.

THE DRIVE FOR QUALITY

Quality has been one of the buzzwords of recent years. There is now hardly an organization left that does not profess to recognize 'quality' as one of its competitive advantages. This has been ably assisted by the wide promotion of the ISO 9000 quality standard as a successful model of quality management. The net effect of this 'drive for quality' has been twofold: more management systems; and increased requirements for product conformity.

The ISO 9000 philosophy is built on the idea of installing management systems to control and monitor those parts of an organization that are deemed to have an influence on quality (in practice, virtually all of it). Its disadvantage is that it is not directly related to the issue of product conformity. This has been addressed by a parallel, and equally strong, trend towards mechanisms that do purport to control the final quality of manufactured goods, such as standardization and the use of more prescriptive product specifications. Most product conformity requirements are consumer-driven – consumer products (electrical goods, motor vehicles, etc) that would have been acceptable to the consumer 20 years ago would today be classed as sub-standard or shoddy. Many commercial services, as well as manufactured goods, would fall into the same category.

The effect of the drive for quality has been a tightening of customer requirements in all spheres of business. Some businesses have become very proactive – continually improving quality levels on their own initiative, thereby leading customers to *expect* better quality goods and services. The overall trend resulting from this has been that manufacturers and service-providers have had to increase their efforts to retain their customers. The economic recessions of recent years have weeded out those whose quality of goods or service are poor. At the business level, the drive for quality has also provided impetus for co-operation between companies that possess top-notch skills – business alliances have taken place specifically to exploit complementary skills of technology and high quality manufacture.

TECHNOLOGY AND MANUFACTURING

As we approach the millennium, the world has a thirst for technology. A continually expanding range of products from basic comfort needs to commercial products seems to be in ever-increasing demand. This march of technology provides the businesses of the world with a valuable source of economic activity – producing business opportunities for sellers, buyers, those who develop the technology, and those who take the role of facilitators and 'enablers' in the chain of commerce. The more dynamic the rate of technological development, the greater the level of opportunities for all. There will always be open questions about whether the rate of technological change is greater now than it ever has been, or conversely, whether it peaked at some (indefinable) time in the past and we are heading for a future of technological stagnation. Despite opposing extreme views, common-sense observation seems to suggest that technology is still moving forward at a fairly constant rate. This rate varies between commercial sectors, and with time, and of course is always subject to the pressures, checks and balances of the market.

With the advance of technology comes the attendant problem of technological complexity. In vying with each other for competitive position in the market, goods and services become more complex. This trend is almost universal – look at the complexity of today's motor vehicles, electrical goods or financial service products compared to those of ten years ago. The effect of such complexity-increase, results in a *multidisciplinary* approach to the provision of goods and services. Previously simple manufactured products now have designers to design them, consultants to advise on shape and styling, and innovative packaging and marketing techniques to present them to customers in the most appealing way. Services follow similar lines. This has encouraged an ethos of joint working between specialist companies, the objective being to produce the very best product or service with the skills and resources available, even if it does mean sharing the profits. This interdependence between skill groups has been an important structural shift in the way that technology and manufacturing coexist; single-discipline specialists still exist, but they have to work with others across technological, regional and probably cultural boundaries as well, if they want to sell to the market.

CASE STUDY 2.2

Technology trends: the entertainment business

It is not only manufacturing industry that has undergone structural shifts due to technology trends. Services such as the entertainment business have undergone major changes eg:

● *Multi-channel digital television*: this is a business driven by the march of technology, rather then consumer demand for more channels. There is a growing interdependence between communications network companies and the sports clubs and programme-makers that produce attractive material for broadcast.
● *Theme parks*: these are no longer the domain of single-discipline operators. They are now a technological mixture of advanced engineering, sound and vision experiences and computer simulation.
● *Film special effects*: the content of many films is now driven more by the capabilities of special effects and computer graphics than the storyline. This is an example of technology 'push'.

ECONOMIES OF SCALE

As well as increasing in complexity, the volume of manufactured goods (and services) is increasing as well. The increases apply not only to 'products' like motor vehicles, consumer goods or foodstuffs, but also to the project and civil construction-related aspects of industrial development such as bridges, airports and roads. This has caused an increase in the use of mass production as a general means of manufacture. Production philosophies which were once restricted to the manufacture of motor vehicles or televisions are now in widespread use for furniture, building materials and a raft of prefabricated and pre-assembled parts for the developing world. Mass production has become the ethic of industrialization.

This trend in manufacturing has not, however, just been 'more of the same'. There has been a clear trend from the labour-intensive mass production techniques of the past to a much more capital-intensive regime. The products of production lines are now made by expensive robots rather than people, with the basic economies of scale of mass production reinforced by a swing to capital-intensive methods. These pressures all push towards an increase in manufacturing volume, in order to fulfil the payback or returns on investment required. Manufacturing support techniques such as flexible manufacturing systems (FMS), just-in-time (JIT) supply, and statistical process control (SPC) have proliferated to try to improve the efficiency of the end process – evidence in itself, that the volume and complexity of the manufacturing world are increasing all the time. Practical considerations apart, the economies of scale of mass production remain as lucrative as when they were conceived nearly one hundred years ago. More products means more profit – if you can get it right.

MANAGEMENT STYLE

It is common now to hear a lot of informed (and sometimes uninformed) opinion about trends in management style. Everyone seems happy to vouch an opinion as to whether management are becoming more or less democratic, or authoritarian, and whether this is somehow 'deserved' or not. The picture is further confused by the almost weekly emergence of newly-discovered techniques and acronyms – each claiming to hold the answer to the Pandora's box of day-to-day management problems. Most turn out to be little more than fashion or, at best, capable of producing only short-term solutions. Confusion reigns.

Thankfully, it is possible to identify a number of management trends that are less affected by 'management fashion' diversions and which keep reappearing as salient management issues that warrant serious discussion. The three most common ones are shown in Figure 2.4 These trends follow the basic cyclic pattern discussed earlier with the timescale of the cycle dependent, as always, on a matrix of outside influences.

SHOULD OUR COMPANY

1. Be authoritarian or democratic (consensual)?

2. Model itself on co-operation or conflict?

3. Value its independence or accept its *inter*dependence?

Figure 2.4 Three perennial issues of management style

One of the predominant trends is the way in which company management perceives the value of organizational *independence* in its business activities. At some time in the business cycle there is a forthright view that 'the company' is a valuable but nevertheless limited part of the world of business and commerce and that its role is to play its true part in the interdependence of all other (nominally competing) companies in the chain. At such times, the search for extreme profit is sacrificed for the easy ambience of coexistence and co-operation. At other times, the cycle produces the opposite – the platitudes and ethos of co-operation disappear, to be replaced by the viewpoint that; 'it's us against all the rest' and that it is competition that reigns supreme, not co-operation.

Whether the prevailing management strategy at any point in time values interdependence or independence (these are quite neat summary terms of what the strategies are) depends upon the compounded result of many outside influences. There is a valid, if controversial, argument that this fundamental strategic issue is not actually the product of conscious strategy at all, but is simply the enforced result of outside events and constraints. It is as if company strategy in this area is almost predetermined by the course of events over which management have no control. Within this framework of constraint and speculation, the management style of any sector of business – and probably that of the business world as a whole – is, once again, broadly cyclic. It swings from being predominantly based on *independence* to a condition of relative *interdependence*, and then back again. Opinions vary as to the length of the cycle but the average seems to be between 20 and 25 years, depending on which sector you look at.

The late 1980s and 1990s were a period of *interdependence* in almost all sectors. The principle of co-operative working flourished, paving the way for strategic alliances and joint ventures. It is fair to say that this trend has been helped along by other concurrent world trends, but the result is the same – co-operation is king (at least for the moment).

FINANCIAL TRENDS

The underlying rationale of any commercial business is the quest for profit – there can be little doubt about that. What can be questioned, however, is whether this profit motive is a permanent, preset factor of the business landscape or whether it itself is cyclic, like so many of the other driving forces we have seen.

Is the profit motive cyclic?

In times of economic growth the search for profit takes priority. People and business will take whatever steps are necessary to obtain their rightful share of economic cake – and are not ashamed to admit it. This is profit as a motivator, slicing through the need for other, less important, corporate objectives. Now consider what happens when the cycle turns and the growth period ends (as we know it must). The quest for profit is magically replaced by the pursuit of stability; it is the survival of the business that suddenly becomes important. At this stage, the eyes of management strategy rotate inwards, looking for methods of cost-cutting and rationalization. Words such as 'consolidation' and 'downsizing' make their unwelcome appearance in the minutes of management meetings. The result, in summary, is that the incentive to make profit takes second, or even third place to issues that are more concerned with avoiding risk than taking it. The profit motive has not of course gone away (it would take a fundamental shift in human nature to do that), it is merely in recession.

The existence of risk is what causes many of the traditional ways of the financial objectives of business to sometimes feel a little unreal. A return on capital employed of 20 per cent may sound good, but if a business feels that the sheer risk of financing an asset to produce this return is too great, the return will never happen – it will be little more than illusion. So, while risk is not in itself a tangible business 'parameter' (you won't see it quantified in anyone's annual report), it is a real and overriding constraint on the financial objectives of a business. The inherent level of risk present in any business environment is difficult to quantify – about the only thing you can guarantee about it is that it is *cyclic*. This is a long-winded way of saying that what looks like a good deal today might look worse (or even better) tomorrow.

It is fine, if a little distracting, to talk about risk in this general and abstract way. It is not, however, very productive. We can learn more by looking at the more tangible parts of the financial territory of business – remember we are looking for those that are subject to *trends*. These are shown in Figure 2.5.

Investment criteria

The central tenet of business investment is the concept of return. The three main interpretations; return on sales (ROS), return on capital employed (ROCE) and return on investment (ROI) are all valid indicators, in their own way, of the financial efficiency (or otherwise) of the business.

The key criterion is of course the return that is anticipated by the management of the business activity, ie the *expected return*. It is a tangible business indicator but because it is based on expectation (in reality it is little

> **All these aspects of financial management**
>
> **are subject to *trends*:**
>
> ● investment criteria (how much return for how much risk?);
>
> ● project appraisal (should we do this project or not?);
>
> ● funding strategy (availability of equity or debt);
>
> ● capital structure;
>
> ● the absolute cost of capital.

Figure 2.5 Trends in financial management

more than a mental construct of managers), it will vary in a way which reflects the relative amount of risk and confidence that is around in the business environment. It is also closely linked to its opposite: the cost of capital – heavier costs of accessing capital result in high expectations of the performance of that capital, once the step has been taken to acquire it. The rational economic view places the value of the expected return higher than the prevailing cost of capital. It is difficult to specify how much higher it should be – it all depends on other factors such as the personal attitude to risk of the involved managers. In practice, the ratio of expected return/cost of capital is itself cyclic, varying from perhaps 25–30 per cent down to 5 per cent during periods when corporate expectations are low for whatever reason. The unavoidable existence of low expectations for some of the time during the business cycle is one of the reasons why companies sometimes feel encouraged – or, conversely, constrained – to take part in certain ways of working at various times in their business life. This means that a business's attitude to financial return (remember, it sets this attitude itself) is a strong determinant of the organizational form or structure that it will adopt. We will see later how this has particular relevance to the expected financial returns from those organizational structures that involve co-operative working, in the form of alliances and joint ventures with others

Funding options

The funding options available to a business determine what it can and cannot do. It is of little use being dedicated to the ideology of global expansion if you don't have access to any money.

The type of funds available to a business are the same as they have always been – the simple choice between debt and equity. Despite the imaginative ways in which the financial industry manages to present these in user-friendly packages, this does not change the fundamental nature of these financial sources – you either sell equity to raise funds or you borrow. The costs of equity capital and debt are quantified and well documented at any point in time, and can be considered a known variable of the corporate financial equation. Although sometimes amalgamated together into the well known weighted average cost of capital (WACC) to a business, the variations in costs of equity and debt are frequently identified separately. Not surprisingly, both have a tendency to follow a cyclic pattern. The cycles for equity and debt rarely coincide exactly, either with each other or with the overall variation in the global economic cycle, but the approximation is close.

The relative availability and cost of equity and debt have a well-defined effect on the way that businesses organize their financial structure. In good times, the basic rule that debt is cheaper than equity holds good and a business can increase its expected return by levering its financial structure to contain more debt. When a recession hits, however, firms tend to lean heavily on equity – everyone wants equity-investors who don't want their return 'just yet', and are prepared to wait until things improve.

These features of the nature of finance mean that the prevalent financial structure of businesses changes with the rise and fall of other cycles – some predetermined and some not. There is nothing new about this finding, it fits neatly with the traditional economists' view (well one of them anyway) of the financial world as an 'uncertain disequilibrium', rather than an ordered and stable equilibrium. The effect of financial structure is almost absolute because it acts as a constraint on the motives of the managers of a business; there is nothing better at tempering the excesses of entrepreneurial spirit then the spectre of having to pay crippling dividends or debt repayments long after a project or venture has gone badly wrong. Taking a more positive view, you can think of the debt/equity structure of a business as an independent balance on the activities of the business, almost a self-checking function, restricting the projects and ventures that the business can enter, and curbing some of its over-zealous decisions. There is not much emotion in the world of equity and debt finance.

SUMMARY

We started this chapter by concluding (or was it a proposition?) that the business world is crammed full of trends; many real but some mainly illusion. In looking at them in a little more detail there is clearly a cyclic nature to them: business fortunes go up and down, as economists and common-sense managers know that they must. So what? The main message of this chapter is that the cumulative effect of business cycles is to form, at certain times, conditions under which methods of joint working and strategic alliance between business are acceptable and *desirable*. This in no way devalues traditional economic or management theories of the business world, it is simply a manifestation of one of its many forms. Strategic co-operation is (and always has been) in the repertoire of all businesses – it just needs the right conditions in which to appear.

The scene is set. The following chapters of this book explore, in detail, the nature and character of this strategic co-operation with particular emphasis on the joint venture across international boundaries, perhaps the most difficult form of them all. We need to start with the first step: the different forms of co-operation.

TRENDS: KEY POINTS

Trends are a feature of the business world. Some are based on fashion or illusion but many are real.

1. *Economic cycles* are well defined and documented, they affect the performance, confidence and expectations of businesses.
2. *Wealth* influences businesses' views on risk: the trend is for wealthy companies and countries to become more risk-averse.
3. *Quality and technology* are influential trends which encourage the search for complementarity and economies of scale between businesses.
4. *Financial management* is affected by unavoidable changes and trends in the cost of equity and debt.

Trends have a cumulative effect on a business. Under some conditions they provide strong pressure for companies to co-operate rather than compete with each other.

Chapter 3

Co-operation

Is the world of business about co-operation or conflict? Sometimes it is difficult to decide which predominates, or even to tell them apart.

CO-OPERATION VS CONFLICT

The basic idea of co-operation infers some kind of venture or alliance between businesses. The inference is that the co-operation straddles parochial boundaries, extending into another business sector or company that would not normally be considered as 'ours'. We looked in Chapter 2 at some of the rationale behind this, conceiving it as being driven by the requirement to agree to a level of *interdependence*. For the mechanics of such co-operation to have even a half-chance of success, the co-operating parties must have:

- a common *vision* (of what it is they want);
- an understanding to share the *risks*;
- an agreement to share the *profits*.

This sounds easy. It is not difficult in everyday business life to hear these sentiments being expressed, either singly or as a set, by company managers who claim to be enlightened to the advantages of co-operation with others. The idea also has the apparent support of the way that organizations themselves are supposed to work – they are claimed to be mechanisms of co-operation between people and systems, so why not extend this philosophy outside the company boundary? In practice, things are rarely this easy because joint operations between business organizations raise the well worn problem of *hierarchy*.

HIERARCHY: THE HIDDEN AGENDA

Hierarchy is part of the territory of business organizations. You could be forgiven for concluding that the word is written on the reverse side of every letter and communication that passes between company managers. The general meaning of hierarchy is well understood – it infers a ranking of people and their ideas, in a way that predetermines who will decide who does what. It also has softer but equally effective influences on the way that an organization moves as a single body, with a sense of purpose (or even a conscious lack of it). Hierarchy is commonly accepted by all those who work in organizations – there are even those who believe that hierarchy is essential and that the only alternative to it is organizational anarchy.

The question is: is the concept of co-operative working likely to be restricted, in application, by the partially hidden agenda of hierarchy? Yes and no – there is undoubtedly evidence that it is, and probably some that it is not. Such arguments have been responsible for wasting masses of management time. Whatever the answer, the issue of hierarchy is a well-proven time- and money-waster: instead, it is more productive to think of co-operative working as the interaction of *groups*.

GROUPS AND CO-OPERATIVE WORKING

Most ventures involving co-operation between business companies are seen as a programme of linking and interaction between companies' structures, as in Figure 3.1 The levels of interaction and the amount of linking vary in each case but the general picture is one of two or more company structures interleaving together, striving towards some common purpose.

Unfortunately this is far too complex to be of any practical use. Most types of co-operative working do not work anything like the intimate way that is inferred in Figure 3.1: this figure is more a theoretical example of a strategic principle than a practical model for business organization. Think of the complexity that would be involved in trying to decide which part of the nominally 'merged' structure does the planning, or who is really responsible for day-to-day management discussions in each little bit of the joint business. Sadly, many joint ventures and alliances start off by trying to do precisely that; soon, however, much of the initially flurry of co-operative spirit fades, and it is back to the old (and expensive) question of hierarchy.

The concept of *limited groups* provides a much better set of starting assumptions. The groups each still 'belong' to their own co-operating parent partner in the venture but they are sidelined away from their main

A-parent company
B-parent company

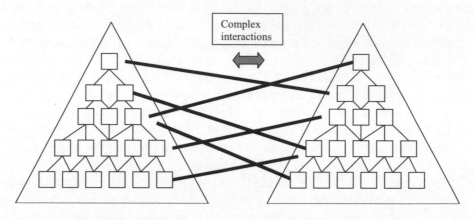

Figure 3.1 Interaction between company structures

organizational structure. In this new role, they develop new objectives in common with their opposite number from the other co-operating parent company. This situation is summarized in Figure 3.2. Note that the principles of shared objectives, risk and profit, are not in any way diluted by this way of visualizing co-operative working; it is actually a method of making them more achievable and less fraught with the issues of hierarchy and other problems that plague business organizations.

A-parent company
B-parent company

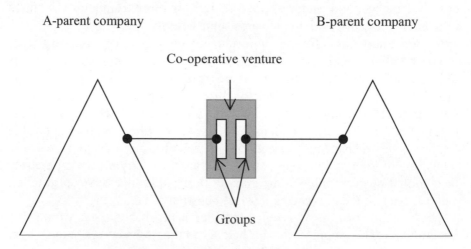

Figure 3.2 The idea of co-operating groups

We decided that methods of co-operative working between consenting organizations can be conceived as a set of liaisons between groups which have been partly hived off from their parent organizations, the purpose of all this being to attain some greater and more global corporate objective. Granted, there is nothing particularly new about this idea: formal group-working techniques have been written about and understood for at least a hundred years, and probably used for a lot longer. The key difference is the way that groups are conceived as fitting into the forms of the parent organizations to which they belong. All organizations are different, although they do fall into identifiable categories. Fortunately, those at the larger end of the corporate scale are easier to classify – it would be almost impossible to decipher the objectives and problems of the millions of smaller organizations that make up the world of commerce. Before starting to analyse the mechanics of co-operative working we need to look at some of the common forms that it can take such as supply chain licensing, divisionalization, strategic alliances and the consortium approach.

STRUCTURE DIAGRAMS

Organizations are complicated things. It is just about impossible to understand the internal relationships and intrigue existing in a group of even two or three people. Once an organization grows, and starts to interact with others, the situation becomes almost infinitely complex. How can you possibly hope to understand, or even describe, such conditions?

One way is by using *structure diagrams*. These attempt to represent complicated organizational forms and situations on a sheet of paper. They are an unashamedly conceptual approach to looking at organizations – they do not pretend to be reality, but they do claim to *represent* it. Structure diagrams are a useful way to portray the shape and characteristic of groups of people who claim to have collective purpose – they are pictures of the organization that cannot be photographed. We will develop the use of structure diagrams throughout the book and see, in Chapters 4 and 6 their use in describing in some detail how parts of organizations work together.

SUPPLY CHAIN LICENSING

The practice of licensing is widespread in business. In its most basic form (see Figure 3.3) a manufacturer enters into an agreement with another company whose job it is to sell the product. A reciprocal arrangement is possible on the supply side, where a large contractor or manufacturer may form a close relationship with dedicated suppliers who can match their requirements on delivery, quality and price. Such relationships are often found up and down the supply chain – either stacked in a neat 'back-to-back' arrangement or sometimes random and overlapping. Licensing arrangements can apply to goods, services and knowledge alike, they do not have to be linked to physical products. These arrangements are typically seen by the participants and outside observers as being a type of joint working, with the inference that the relationships are somehow closer than a normal commercial transaction, maybe even a little bit 'secret'.

Licence agreements can exist almost anywhere in the chain.

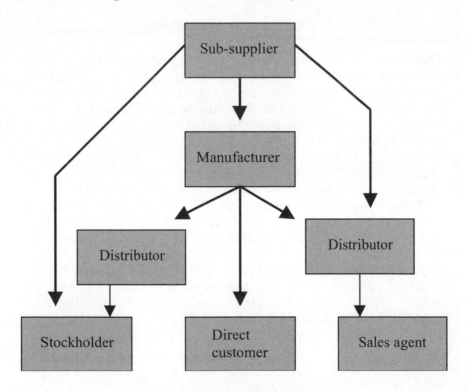

Figure 3.3 Supply chain licensing

Most of this is not true. In most businesses, licensing agreements turn out to be temporary, with few genuine features of management co-operation or joint-venture working. We can examine this a little further by looking at four features of these supply chain licensing agreements:

1. *Formal structure*: organizations involved in pure licensing rarely merge with each other or change their formal structure. They may deal with each other continually, often exclusively, but they remain separate and independent.
2. *Division of tasks*: licence agreements do not involve great subtlety in the way that they allocate the various business tasks. It is often a simple arrangement whereby company A designs a project or product and companies B, C and D agree to make it, passing it on to company E to market and sell it. This nominally straightforward plan is frequently dressed up to look more complicated and sophisticated than it is, or swamped with heavy contractual conditions; or both.
3. *Financial co-operation*: frequently there isn't any. In straight supply chain licensing agreements, the parties retain their financial independence from each other. They keep their own financial structure and experience no significant change in their financial practices as a result of being involved in the licensing agreement. This holds good irrespective of their position in the supply chain. It would not be true to say that participation in the licence agreement has no financial effect on the companies involved (they are clearly involved to try to increase their profit) but these effects are unlikely to be far-reaching, in a financial sense. Many companies have created healthy revenue streams from licence agreements, but it is difficult to find one that has increased its overall capitalization value by more than a few temporary per cent.
4. *Shared objectives*: don't expect to find many of these either. All participants in a supply chain want to maximize their profit and net cash flow, but it would be facile to suggest that this was a direct result of being involved in simple licensing agreements, exclusive or not. Apart from the objective of maximizing profitable sales (a statement of the blindingly obvious), it is generally difficult to find evidence of real shared objectives of the participants.

How do these observations affect the business validity of licence agreements? It certainly doesn't mean that licence agreements are a poor way of doing business, or that they necessarily produce mediocre profits – there are many successful supply chain structures that would soon invalidate such arguments. The point is an organizational one: *licence agreements are fine – but they are not true examples of 'co-operative' working*. This can be a little controversial because many licence agreements provide the illusion of co-operation. Assembled behind closed doors and then announced to the market in a deluge of publicity, licence agreements (especially international ones) are heralded as deep co-operative ventures. The participants may honestly believe that they are entering a spirit of shared objectives with their licensors or licensees, until the reality slowly dawns, sometime later, that the level of co-operation was little more than traditional interaction between buyer and seller. In-built management prejudices such as 'joint ventures don't work' often stem from experiences like this.

CASE STUDY 3.1

Supply chain licensing: electronic assemblies

The early days of the electronics industry in the Far East were characterized by supply chain licensing. Instead of investing heavily in new manufacturing plants in Taiwan or Hong Kong, electronics companies from the United States, Japan and Europe simply subcontracted the component supply and assembly of parts of electronic goods to these countries. This period of conventional buy–sell relationships was used to achieve high quality levels and cost reductions before more formal agreements were put in place. Everyone learned from the experience but there was little structural integration of the businesses in the early years.

Supply chain licence agreements do have some positive points. In theory, they can form a useful introductory stage of co-operation between companies, allowing them to find out how well they work together before entering into a greater commitment with each other, involving merger, sharing of resources or equity, or whatever. This can seem like a good idea; caution and indecision are closely interlinked in some companys' strategies. It *can* work in practice: Case study 3.1 gives an example of a particular industry sector that has developed its strategy of international business co-operation as a series of careful steps. As a strategic tool, however, the idea of using supply chain licensing agreements as an 'easy introduction' to proper strategic co-operation between businesses is probably flawed. Commercial buy-sell agreements involving a lot of day-to-day interaction at all management levels are a fertile ground for the myriad of communication, cultural and niggling contractual disagreements that live in these types of relationships. It is hard to keep a strategic focus when your people have spent three months bickering over the number of work hours or widgets that were invoiced for a supply contract two years ago, and for which you still haven't been paid.

In summary, supply chain licence agreements have little strategic strength and are a breeding ground for minor practical difficulties. They can look, and feel, like a genuine mechanism for co-operation between organizations but are usually little more than commercial buy–sell arrangements obscured by a bit of well-intentioned publicity and public relations gloss. Feel free to implement them, by all means, but don't confuse them with true strategic alliance or joint-venture ways of working.

CASE STUDY 3.2

UK electricity industry privatization

The announcement of UK electricity industry privatization in the late 1980s was followed by a flurry of activity between the twelve Regional Electricity Companies (RECs), large-scale electricity users and generating plant contractors, all eager for a slice of the new post-privatization market. More than 40 alliances were formed, most consisting of multiple parties, each contributing a small equity investment. The idea was generally that an alliance 'group' comprising an REC, a lead financier and a plant contractor would invest equity in a new or existing power station, raising the remainder of the funding via debt finance. A small group of industrial electricity consumers would join in later equity rounds and all would share the profits from the venture.

This was a classic case of supply chain licensing agreements in disguise. The main interest of all the parties lay not in equity investment in a power project, but the opportunity to supply their services to the project. Their strategic objectives were not capable of being merged for anything other than a very short period of time, certainly not the 5–6 years necessary from the initial project structuring phase through to the payback horizon of a power station. Some of the alliances became too large – one almost attained the status of a national co-operative, with 10 members. The environment also changed, with the introduction of the regulated electricity market and overseas take-overs of many of the RECs. Just about all of the 40 alliances proved to be temporary, with more than half disappearing or being restructured within 18 months of their formation.

DIVISIONALIZATION

The term 'divisionalization' covers several types of corporate structure. The existence of a division infers a part of an organization that has a certain level of autonomy in its business area. This in turn infers that it has specialist knowledge of its own area and is big enough to be self-supporting. This last point is an important one – perhaps the only true feature that divisions have in common is their ability to lead a separate existence – to have the property of *viability*. Apart from this, the exact corporate form of 'a division' is open to some freedom of interpretation. The following structures can all be classed as divisionalized:

- a single-location company divided into different business units, either by product or market, eg fresh food division, frozen food division etc;
- a multi-location company split by product area and region, eg investment services (Far East) and pension services (UK);
- a holding-company structure, where a small company owns a network of diversified, often unrelated, businesses such as shipping, property and investment services.

These structures all contain the necessary 'self-supporting' parts that can be broadly classed as divisions. There is no central edict that says they have to be called divisions (they often aren't) but the structure is, nevertheless, still divisionalized. Given the diversity of divisionalized structures it is not surprising that it is possible to find a few well-defined trends in the way that they develop. Figure 3.4 shows one which is a feature of several fields of business including manufacturing, transport and some types of retailing. The main characteristic is the trend for small and specialized (and successful) businesses to be acquired by larger conglomerate 'groups'. Sometimes this happens as a result of the group extending its chain of supply (*integration*), if it is actively involved in business operations, or merely acquiring them for their revenue potential, as a true holding company. The whole process is helped along by the general managerialist belief of large companies that 'bigger is better (we think)' and 'we can manage them all – no problem'. Perversely, once the central core organization reaches a certain size, the old problems of management control appear. It is then decided that the business must be rationalized, control must be apportioned – specialists allowed to specialize, while everyone addresses the part of the market that they know best. It seems as if almost overnight the word 'control' disappears, to be replaced by its opposite: autonomy. What is the result? Divisions.

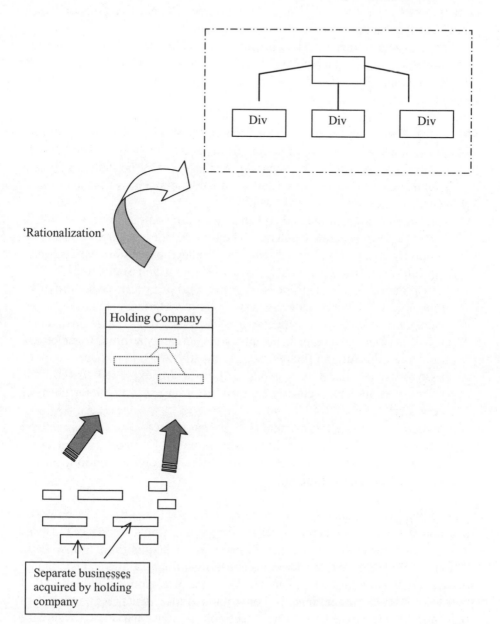

Figure 3.4 The trend towards divisionalization

Divisions create autonomy or at least provide the environment for autonomy to develop. The result (as we saw in Figure 3.4) is a corporate structure which is divisionalized. It is not necessary, remember, for the autonomous self-existing bits to be *called* divisions, they just need to act like divisions to fit the general model of what divisions are, and do.

The message is that divisionalization is a widespread, but nevertheless interpretable way of organizational working – you can track it, and understand its rationale and form. Despite its variety, a divisionalized structure has the following general characteristics:

- *Formal structure*: a central management core which has responsibility for a span of operating divisions or separate businesses. The span of control can be wide. The separate businesses may be called associate companies, subsidiaries or affiliates, depending on who owns their shares. These names are often used loosely.
- *Division of tasks*: divisionalized structures are composed of parts which are capable of separate existence. They could, if necessary, be viable by themselves. There is little sharing of management resources; each part concentrates on solving the day-to-day problems that matter to itself. The group generally claims to possess some kind of synergy which may, or may not, be visible outside the very top levels of management.
- *Financial co-operation*: expect consolidated accounts. Divisionalization involves amalgamation of financial results but rarely as much togetherness on the re-allocation of finance back to the divisions. In the true nature of autonomy, the parts of a group structure are expected to fend for themselves and meet sales revenue and ROI targets which have been set centrally.
- *Shared objectives*: the existence of shared objectives in divisionalized structures can be tenuous. Everyone's financial objectives tend to be similar but strategic objectives can differ widely, depending on the business pressures of the day.

On the basis of this analysis, there seems to be precious little to recommend divisionalization (in all its forms, remember) as a healthy example of business co-operation in action. The typical activities of acquisition, followed by rationalization into separate divisions are more a financial mechanism than a management strategy. It is a sad fact that many acquired companies find themselves subject to the financial constraints of their new parent, rather than reap any benefits of access to new technology, new markets or visionary management. The corporate outlook at high level is centred on financial mechanisms, not just in true investment-orientated holding companies but also in single companies that have taken the step to split into divisions. It is also not uncommon for more discussion and management effort to be spent on these mechanisms and techniques of finance, rather than the levels of sales or profit that they are there to serve.

In summary, divisionalization is not a system that necessarily results in good quality co-operation between businesses. It is similar in effect to the idea of conventional licence arrangements whereby businesses are in theory encouraged to work closely together but rarely do so. Two points follow on from this: first, divisionalization may not be a bad idea; but second, it is not a good model of business co-operation – even if it sometimes looks like it could be.

STRATEGIC ALLIANCES

Strategic alliances are now commonplace as a model for business co-operation between large companies. Over the past 20 years they have attained the status almost of an ideology in technology-driven business sectors such as motor vehicle manufacture, airline operation and pharmaceuticals.

What is a strategic alliance?

A strategic alliance (SA) is an agreement between two or more 'partner' organizations, committing them to pool their efforts and resources in some way. The level of agreement can be either 'overall business' or project-based, but stops short of requiring full commitment by the partners, so allowing them each to retain their separate identity, as illustrated in Figure 3.5. The driving force behind SA formation is that of organization *capability*, ie the partners wish to achieve something that they feel is not achievable by other means in the time that they want. This concept of time is important; it is rare to find a situation where each partner could not eventually achieve their aim by themselves, but it is the desire to achieve it more quickly which drives them into an alliance. This is different to some other forms of business co-operation where the emphasis is on avoiding risk – SAs do not necessarily take place in high-risk parts of the business environment. This consideration of the driving force behind SA formation is an important area of strategic thinking, and responsible for a lot of *mis*conceptions and problems for organizations that get it wrong.

SA characteristics

SA partners display a surprisingly constant set of characteristics:

- *Dependency*: the concept of an alliance is clearly linked to a mutual dependency between the allies in the way that they interact with the market.
- *Size restriction*: each partner organization wants to be bigger than it is but usually faces some restriction why this cannot happen.
- *Technical competence*: this is generally high. It is rare for successful SAs to be forged between organizations that do not have some kind of specialist technical input to offer. Simple commercial knowledge and enthusiasm alone are not enough at this level.
- *International capabilities*: they all suffer from aggressive international competition and operate in highly price-sensitive markets.

The markets of the A- and B-parent companies overlap.

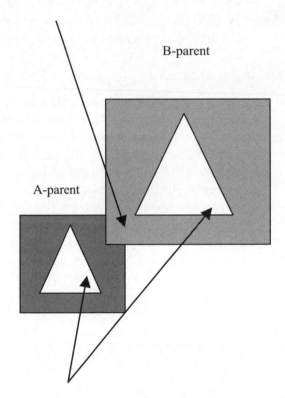

The company structures of the A- and B- parents remain separate

Figure 3.5 The strategic alliance model

These characteristics feed forward into the two main types of strategic alliance that you will see: scale alliances and complementary alliances. These forms have developed in a series of steps since the early 1980s and are found distributed fairly evenly across business sectors.

CASE STUDY 3.3

Successful alliances: Airbus Industrie

Airbus Industrie has been a success story of European business since its formation in 1967. It consists of UK, French, German and Spanish partner companies and has become the second largest aircraft producer after Boeing of the United States. Although it has modified the detail of its alliance structure since its formation, the basic concept of the alliance has remained sound.

Intra-European alliances

More than 80 per cent of intra-European alliances are based on economies of scale rather than complementarity of skills. Airbus Industrie is an example that has elements of both types and has managed to remain among the technological leaders in its field.

Scale alliances

Scale alliances are driven (as their name suggests) by the search for economies of scale in the goods or services that the partners provide to the market. There are only a few cases where pure purchasing power is the major issue. The desire for increased business volume means that scale alliances are found in areas of business that involve mass-market sales and where sales take place through agents, dealerships and other intermediaries in the commerce chain. The products or services are high-tech, but not *too* high-tech – a situation which would dilute the competitive nature of the market, reducing some of the primary driving force that an SA needs in order to form.

Scale alliances can have a long life. Many have continued over 20 years or so in an atmosphere of apparent serenity but some others have been only temporary. One of the key characteristics of scale alliances is the way in which the partners rarely transfer their technical specialism to each other. There is good reason for this – scale alliances tend to form between partners that have similar useful skills from the beginning, each considering that they have little to learn from the other. It is economies of scale they are looking for rather than transferable technical skills.

Complementary alliances

These are almost the opposite of scale alliances. The purpose of the alliance exercise is for the partners to complement each other's technical skills. There is a strong learning basis – both partners in a complementary alliance can be heard proclaiming loudly the benefits of organizational learning. Organizational learning, they will tell you, is the key to just about everything.

In practice, it rarely works like this. Unlike the purest scale alliances, complementary alliances do not possess a permanent rationale for their existence. From the day they are formed (and the learning starts) the mutual dependence between the allies starts to decrease – the faster the learning, the more quickly the real need for the alliance recedes. People and organizations learn quickly, which means that: *complementary alliances are always temporary*.

This view of a strategic alliance as a transient organizational form is not an easy one for managers to accept. Finely polished strategic business plans rarely concede that such alliances result in an injection of instability into the organization's future; they are more often couched using the opposite terms: better stability, maintainable profits and a solid customer base. Isn't this what every board of directors is looking for? Sadly, it is rarely found in complementary alliances. Neither is it found in complementary alliances that pretend to be some other type. The truth is that strategic alliances that are based on complementarity are a *transient* form of organization.

Of the two pure types of strategic alliance, there are not many that are intimate mixtures of the two. Of those that are commissioned on this basis most never get past the starting block – there is confusion and lack of direction from day one. The rest fail after a short time and spend the next few happy years trying to decide who was at fault. The proper answer is, of course, that the activity lacked clear strategic direction and was simply waiting innocently to become the victim of the mixed-up strategies, accompanied by the inevitable fall off in 'complementarity' driving force.

The problem of control

Once an alliance reaches a size where it attains the characteristics of an organization, ie it can be said that it has an organizational form, along comes the old problem of control. Control is part of the territory of organizational management – a subtle mix of vision and understanding, laced with a bit of confidence. Alliances of any type are difficult to control. Any mechanism of co-operation between businesses where there is dependency (as we have seen that there is) carries with it the issue of hierarchy and its overtones of who is in charge. This raises problems for management at all levels, making the enterprise difficult to control. You cannot expect, therefore, the management of any kind of joint enterprise or alliance to be easy. The situation is compounded by the problem of reconciling the corporate objectives of alliance partners. It is difficult to get agreement on a practical set of objectives that suit two organizations that themselves choose to be linked, rather than have it imposed on them by formal merger or acquisition. Later we will see some ideas on how we can achieve control, without swamping the individual management discretion that is so essential for the venture's survival.

So how should we view strategic alliances? They are in successful use by large international businesses as a strategic weapon – their power in the motor vehicle and airline sectors is well proven. In contrast, they have failed, in their thousands, in smaller companies, or when they have consisted of nothing but a collection of problem companies, desperately pieced together in a process of organizational patchwork. From the viewpoint of a model of business co-operation, SAs vary in merit; neither scale nor complementary alliances are a guarantee of business harmony, or the ever-elusive synergy. They both have their problems. Strategic alliances are, however, much closer to a usable model of business co-operation than the earlier examples of licensing agreements or divisionalization. They can provide useful pointers towards an effective method of managing joint ventures.

THE CONSORTIUM APPROACH

Along with strategic alliances the growth of the 'consortium approach' has been a business trend since the early 1980s. In some sectors of commerce it is difficult to find an organization of more than about 500 people that does not claim to be involved in a consortium of one type or another.

Consortia are common in large construction and infrastructure projects for bridges, airports, railways etc, through to the purely commercial sectors of banking and investment. Their lowest common denominator is that they are normally formed on a project-by-project basis rather than as a instrument of organizational strategy. As a general rule, it is businesses that are centralized and a little risk-averse that have the tendency to form consortia. The rationale behind the formation of consortia can be surprisingly wide: there are four main threads to it:

1. *Shared risk*: participation in a consortium gives the appearance of less risk exposure. In practice, this is often true – the risk in, say, large construction projects can be shared if the contracts are carefully written. This is particularly important in the modern design of project agreements in which the trend is for the project contractor to be expected to share risk with the purchaser or end user.
2. *Pooled R&D*: high technology-based business such as the large chemical and pharmaceutical companies sometimes pool their R&D resources for the joint development of a potentially lucrative new product. The depth and expense of the R&D required act as the driving force for this, rather than any great managerial belief in sharing.
3. *Allocation of staff resources*: infrastructure projects demand staff numbers which are frequently larger than one organization can handle. Joining resources on a temporary basis is a way to alleviate this problem.
4. *Financial capability*: projects that are constructed using limited resource finance often have to be partially underwritten by the organization executing the project. This can stretch the finances of an organization trying to act on its own.

There are two common factors in these characteristics of the consortium approach. First, they are all temporary mechanisms – once the project or venture has finished, everything can return to the way it was before without too much trouble. Second, along with their short-termism, they are practical business manoeuvres, rather than parts of a coherent strategy. There is nothing strategic about them at all in the temporary context in which they present themselves. In terms of the extent of close business co-operation, recent history shows that the consortium approach gives poor results. There are many business consortia (even successful ones) that have started, and ended, without the slightest real consensus of the organizations involved. The consortium approach can accept, perhaps even encourage, low levels of management consensus about issues outside the immediate boundary of the project under consideration. Perhaps 40 per cent of consortia are formed simply to *bid* for a project, then disbanded the minute the bid is unsuccessful (see Figure 3.6).

SUMMARY

We have looked in this chapter at the various ways in which organizations co-operate with each other in carrying out their businesses. We have seen that this co-operation can take several forms, from the close working relationships of complementary strategic alliances through to the low level

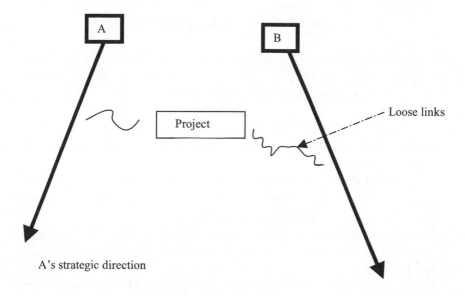

A's strategic direction

B's strategic direction

Figure 3.6 The consortium approach

'pretence' co-operation that is a feature of scale alliances, licence agreements and some types of divisionalization. The search for a good system of business co-operation has revealed some of its more difficult facets, such as the ever-present potential for argument, and the rather temporary nature of it all.

What does this mean for the general concept of *joint ventures*? Our understanding can be hampered by the fact that the terminology is used loosely; you will see licence agreements, divisionalization, strategic alliances and the consortium approach all referred to as 'joint ventures' by the participants and outside commentators alike. This can make for a confusing picture. Some of the answer lies with those models of business co-operation that have been successful. These are in the minority – it is a sad fact that large numbers of such ventures have been markedly unsuccessful. The common factor in the successful ones seems to be that the venture has simply been well thought-out and organized, and a good fit with the strategic objectives of the participants. This is worth repeating: *a successful joint venture needs to be assembled as part of a strategy and then well organized.*

There is nothing random about those joint ventures that do succeed, but they have to be planned and organized properly with attention to the difficulty of getting the objectives right and the task of controlling the venture when it is in operation. In the next chapter we start to look more carefully at the core idea of a joint venture.

CO-OPERATION: KEY POINTS

The idea of business co-operation infers some kind of joint venture or alliance between businesses. It works on the premise that there is interdependence between business organizations. The main forms of co-operation are:

1. *Supply chain licensing*: a contractual agreement to buy or sell each other's goods or services. This is a very loose form of co-operation with little strategic significance.
2. *Divisionalization*: a divisionalized structure consists of largely self-supporting organizational parts reporting to a central core. It is a common, but poor, model of business co-operation.
3. *Strategic alliances*: a common method of joint working of airlines and automotive manufacturers. It is an alternative to a full merger. There are two types:
   (a) scale alliances whose objective is to acquire economies of scale. They can be long term.
   (b) complementary alliances: the driving force is the complementarity of the partners' skills. They are nearly always temporary.
4. *The consortium approach*: basically a risk-sharing mechanism for large R&D-based or infrastructure projects. A transient form of organization without much real internal consensus.

All of these forms of co-operation are frequently described loosely (and incorrectly) as joint ventures.

Chapter 4

IJVs: The basic idea

Historically, the different types of co-operative working seen in the last chapter have been called various things. The trend of the past 10 years or so has been to bring many of them under the umbrella term of joint ventures. Some sectors (motor vehicle manufacturers and airlines) have been focused enough to retain the term 'strategic alliances' but others have followed the trend to label almost any type of business co-operation as a joint venture. This has been particularly prevalent in the context of international business – the idea of the International Joint Venture infers participation in the trend of globalization – and sounds good to the shareholders. The reality, however, is that many of them are not really joint ventures at all; they can be a type of business co-operation, granted, but they would not meet the particular organizational form that a joint venture must adopt if it is to survive. This is less organizational theory than economic fact; any quick study will show that the majority of so-called 'joint ventures' fail. Although the mechanisms of this failure are the traditional ones: lack of orders, increasing production costs etc, these things are the symptoms, not the disease. The final chapter of all failed joint ventures reads much the same and many of the unanswered questions are to do with the issues of purpose, structure and organizational design.

WHAT IS A JOINT VENTURE?

The answer is the same whether we are discussing a small regional joint venture (JV) or a large-scale international joint venture (IJV). It is: *an IJV is part of a strategy*. It is part of a strategy because it has to be, if it is to stand even a half-chance of survival. Note how this is more than saying that an IJV is simply a type of co-operation between organizations. We saw in Chapter 3 that there are perfectly acceptable ways of co-operative working that are not really part of an organization's strategy. Strategy infers a level of thinking; development; knowing where you are going rather than being troubled by the day-to-day purchasing problems of the company or its internal political games. To reinforce this concept of an IJV as a strategic tool it is worth reminding ourselves of one of the downsides of IJVs: *IJVs are absolutely full of problems for management* (that's you).

At times, IJVs can be an organizational burden, stressing and testing a business in its most sensitive areas. Because of their difficulty, there would appear to be little point in initiating IJVs in response to myopic organizational problems – this would only make things worse. The benefits of co-operation between businesses only become clear when considered at the higher strategic level, which reinforces their position as being part of a strategy, rather than a knee-jerk response to some problem or insecurity in day-to-day business life.

If IJVs are to be part of the strategy of an organization, it follows that they must have strategic *objectives*. This can prove difficult – IJVs can be a fertile source of disagreement between sets of senior management, so you cannot expect objective-setting to be easy. We will look at objectives in detail in Chapter 5, please accept for the moment that proper objectives are the imposed currency of IJVs, and you cannot have a business venture without any currency.

DEFINING CHARACTERISTICS

The defining characteristics of IJVs have gradually emerged over the collective business experience of the past 20 years. The main ones form the skeleton of the later chapters of this book. The defining characteristics are:

- IJVs need *strategic* objectives.
- IJVs are full of management problems.
- IJVs need to adopt a viable organization form.
- IJVs are always transitional structures (yes, always).
- You have to inject stability into IJVs – it is not there naturally.

The last three are interesting. The message is that IJVs need a high degree of organizational understanding if they are to be successful. The instruments of this understanding involve incisive thinking about how organizations work within themselves and with others. Don't confuse this with the subject of organizational *theory* (there are much better books about that than this one), the characteristics of IJVs are such that they need seriously practical ways of looking at their organization and management. This can seem a difficult task, so we have to start by developing some tools. These tools are not unique to IJV situations, and are certainly not new, but they have a certain simplicity and accuracy about them. They can help you think about, and decide the characteristic of IJVs in a clear way, without confusion. They are: viability, stability, structure, and the ruler of them all: the management of *complexity*.

Viability

All managers involved in IJV activities would no doubt concede that their IJV has to be viable. They would talk of it needing to be economically viable by producing a profit; or technically viable, with the ability to produce the goods or services from which the venture will reap a benefit. Some managers will see things from an organizational perspective, defining viability in terms of the acceptability of the IJV partners to their clients, and to each other – to them, viability means harmony. In short, you can expect to see (and hear) a lot of different ideas as to what constitutes viability. While the above definitions are not wrong, they are little too shallow and well-worn to be of any real use. Try this one. Viability means: *capable of separate and continued existence*.

Under this idea, an IJV has to be able to support itself when separated from its parent organizations. It must be able to plan its own strategy and be self-managing. Note how this simple definition starts to bring focus to the idea of what an IJV actually is: the models of divisionalization and strategic 'scale' alliances in Chapter 3 cannot meet this simple test of viability that we have just set. Figure 4.1 summarizes the state of viability that we want. Note how there is no overt mention of independence, as such; it is the ability to maintain a separate existence that is important, not whether the IJV gives itself a new name and proclaims itself to be independent of its parent organizations.

A venture which is *viable* can:

- plan for itself (and react to the business trends in chapter 2);

- manage itself;

- solve its own internal problems;

- **Survive** – over a period of time.

Figure 4.1 The idea of viability

Many IJVs have problems with viability. This is because they have to be *designed* to be viable. It is little use commissioning a complex IJV in the hope that it will be viable; that it will somehow develop this viability itself. Viability has to be built in to a system from the beginning – it will not design itself. This simple fact is responsible for the meagre financial performance of many IJVs; those that waste their time in internal bickering and the ones for whom profitability proves ever-elusive – whose first real profitable deal is always 'in the pipeline'.

Stability

IJVs are, at best, a transitional form of business organization. Even the best-performing ones have a life cycle which eventually will expire, ending the venture. Our previous concept of viability accepts this, and places the onus on management to design the venture to retain its viability for as long as possible, this is sound business practice. For a venture to be viable it needs to be *stable*. Any organization composed of a number of departments or groups has the tendency to become unstable. Ventures that operate in a challenging business environment (as IJVs do) have high inherent *in*stability because the effect of interaction between groups with different roles and cultures will soon start to cause problems. These problems usually manifest themselves as arguments between those parts of the IJV that have roughly equal 'seniority' so it is not strictly a hierarchy problem. The effect is eventual mistrust between sales, marketing, production and centralized corporate function such as IT, finance and personnel – all the functional parts on which the IJV depends for its continued existence.

One positive way to think about stability is as the ability to adapt to changes and new surroundings, while maintaining the venture in its organized form (see Figure 4.2). The international perspective of IJVs guarantees an environment which will be in a state of almost constant change and a venture which is not designed to self-stabilize under such conditions will experience problems. Unfortunately, stability is rarely transferable from the parent companies of the IJV to the IJV organization itself. There is a rationale behind this – the most stable parent organizations have often achieved this condition only after many years of gradual organizational development using conservative and incremental strategies. Typically, such organizations *possess* stability, but do not understand it, and so are in a bad position to try and implement it in their offspring. This is one of the classic weak spots in IJV management – it is practically difficult to build an IJV that is self-stabilizing.

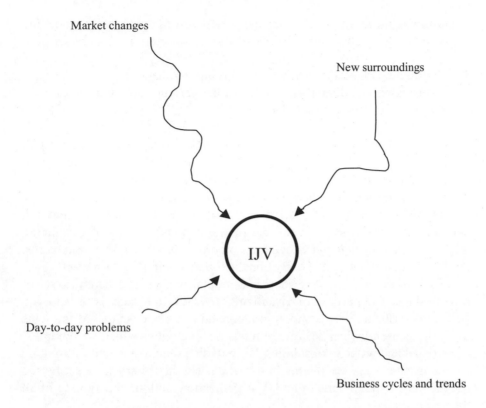

Figure 4.2 Threats to an IJV's stability

Structure

Even the simplest form of organization needs a structure. In most cases, IJVs are built along traditional lines using the conventional ideas of departments, functions and job roles, all expressed in a 'block' organization chart that is meant to represent how the IJV works. In practice, the organization chart is a poor way to describe the happenings in an organization and almost worthless as a way in which to prescribe the actions of managers at the various hierarchical levels. One of the weaknesses is that the organization chart is purely hierarchical; it may defer to conventional management techniques such as matrix management or 'group working' but its only proper point of reference is that of organizational hierarchy. For a complex and changing organization form such as an IJV, the main purpose of the traditional organization chart seems to be to decide who to blame when something goes wrong.

Designing the structure of an IJV is more involved than merely producing the type of organization chart described above. Structure is also about:

- the framework of an organization – giving it a shape;
- independence and interdependence of the various parts of a venture;
- tangible communication links.

This last one forms the basis of the detailed look at IJV structure that we will develop later in Chapter 6. We will look at an IJV as a network of communication links between its own parts, and between itself and the business world outside. There is nothing theoretical about this model, the communication links carry all manner of information about financial, personnel and business matters – the model is merely a way of visualizing the links, helping you to piece together a picture of how the IJV system works. We have made an important early conclusion here: *an IJV is a system*.

So what is a system? A system is a mental picture of a complex set of relationships. The purpose of visualizing an IJV as a system is to help you first, to describe it and, second, to understand it. This technique of 'systems thinking' is useful when dealing with business activities which are complex, transitional and prone to instability. We will also see this method of thinking in use in later chapters of this book when it is necessary to describe the interactions between parts of an IJV organization, and the functioning of all the sub-parts.

Systems thinking is a valid response to the problem of complexity in IJV organizations. Complexity can be defined simply as 'the number of states that something can be in'. It makes things difficult to understand and awkward to organise. Complexity is the main reason why people in organizations behave and do what they do, rather than what they should be doing. Increasing the number and diversity of the parts of an organization (as in an IJV) multiplies the complexity to the point where it can make a venture next to impossible to control. When this happens you can wave goodbye to the ideas of stability, structure and the ever-elusive viability. Systems thinking is a response to this problem, a way of trying to make sense of the complexity, rather than pretending it doesn't exist. One of its strengths is its applicability to a wide variety of problem situations – it is equally comfortable with questions of strategy, structure, communication or political interactions between people. Systems thinking does not presuppose any particular management 'theories' – its only purpose is to help address the complexity that exists. We will see later that this can be a useful ally in solving (and preventing) difficult IJV problems.

CASE STUDY 4.1

Insurance IJVs: sources of complexity

Insurance industry IJVs provide a good example of how IJV organizations can benefit from a 'systems' approach to handling their complexity. Several UK and European insurance companies have established IJVs, with established product portfolios being sold by an overseas IJV partner.

Some of the companies experienced difficulties in communicating product information across the international boundaries. It became clear from the early days that it was not sufficient simply to send all the product information and customer literature in a batch and expect the overseas partners' staff to successfully sell the insurance products – this approach didn't result in enough sales. Sales staff blamed their poor results on the fact that they felt unfamiliar with the new products, and so couldn't make convincing arguments to potential customers.

Better results were experienced by IJVs that installed systems of communication between the new sales force and the product managers in the home partner's head office. Systems were designed to disseminate product information on a regular basis, to deal quickly with technical enquiries and provide a 24-hour helpline service, to get round the problem of the 6-hour time difference between the two countries. The system had rules and procedures to make it run smoothly and a programme of audits and internal assessments to ensure that it was doing what it was designed to do. The result was to improve the efficiency of the sales force *and* help the internal harmony of the IJV organization.

BASIC IJV MODELS

Despite the obvious variety of IJV forms, they all fit into a few well-defined categories. The most useful way to divide these categories is by reference to the relative business strength of the partners. There is sound rationale for this – the idea of a *joint venture* (as opposed to a strategic alliance or other, looser, business agreements) infers the existence of a true jointly owned organization with separate legal identity. An implication of this joint-ownership model is that the nature and characteristics of the resulting organization are derived predominantly from the relative strength of its partners. Put crudely, it is of little use having a good product and demanding market if the supplying organization cannot organize itself well enough to produce and sell its product or service in an effective way. The concept of relative strengths of the IJV parties contain two elements: ownership influence and management strength:

- *Ownership influence* is simply the relative amount of influence that an IJV partner can exert by virtue of its legitimate ownership of the IJV company. This is not necessarily exactly the same as its equity interest, but usually is.
- *Management strength* is a measure of the relative strengths of the management teams that each parent organization allocates to the task of managing its IJV activity. It is a heady mixture of role, responsibility and personality and hence makes for a less pure type of management model.

It is easy to confuse these two aspects or to mentally combine them into one. This can be a seductive path – to believe that management and formal ownership are necessarily in harmony, or even synonymous, and can be included in this combined form as the basic building block for a 'model' of an IJV. In some cases it may be true, but there are numerous IJVs which have foundered on the rocks of the ownership vs management argument. It is better to think of them as being separate even if this is a less-than-perfect simplification of the truth.

The four basic models are:

1. the independent model;
2. the dominant parent model;
3. the shared management system;
4. transplants.

Figure 4.3 shows three of the basic models of IJV, each with its separate ownership-v-management strength 'structure'. Note the key features of the structures; the relative sizes and strengths of the parts, their subdivision from their parent organizations and the common factors of *dependency* between the parties. All three are legitimate models of IJVs which can be found in the business world. At this early stage, it is enough to understand the different forms without a value judgement as to which ones are right or wrong (that comes later). Accept, however, that in the way of things, they will have different strengths.

(1) Independent roles

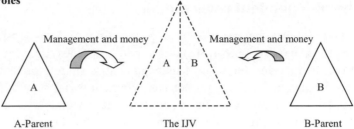

Management and money

Management and money

A

A   B

B

A-Parent

The IJV

B-Parent

(2) Dominant parent

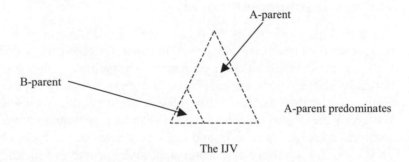

A-parent

B-parent

A-parent predominates

The IJV

(3) Shared management

Equity holding, money and management
are shared between parents A and B.

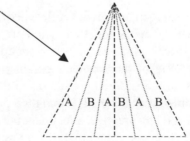

A B A B A B

Figure 4.3 Three basic IJV models

The independent roles model

This is where the parents have 50:50 financial ownership of the IJV organization (see Figure 4.3 (a)). Each party provides some irreplaceable input to the venture and the task of management is shared, or that is the general idea. Such ventures are often seen as being a low risk way of forming an IJV, each parent organization keeping control of its own management and financial input to the shared organization. Despite the laudable idea of shared management, IJVs based on this model tend to develop a management style which is a hybrid of those of the parent organizations. Paradoxically, this is accompanied by sharing of organizational resources but poor interlinking of ideas. Perhaps the most distinguishing feature of the 'independent roles' model of IJV is the continuing management discord within the organization as to its objectives and how it should be achieving them.

The dominant parent model

The main characteristics of the dominant parent IJV model (see Figure 4.3 (b)) are unequal (majority : minority) financial ownership and a domineering management style, led by the larger partner. The partners' parent organizations normally differ in size, technical skill and business capability. When one parent is much larger than the other, there may be almost full 'stakeholding' of the venture by the larger parent with the minor parent subordinated to a specialist technical area, or a pure sales and marketing role. Surprisingly, these types of IJV exhibit a variety of management styles; some are hierarchical and authoritarian, reflecting the dominant partner's position, while others are softer and paternalistic. Despite the obvious power imbalance within the IJV itself the relationship between the parties is still based on dependency – hence distinguishing it from looser co-production or licence-based co-operation agreements.

The shared management model

The shared management model reflects some of the purer ideas of the way that organizations work together. The concept is that the task of managing the venture is truly a *shared task*, irrespective of the relative size, strengths or equity holding of the partner's parent organization (see Figure 4.3 (c)). These issues are considered peripheral to the fundamental job of deciding a clear set of objectives for the IJV and then pushing them forward to make the venture succeed. In practice, the financial split follows the common 'near equal' distribution common in wholly owned subsidiaries, ie 51 per cent : 49 per cent or similar. The resulting difference in voting rights is used only in the event of major policy issues and is not a day-to-day issue within the management boundaries of the IJV organization itself. There are different variants of this model, depending on the nature of the IJV's business and the exact form of the marriage between the parents' management, but the common denominator is the complete, almost immutable, belief in the value of *sharing* the management tasks between the IJV partners. In common with the other models, the structure still relies on mutual dependency between the participating organizations – each must possess some vital resource needed to enable the venture to work.

Transplants

Transplants are a generic feature of IJVs, rather than being restricted to a single model type. The basic idea (see Figure 4.4) is to take a proven 'host' business formula and transplant it into a remote business environment normally in another country. Note that it is the business formula that is transferred rather than the entire operation itself – the objective is to transplant the successful *ideas and practices* of the host business, not its physical assets and resources. These key ideas can be a mixture of:

- technological aspects;
- personnel practices;
- management style and ways of working.

When the ideas and practices are transplanted into the new location it is common for the other partner of the IJV (in the 'receiving' country) to help in the setting-up procedure. In this way the transplant becomes a shared activity of the IJV. It is rare to find a transplant that does not utilize some of its partner's facilities in the new location. Transplants may be single location or multi-location, in which several transplant operations are started simultaneously or in quick succession. In the manufacturing sector, transplant operations favour greenfield sites where plant layouts can be designed without constraint and there are no historical precedents in working practices. New manufacturing businesses have a similar preference for greenfield sites, as it is much easier to transplant a new culture into an 'open space' than to have to impose it on top of existing procedures and practices.

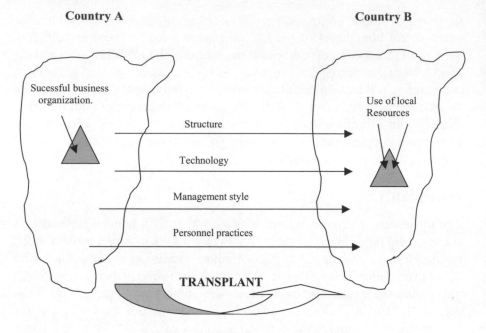

Country A

Country B

Figure 4.4 The idea of a transplant

CASE STUDY 4.2

Transplant IJVs: Japanese–US automotive businesses

Towards the end of the 1980s Japanese automotive industry suppliers were moving focus away from their traditional home markets towards foreign investment. Over a period of about five years, more than 200 Japanese-based automotive component companies opened 'transplant' ventures in the United States. Most were direct suppliers to automotive assemblers and were opened on greenfield sites, separate from the US partners' existing manufacturing facilities.

The most common ownership model was an equal split of equity between the Japanese and US partner. Most of the transplant operations involved the use of Japanese personnel practices and working methods with a predominantly US workforce.

THE IJV LIFE CYCLE

It is a well-known feature of the business world that nothing lasts for ever – we saw in Chapter 2 the idea of the business environment as being made up of a series of overlapping trends. Business operations and structures that involve mutual co-operation are a good example of this – there may be trends and pressures for the formation of joint venture activities but these are always accompanied, in the background, by negative forces trying to destroy them. When the mutual desire for co-operation is strong enough, IJVs can flourish, but when it starts to fade, the negative forces take over, threatening their survival. All this adds fuel to the argument as to whether a joint venture may be a temporary form of business or whether it *has* to be. Fortunately, the answer is clarified by looking back over recent business history. It is: *IJVs have been shown to be transitional*. This is not quite the same as being temporary, or doomed to failure. A better explanation is that although a joint business venture may be profitable, or desirable at one point in time, it is never guaranteed a continued existence – IJVs are, almost by definition, a *transitional* organizational form. There is always likely to be a limit on the 'newness' of an IJV, and hence the pressures that worked to cause the formation of the venture cannot be expected to last. This means that IJVs are not very durable.

The life cycle of an IJV is surprisingly well defined, following the six stages shown in Figure 4.5. There is nothing theoretical about the contents of this figure, it shows the condensed experience of many type of IJV. Consideration of this life cycle is an important background consideration to the task of managing IJVs – it can help you know what to expect.

Stage 1: Initiation

Initiation is a discrete stage in the formation of an IJV. It is more than early discussion between the parties. You can think of it as a response to the business and market conditions that are pressurising the JV to form. IJV initiation rarely happens bilaterally, it requires one of the parties to take the lead.

Stage 2: The early partner agreements

This is the first set of formal agreements struck between the contracting parties of the IJV. The agreements are often a precursor to the splitting off of the pieces of the parent businesses to form the organization with the separate IJV identity. There is no guarantee that these agreements will last into the operational stages of the IJV – they are best thought of as agreements of the initiation stage.

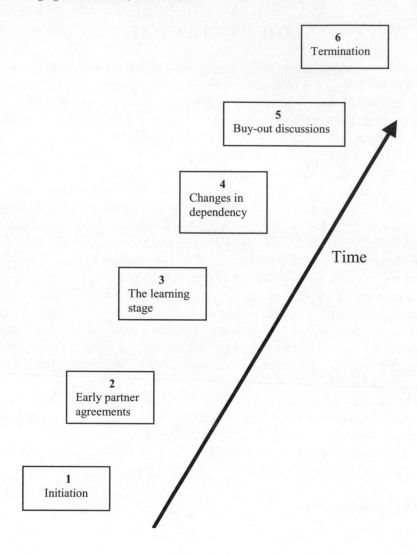

Figure 4.5 The IJV life cycle

Stage 3: The learning stage

The learning stage is one of the fundamental parts of the life cycle of an IJV. The activity of organizational learning – the way in which an organization gains knowledge from its partners – has both positive and negative influence on the prospect of joint ventures as time progresses. At the beginning of an IJV when there are large gaps between the capability of the partners, learning happens rapidly. Their rate of learning tails off quickly as the parties continue to interact to a point where, later in the IJV's life, the differences in capability become eroded. In theory, organizational learning takes place between IJV partners in both directions simultaneously – an idealized situation in which each organization has something to learn from the other. Real IJVs rarely follow this model; it is more common for the knowledge and learning activity to flow mainly one way, ie for the 'technical dependence' to be predominantly on one side of the IJV.

Despite its imperfections, the concept of organizational learning remains a key element of IJV strategy. Features of ventures such as the 'complementary skills' strategic alliance model carry over easily into the field of IJVs with organizational learning having a big effect on the way that IJV partners adapt to working with each other. It is, frankly, rare for the rate of learning to increase as the IJV timescale progresses; a characteristic of mature IJVs is accompanying maturity of the partners' own technical capabilities. They feel they have less to learn than at the beginning of the joint venture.

Stage 4: Changes in dependency

Organizational learning produces a change in the level of dependency of IJV partners. What may have started out as a clear dependency of one partner on the other's technical skills or market knowledge soon changes. IJVs based largely on financial dependency display a similar characteristic which can manifest itself in several ways. First, when the initial dependence is based on heavy capital investment by one partner, the dependence starts to decrease once the investment has been made and the new premises, plant, or whatever, is in use. It tends to be the *existence* of the investment that triggers the reduction of the dependence, rather than the issue of which party legally owns it.

Second, if the availability of revenue expenditure is the predominant dependence of one of the partners (common in economies of scale ventures), the reduction in dependence occurs more slowly. Unlike capital expenditure, revenue expenditure commitments are made gradually, are subject to changes of mind, and can be cancelled. The dependence therefore continues to exist for as long as revenue expenditure remains a scarce resource to the IJV organization. In practice, this type of dependency still changes over time, either by the success of the venture (in producing revenue to fund its own expenditure) or by changes in expectations of those ventures that are unsuccessful in their early life.

Changes in dependency are a feature of all business ventures that rely on co-operation between different parties. It does not have to be a negative feature, but you do need to make sure it is an expected one. Its main capacity for causing problems is if it is allowed to become a surprise to either of the venture partners.

Stage 5: Buy-out discussions

In the later stages of the life cycle, along come discussions about changes in financial ownership of the IJV business. The usual format is for one partner to want to 'buy out' the other. Buy-out discussions can be an emotional subject – it is often seen as indicative of a venture that has failed commercially, or that the parties cannot agree on some important technical or commercial matter, or simply that the management teams have become tired of each other. None of these are necessarily true. The nature of the IJV as a transitional organization means that it is *not expected* to be permanent in a single form, so changes of ownership discussions can be seen as a stage of development – a function of the inevitable life cycle of an IJV. This means that you can approach these discussions in a positive frame of mind, rather than class them as crisis discussions in which both parties need to adopt defensive positions, protecting their own future interests at the expense of the others.

Buy-out discussions don't 'just happen', they are initiated by one of the partners, often as a response to poor technical or commercial results accumulated over a period of time. You can expect the need for these discussions to be cloaked in the pretence that they were requested by both parties, secure in the knowledge that they rarely are. The reason for the pretence is normally to avoid management embarrassment, which is fine. It is worth repeating that although they may be sensitive, there is no need for buy-out discussion to be seen as an admission of failure by either party – they are merely a part of the IJV life cycle. Even viable, profitable IJVs end up in buy-out discussions.

Stage 6: Termination

Given the inevitability that IJVs all have to come to an end, there are a variety of ways that this can happen. Some are ended by formal written agreement, with all the details of dissolution of the management team and division of the joint assets clearly spelt out. This can be a long procedure if done properly – intangible assets such as marketing practices, commercial brands and business goodwill are notoriously difficult to apportion. A larger number of IJVs are terminated in a less formal way, simply by allowing the joint organization to wither, by not developing new products or projects. Surprisingly, some of the largest IJVs involving international corporations have ended by fading into insignificance in this way. It is understandable that these receive little in the way of promotion or publicity – organizations do not publicize the end of their business relationships with the same enthusiasm with which they announce their formation.

In summary, just about all IJVs exhibit these six basic stages of the life cycle. The cycle varies in timescale between about two and 15 years, depending on the characteristics of the business sector, the corporate nature of the parties involved and a myriad of other variables, many of them unpredictable.

So what is the message about the IJV life cycle? Granted, it is difficult to predict; even more difficult to manage, and is composed of interrelated elements, some of which attract more than their fair share of public relations gloss and good old corporate pretence (well-meaning, of course). The import-ant point is: *don't let the IJV life cycle come as a surprise.* From a manager's viewpoint, a knowledge of the form that the life cycle will take, and a tacit acceptance of its inevitability, are a step on the right path to effective management of an IJV. Experience shows, sadly, that the opposite is also true.

SUMMARY

An IJV has to be part of a well-constructed strategy – it is a strategic tool rather than a quick-fire solution to getting more orders or solving awkward management problems. Three things need to be built in to the design of an IJV:

- *viability*: the capability to maintain a separate and continued existence;
- *stability*: because IJVs are a transitional organizational form which have a tendency to become *un*stable;
- *structure*: the best way is by building an IJV structure using 'systems' principles incorporating an organizational framework showing areas of independence, interdependence and tangible communications links.

Basic IJV models

There are four basic IJV models, based on different arrangements of ownership influence and management strengths. They arc:

- *the independent roles model*: a low risk solution with 50:50 split of ownership and management responsibility;
- *the dominant parent model*: a dominant and subordinate partner with an unequal balance of ownership and power;
- *shared management models*: these can take several forms, all involving an intimate sharing of management tasks between the IJV partners;
- *transplants*: a model in which a successful business organization formula is 'transplanted' into another country.

The IJV life cycle

The life cycle of IJVs is well defined, consisting of six steps:

1.   initiation;
2.   the early partner agreements;
3.   the learning stage;
4.   changes in dependency;
5.   buyout discussions;
6.   termination.

An understanding of the IJV life cycle is an important background consideration to the task of managing IJVs.

Chapter 5

Objectives

RETHINK: CORPORATE OBJECTIVES

Corporate objectives are the product of individuals rather than 'the organization' as such. Many managers see the corporate objective of forming an IJV as being linked in some way to the growth of their organization. There are many and varied reasons for wanting growth: it may be seen as a way of keeping ahead of the competition, providing access to bigger profits or achieving economies of scale. Sometimes, reduced to a more personal level, growth is felt amongst managers to be a natural and almost instinctive state of affairs.

In reality, IJVs and growth do not always fit easily together. Two parent organizations that work together to start a separate entity IJV business do not necessarily 'grow', as they would do if they joined in a formal merger. In a few cases an IJV will produce cheaper or better quality goods or services that replace those of their parent organizations, thereby causing both businesses to contract. Formation of an IJV is part of a business's strategy undoubtedly, but not one which *necessarily* involves growth.

WHAT ARE THE OBJECTIVES OF AN IJV?

Why do businesses enter into IJVs? Despite the downside of financial risk, management difficulties, and the ever-present problem of operating a form of organization which is inherently unstable, the number of IJVs world wide continues to increase. It is not limited to particular sectors; companies from all areas of business and commerce can, seemingly, hardly wait to embark upon the difficult path of forming and operating an IJV of some sort. Of those that never really get off the ground or fail within their first year of business, most have had problems with poor definition of the objectives of the IJV. The fact is; *many IJVs lack proper objectives*.

The simplicity of this statement belies its hidden content. It is easy for managers intending to commission an IJV to be lulled into complacency about the real corporate objective of entering into a joint venture with another organization. The final chapter of failed IJVs reads much the same: 'we started out looking for better market penetration, global coverage and access to technology, but it just didn't come our way.' You may even hear the ever-elusive *synergy* mentioned as the prime objective of the venture. Some of these were no doubt true, in their day, but there are just as many failed IJVs that didn't have any objectives at all – or at least none that would stand close scrutiny. The mere existence of an IJV does not qualify as a business objective in itself.

IJVs need a *purpose*. There is nothing new in the general principle of setting objectives for business organizations. There are, however, large numbers of apparently viable organizations that seem to operate without any tangible market-orientated objectives at all, except perhaps the continuing presence and capability for self-reproduction of their own internal hierarchy. We all know organizations like this. Unfortunately, this doesn't work for IJVs. IJVs are unstable, racked with the potential for internal conflict and, frankly, just waiting for the chance to lose direction. In such an environment, corporate objectives whose reference are solely 'internal' do not have the capability to give the IJV a clear business direction. The result will be that the venture will collapse in on itself, succumb to the temptation for internal conflict (fuelled by the inward-looking corporate objectives) and waste the energies and abilities of its managers on internal political arguments of ever-decreasing diameter. Business failure soon follows.

To counteract this, IJVs need objectives which are outward-looking – referenced to the world of business outside the organizational system of the IJV. They have to refer to what the organization is trying *to do* rather than what it aspires to be. There is nothing easy about setting objectives like this. They can be difficult to mesh with the existing corporate objective of the IJV's parent organizations – they can clash in either content or timescale, both a fertile source of potential management disagreement. Timescale in particular is often a problem, the finite life cycle of the IJV form can encourage disharmony between short-term and long-term views about what the venture should be doing.

CASE STUDY 5.1

Oil industry IJVs: the view from HQ

Some notable mergers in the oil industry have been preceded by IJVs between already globalized companies. The general pattern is that the IJV organization(s) are absorbed into the combined company during the merger operation.

The 'view from HQ' of the merged company is that the strategic logic of the pre-merger IJV was as a 'tester' to see how (or if) the companies could work successfully with each other. HQ central function managers in particular, saw the IJV activity as a way of combining functions such as accounts and personnel, making the joint organization more efficient than the parents it would eventually grow to replace.

Views like this suffer from being too internally focused. The objective of most oil industry pre-merger IJVs is more to do with external capabilities, for instance access to supermarket petrol stations or service-station sites. These are better outward-looking objectives – better at guiding the business activities of an IJV.

Elusive though they may be, the objectives of an IJV are fundamental to its potential for business success. The first step to understanding this important area of IJV management is to think in terms of the structure of an IJV's business objectives. A quick look at Figure 5.1 shows that they come as a set of three complementary objectives, each of which is referenced clearly to the environment or market in which the IJV operates, rather then being self-referential. Compare this with the self-seeking flavour of many corporate mission statements that are often published outside and inside organizations, purporting to represent the 'objectives' of that organization. The basic set of three complementary objectives: commercial, development, and technology, apply to just about all types of IJV and represent a way of thinking clearly about what your IJV is trying to achieve. We will look at them in turn.

The 'set' of IJV objectives

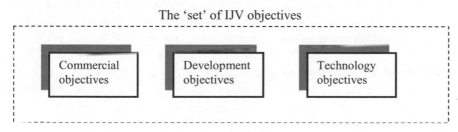

Figure 5.1 IJV objectives

COMMERCIAL OBJECTIVES

There are five of these:

1. the search for legitimacy;
2. value creation;
3. risk sharing;
4. economies of scale;
5. pure financial targets.

The search for legitimacy

For a new IJV to have any chance of success, it has to be seen as a 'legitimate player' in the market. The process of transporting the corporate success of a technology licensor, for example, to a country with lower technological status, but a large and untapped market for technological products can be fraught with difficulty. You can expect the following to cause problems in the early days of the attempt:

● different business practices and customs;
● cultural misunderstandings;
● corporate image (an image classed as wonderful in one country can be mediocre or even offensive in another);
● legal and bureaucratic constraints.

All of these reflect the problem of attaining legitimacy of a business activity in a different country. The formation of an IJV has traditionally been seen as one way to achieve this legitimacy in a short time. Case study 5.2 gives an example of emerging business in Brazil and other Latin American countries and the legitimacy objective used in the early stages of IJV formation.

There is little hard evidence to suggest that the formation of an IJV is alone sufficient to guarantee legitimacy, particularly in difficult host countries. Much depends on the form and structure of the venture itself; a venture that involves little tangible investment or employment opportunities in the host country will soon be dismissed by local customers as little more than a 'sales arm' of some powerful foreign business. Such ventures can suffer labour problems, as well as poor sales. Some of the largest corporations from the United States and Europe suffered from this in their early IJV activities. The search for legitimacy is a justified objective of an IJV, but not always an easy one to realize.

CASE STUDY 5.2

Regional IJVs in Latin America

Businesses in Argentina, Brazil, Columbia, Mexico, Peru and Venezuela are increasingly involved in IJVs with overseas multinationals looking to obtain a business presence in Latin America. The main sectors are food and packaging, energy, coffee, cement and construction. Latin American business is in the grip of privatization, trade liberalization and regionalization with a change in the role of federal and state governments from ownership to regulation.

Despite the positive changes, outside corporations still find difficulty in penetrating the market because existing Latin American companies remain resistant to regional competitors; in Brazil, for example, regional companies are able to mount strong pressure against 'outside' businesses trying to enter their region. The legitimacy objective of IJVs works well in such situations – once an overseas multinational has formed an IJV with a Latin American parent, many of the business restrictions slacken, leaving room for investment into the regions. In Brazil this has resulted in successful 'clustering' of joint venture businesses (eg the vehicle component industry in São Paulo) increasing the entire economic integration of the region.

Value creation

There is nothing new about the concept of value creation. The language of economics identifies 'the firm' as an entity whose job it is to create value, thereby contributing, with all the other firms, to the economic activity of society. There is no reason why an IJV should be *that* different, just because it consists of parts of two or more firms joined together across regional boundaries.

The above statement is only partly true. By their transient nature, IJVs are rarely suitable for value creation in terms of market capitalization of the joint organization. In most cases any growth in capitalization is siphoned back to the IJV's parent organizations via the accounting structure, in fact, it is rare to find an IJV which actually has a market capitalization, as such. It is best to think of the potential value creation of an IJV as being related to its revenue-earning potential. The net present value (NPV) of the venture over its life cycle is a useful approximation to value created. Don't worry about the impurity of this – an approximation is all it is.

In more formalized economic terms, any business venture involving co-operation between two potential competitors represents a worrying trend towards monopoly. In reality, the risk is better described as the tendency towards market sharing by a small number of powerful companies – known as a state of *oligopoly*. Microeconomic theory, being based on the concept of choice between alternatives, generally does not fit easily with the practice of co-operation between competitors, however temporary the venture purports to be. The net result of this is that IJVs are considered, by some, as degenerators of value creation, because of their apparent tendency to distort the market structure. Developing countries, particularly those attempting to run their economies to rigid economic theories (with the odd convenient distortion) are the most likely place for this to happen. It can be very difficult to operate an IJV under such conditions.

What effect does this have on using value creation as a valid objective for an IJV? The answer: not much. It is very difficult to *prove* whether an individual IJV (even a profitable one) creates net value for the economy in which it resides. There is colloquial evidence from research work done in the United States that much of the economic benefit from IJVs is reaped by the country of the B-parent with little tangible benefit to that of the A-parent 'licensor' partner. This, of course, is a macroeconomic conclusion – it doesn't say whether either of the partners made a clear financial profit from their venture.

In summary, there is nothing wrong with using value creation as an overt objective of an individual IJV. It is best treated, however, as of more strategic than practical value, unless it is linked to the purely financial objectives discussed later in this chapter. It looks good in press releases though.

CASE STUDY 5.3

Creating value: ABB in Eastern Europe

ABB is a large engineering corporation with over 200,000 staff world-wide. Recent expansions via IJVs and strategic alliances in Eastern Europe have been based on the clear objective of creating value by participation in the emerging industrial countries of Hungary, Poland and the Czech Republic. The value comes from introducing lower-cost manufacturing from these countries into the existing world-wide manufacturing network, thereby increasing ABB's competitiveness and market share. In some parts of the power generation and distribution market ABB and their rivals, following a similar strategy, have put the market into a state of near-oligopoly because of their success.

Risk sharing

Figure 5.2 shows the basic idea of risk sharing in the structure of an IJV. It works on the well-worn theory that in any business venture involving co-operation between organizations, the risk can be shared out between the parties in a predetermined way. There are three practical weaknesses in this argument:

- *Profit distribution*: there is a firm link in any area of business between risk and reward. An organization that wants to limit its risk must accept the resulting constraint on the reward (or profit) it can expect from the venture.
- *Risk sharing*: this doesn't always sit easily with the profit-motivated strategies of organizations which are financially successful.
- *Internal conflict*: the apparently simple agreement to 'share risk' in a joint venture business is inevitably a source of management problems. At times it can be a licence for internal argument and conflict between the parties. The situation is made worse by the international character of the IJV, making it necessary to negotiate across geographical and cultural boundaries.

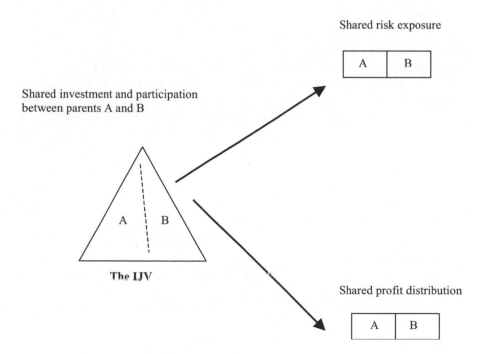

Figure 5.2 Risk sharing in IJVs

In practice, the first of these seems to have the greatest underlying effect on the way that IJVs work (and fail). Internal disputes apart, the fact that risk and profit are to be shared between strong, and forward-thinking organizations (which are almost by definition potential competitors) is guaranteed to cause problems. The main rationale of the problem is an economic one – if a business has the ability to make a profit on each marginal unit of output it produces, then why share it? This holds for all situations in which the net profit is greater than the cost of capital needed to obtain the facility to produce that output. By definition, any venture which is genuinely profitable contains strong internal pressures towards single-party ownership of the venture.

With these practical considerations ranged against it, the idea of risk sharing being a 'design' objective of an IJV has serious limitations. It is wise therefore not to consider it as a primary objective. It is better thought of as a part of the IJV's environment with a role in helping the other objectives work. In formal systems-thinking terms (to be developed in Chapters 6 and 7), it has a function as a *regulator*. The key point is worth repeating: *Risk sharing should not be a primary objective of an IJV*.

The counter-argument

There is one special case in which risk sharing takes more of a primary role in the structure of IJV objectives. This is for IJVs which are predominantly project-based, typically, large infrastructure construction projects such as tunnels, bridges, etc, or those which need heavy research and development expenditure (communication and pharmaceuticals are good examples). In these cases, IJVs are often formed with the specific intention of building an organization large enough to raise the financial capital needed to fund the project. This is not quite the same as sharing the financial risk of a venture – it is more a way of achieving the financial 'critical mass' necessary to realize a profit. Smaller IJV parent organizations are often pressured into acting in this way as part of the conditions for access to funding. At higher management level the argument still applies: risk sharing should not be the *primary* objective of forming an IJV.

Despite its lack of strategic rationale, risk sharing still forms part of the operational objectives of many IJVs. It is normally found concealed beneath the various financial mechanisms used in the operation of an IJV business and influences decisions made between the partners, ie:

- the split of start-up equity;
- apportionment of capital expenditure;
- loan security.

You can expect to see these stated in formal IJV agreements – just be careful not to confuse them with the primary objective of the exercise.

Economies of scale

There is a certain amount of misunderstanding about the role of economies of scale in IJVs. Many types of strategic alliance (as opposed to formalized IJVs) have, at their root, the search for business critical mass – the point at which an organization becomes large enough to be competitive. This requirement to reach critical mass is a feature of business sectors that exhibit one or all of the following features:

- similar products, incapable of much further differentiation;
- competitive pricing;
- reliance on large sales and marketing network in order to sell their goods or services.

Airlines, motor vehicle manufacturers and retail supermarket outlets are among the best examples of these. They operate in a business environment that comes very close to traditional perfect market assumptions with the always-present trend towards oligopoly. One feature of this type of business is the predominance of return on investment (ROI) as a key criterion of financial performance. Airlines, in particular, are very good at calculating the ROI on apparently minor capital assets such as baggage conveyors and fork lift trucks, as well as aircraft.

It follows that these types of organizations are the ones that have been active in forming strategic alliances over the past 15 or 20 years. Figure 5.3 shows the concept: amalgamation of overhead and support functions such as sales and marketing, IT and operations management, eliminates duplication and reduces the overhead burden per 'producing' unit. The critical mass is, in effect, these overhead functions – it is clearly uneconomic to maintain a full set of support departments and managers if there is not enough revenue-earning units for them to serve. The question is: does the experience of strategic alliances transfer to formal IJVs, where there is a separate organization spawned by the two or more IJV parents? Casual research on the structure of IJVs in the United States and Europe shows that only 10–15 per cent actually operate in a business sector that persistently shows a trend towards perfect competition and oligopoly – the conditions which provide the most pressing need for economies of scale if businesses are to retain their competitive position. Most of the remaining 85–90 per cent are not in a business where economies of scale are going to make much difference. This means that of those (many) IJVs where economies of scale is flaunted as the great objective and *raison d'être*, some of them have misconstrued the situation. Sadly, the reality only reveals itself some time into the IJV life cycle, by which time investments in effort and hard cash have already been made. The mistake has usually started with the misconception, by the managers of the IJV, that a joint organization behaves as an integral part of its parent organizations and can therefore reap the benefits of the combined size and resources. We know (from the hard experiences of chapter 4) that this will not always be true.

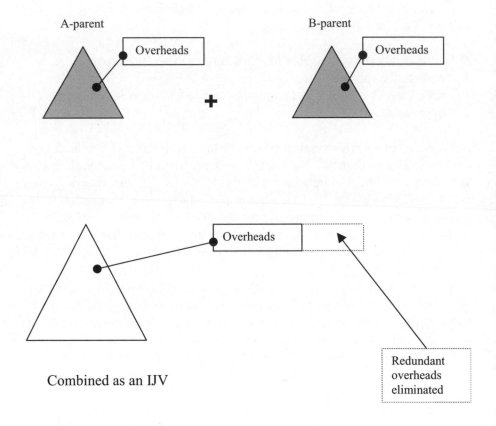

Figure 5.3 Economies of scale: the idea

CASE STUDY 5.4

Airline alliances: reality vs symbols

Picture an airline industry in which every company maintains absolute independence from the others. As well as its own symbols and logos, each one would need its own baggage handling, booking and ticketing systems and its own set of dedicated suppliers of the hundreds of goods and services needed to enable their aircraft to fly. Independence would be possible, but only at the expense of efficiency – the business would be full of duplication.

The reality of the airline business world-wide is that joint ventures and strategic alliances are a natural objective for both developed and developing countries' airlines. Developed country (A-parent) airlines gain direct access to economies of scale in their ticketing and logistics operations while developing countries obtain the same, coupled with access to better operational facilities such as aircraft maintenance and staff training. The same applies when both partners originate from developed A-parent countries but here the objective is directed also towards achieving pure economies of scale. These are good, outward-looking corporate objectives, designed to increase the participants' competitive performance in the market-place.

As IJV managers, you have to treat the search for economies of scale with care. Some will be real but difficult to attain while others possess more than their fair share of illusion. Every time two, albeit successful, organizations spawn a third be prepared to look first for *dis*economies of scale caused by the fragmentation – then decide whether there are any real economies of scale *for you*.

Pure financial targets

Financial results play a big part in the way that an IJV's performance is assessed by its own management, the parent organizations, and the business world outside. This is because financial results are tangible and visible, and because the general ethos of business is that an organization's role is to make a profit. It makes sense therefore, to recognize financial targets as part of the structure of objectives set for an IJV at its conception.

It is important not to confuse the idea of financial *objectives* with that of financial structure or, even worse, accounting practices. Objectives are firmly about the financial reality of business rather than a set of conventions that have to be blindly followed to comply with the sometimes obscure requirements of accountants or their auditors. Accounting techniques, honourable and accepted though they may be, can easily be misrepresentative of the real financial performance of a business venture. The situation is further confused when the business structure allows consolidation of individual figures into group accounts. Published accounts are, at best, distortions of the real financial situation of a business unit – not a good premise under which to formulate a set of financial objectives for a budding IJV. The important criterion is therefore that objectives must be set in a way that allows them to be clearly and accurately *assessed*, when it becomes necessary to make decisions based on what they say. Unfortunately, IJVs are one of the most difficult forms of organization for which to specify unambiguous financial objectives. The first step is to look carefully at the structure of the organization to which the objectives apply.

Financial objectives of what?

Even in well-developed IJVs, the structure is sometimes not too clear. Figure 5.4 shows the problem – because the IJV organization evolved and was funded from several parent organizations, their financial interests remain inextricably linked together. Even when the IJV is structured as a separate organization (see Figure 5.4 (b)) there is still a residual financial responsibility between the parties as the parent organizations strive to account for their initial start-up investment in the IJV. What is needed is the least imperfect model on which to base a structure of financial objectives.

One method is shown in Figure 5.5. In this model, the parent organizations and the IJV retain the legacy of their financial interdependence but with the distorting effects of transfer pricing, overhead apportionment and creative accounting techniques stripped out. Look how this also accepts the status of the IJV as a separate corporate body with its own accounting system and tax responsibility in its host B-parent country.

A suggested pattern of financial objectives

The problem with financial objectives is that there is no single monetary target or mechanism that will alone ensure the 'success' of the IJV. The following points are worth bearing in mind:

- Many IJVs have few real fixed assets and operate in a condition of 'acid test' technical insolvency;
- IJVs can have healthy liquidity because of their parents' funding but have difficulty in producing a net profit in their balance sheets or vice versa;
- The net present value (NPV) of large IJV projects can be negative, while liquidity is good.

(a) Full funding from parent organizations

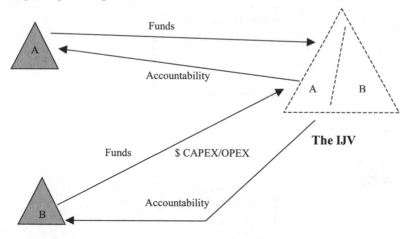

(b) Initial funding only from parent organizations

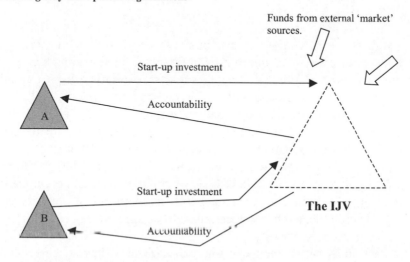

Figure 5.4 IJV funding and accountability

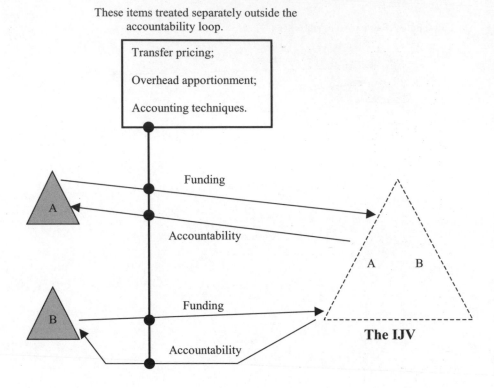

These items treated separately outside the accountability loop.

Transfer pricing;

Overhead apportionment;

Accounting techniques.

A

Funding

Accountability

B

Funding

Accountability

A   B

The IJV

Figure 5.5 IJV funding and accountability: a better method?

These statements apply to any business organization but are particularly relevant to the type of decentralized financial relationships that exist within the structure of an IJV. The fact that the relationships extend across international boundaries, with different financial systems and practices, is sufficient to expose the inadequacy of a single level of financial objectives.

An over-complex structure of financial objectives can be an equally *in*efficient way to manage the performance of an IJV. Figure 5.6 shows ones that are most commonly used, in various combinations and permutations, as a framework for financial behaviour of complex business organizations. Too many used together soon bring paralysis to the most cleverly conceived organization, once it has to face the realities of operating across geographical and cultural boundaries.

As well as this problem of complexity, IJVs also have to suffer the realities of their business life cycle. We saw in Chapter 4 that the IJV's organizational form is, by definition, transient and temporary. All IJVs exhibit this to a greater or lesser degree, irrespective of their type or individual characteristics. This life cycle affects the priority of the financial objectives of an IJV organization

NPV	IRR	ARR
PROFIT	PAYBACK	LIQUIDITY
ACIDTEST	ROS	ROCE
ROI	VALUATION	FFA

ARR = Actual Rate of Return; FFA = Finds Flow Analysis;
IRR = Internal Rate of Returns.

Figure 5.6 The choice of financial objectives – take your pick

throughout its life. An understanding of this life cycle provides the clue to a meaningful system of financial objective. Figure 5.7 shows the situation.

Stage 1: Liquidity objectives

During the early life of the IJV organization, the most important financial objectives are those related to *liquidity*. Once the initial seedcorn revenue funding from the parent organization ceases, most IJVs can expect to face liquidity challenges until their volume of business develops. There are no particular criteria unique to IJVs – the standard liquidity criteria of current ratio, cash flow and 'acid test' are used as a measure. The point at which liquidity starts to recede as a strategic issue is, of course, different for all

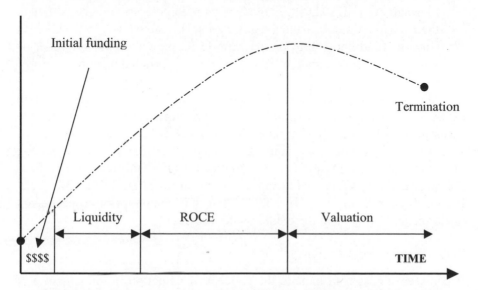

Figure 5.7 Predominant financial objectives during the IJV life cycle

IJVs. It is not unknown for larger ventures to be still experiencing unstable cash flow on a current ratio of less than 1:2 well into their life cycle. Most IJVs will actually have a negative acid test (debtors + cash-current liabilities) ratio over the same period.

Stage 2: ROCE objectives

In adopting ROCE as a guiding financial objective, an IJV is starting to behave like the established and stable organizational form that it no doubt would like to be. ROCE has stood the test of time as a measure of the overall financial health of a business and can be used when the IJV is considered as the type of devolved business entity shown earlier in Figure 5.5. It is subject to a few distortions, however:

- *Equity distortions*: the fact that parent organizations provided the start-up equity for the IJV means that the return on shareholders capital (ROSC) must be considered, as well as ROCE.
- *Tax distortions*: ROCE is traditionally calculated by expressing the profit before long-term debt, interest and taxation, as a proportion of capital employed in the venture. IJVs are typically subject to tax on profits in their host country, under tax regimes which can be rather unpredictable. It is wise to build a margin into the ROCE expectation to allow for unexpected distortions.
- *Leverage distortion*: again, the ROCE calculation traditionally excludes interest payments on debt, hence should be independent of the degree of leverage of the IJV during stage 2 of its life cycle. In practice, although there may be little formal debt, a fledgling IJV often has to set aside cash sums to fund short-term repayments to its parent organizations. This reduces the headline rate of ROCE, if not the formal accounting value.

In addition to these distortions, ROCE suffers from the general malaise of all ratios in being more meaningful as a comparison measure than an absolute assessment of business performance. This causes difficulty in IJV situations where ventures are new and innovative, making comparisons with existing businesses difficult. Despite these limitations, ROCE still provides perhaps the best measure of financial health of an IJV during stage 2 of its life cycle. Figure 5.8 shows some typical published ROCE objectives (and subsequent performance) for IJVs in different business sectors.

Stage 3: Valuation objectives

It can seem unusual to include the concept of valuation in the structure of financial objectives of a business. Some notable IJVs have ended up being

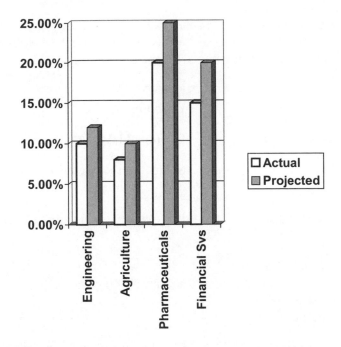

Figure 5.8 Typical IJV ROCE objectives and performance

riddled with insecurity by the mere mention of the venture having to have a financial *valuation* placed upon it. For this reason, IJV managers often feel justified in keeping well clear of the subject – it is just that little bit too uncomfortable. The reality is different. More than 85 per cent of IJVs end up being split up or re-apportioned in some way. This is not necessarily an indication of business failure; rather an acceptance of the necessary structural changes brought about by the natural life cycle of the IJV organizational form. Put bluntly, it means that the endgame of most IJVs is a buyout of the IJV, either by one of the partners or their parent organization. This leaves two options for planning the objectives of an IJV: pretend the end game does not exist; or plan for it.

The first option is the easier – all you have to do is to wait (and prepare to be surprised). The second is simply good management – it makes sense to anticipate the endgame of the IJV life cycle, then plan to make it easier. This is where valuation comes in – the forerunner to the eventual buyout of an IJV is discussion about valuation of the venture to decide how much it is worth.

The mechanism of valuation is difficult – there is no single technique that will guarantee 'the correct' valuation. Figure 5.9 shows the five main ones that can be used – in theory, financial objectives could be centred around any of these. Note the problems that accompany each area. While these problems no doubt weaken the accuracy of each valuation activity, they do little to compromise their validity. A clear set of valuation objectives is essential as an IJV enters the later stages of its life cycle.

Option	Problems
Market capitalization	Unquoted IJVs do not have one
'Book' value	Subject to the unreality of historical cost accounting
Earnings potential	It is always a projection, rather than a fact
Split-level capitalization (using some convenient convention ie by plant area, business unit etc)	Difficulty in finding a mutually acceptable convention
Funding proportion (partners get back what they put in)	Simple but defeatist – the objective of a business is to make profit, not just cover its costs

Figure 5.9 Five possible IJV valuation objectives

CASE STUDY 5.5

Introduction: International Technology Partners IJV

International Technology Partners (ITP Ltd) is a joint venture between a technology licensor from the United States (the A-parent) and an existing manufacturer of consumer goods based in China (the B-parent). The idea is to build A's products in B's manufacturing works for sale to the large and rapidly expanding Far Eastern market. The B-parent already manufactures and sells a range of consumer products but they are of dated design and of poor quality compared to their competitors from Japan, Europe and the United States.

The parent organizations have formed an IJV located in China with the intention of co-operating with each other in all aspects of design, production and management of the joint business.

Financial objectives

'Their financial objectives have the lifespan of your average mayfly', the A-parent IJV project director continued. 'Once they failed to meet the liquidity objectives they tried to argue they were cutting revenue expenditure to shorten the payback period and when that didn't work they started to ring-fence their own assets, presumably to preserve the break-up value – and the IJV has only been in existence six months.'

The financial objectives of International Technology Partners IJV were giving cause for concern. The Chinese B-parent side were having difficulty in disaggregating revenues and expenses for the new extension to their manufacturing plant and had collectively decided that the best way to avoid these new and unforeseen complexities was to ignore them. The concept of liquidity was foreign to them anyway. Payback proved easier to understand – the less you paid out, the shorter time needed to earn back what you had spent, and the better you looked in the eyes of your A-parent partners. The plant director responsible for accounting agreed entirely with this approach and had rationalized the actions to reduce expenditure on the proposed new parts of the product assembly line by selling it internally as a move towards prudence and conservatism. As he put it: 'Prudence has always been a quality of this company and we're not intending to sacrifice this for the sake of satisfying a foreign partner – anyway, all foreign partners are known to be greedy, aren't they?'

What has gone wrong here?

- The overseas (A-parent) partner has not communicated properly the three phase pattern of IJV financial objectives shown in Figure 5.7.
- The B-parent partner has misunderstood the principles behind the early liquidity objectives that it has undertaken because no-one has *taught* them.
- The technology objectives of the IJV (ie improving the product line) has been sacrificed. This is everyone's problem.

The message

This simple scenario illustrates that, despite their apparent clarity, financial objectives can be misconstrued by IJV B-parent partners.

Well-managed IJVs incorporate training programmes to stop this occurring. A-parent partners can also make mistakes by presenting the need for compliance with financial objectives as overriding the importance of co-operation within the IJV. This can be misinterpreted by developing-country partners as greed.

DEVELOPMENT OBJECTIVES

Development objectives are often cast as the softer side of the strategy of an organization. In the context of a well-established organization this has some validity – development is seen as something that an organization does when it doesn't have to worry about its survival or its profits. The situation is a little different for IJVs. The collaborative nature of the IJV form produces an unusually high level of potential for the parties in the IJV to learn from each other. In many cases it will be this complementarity of skills and experience that is one of the driving forces behind the formation of the venture. This fixes *organizational learning* as the predominant development activity in many IJVs.

Organizational learning

The way in which IJV partners learn from each other and their parent organizations has a knock-on effect on the general business performance of the venture. This applies to all three stages of the life cycle shown in Figure 5.7. Organizational learning is therefore a necessity rather than a luxury and is sufficiently important in some types of IJV to be treated as a primary measurement of an IJV's effectiveness. There are two main practical advantages for an IJV in effective learning:

- the IJV becomes properly *flexible* – able to take the actions it wants to;
- knowledge transfer encourages *stability* (an elusive concept in IJVs as we saw in Chapter 4).

Both of these have a positive outcome for the health of the IJV organization. The form of learning particular to the IJV form is twofold: that based on past experience and that to do with business capabilities.

- *Past experience*: IJV parents will have had differing business experiences in their particular field. These will likely be related to all aspects of organizational life, not just the particular business sector in which they operate. The transfer of such experiences is a valuable objective of the new IJV, helping with the integration of the parties.

- *Business capabilities*: The most important areas here are marketing, pricing and supplier-customer relationship. Parent companies in the same market often have surprisingly different ways of operating. The idea of a joint venture is to merge these capabilities to give the resulting organization a much wider view and capability. This starts to exploit the complementarity of the partners – one of the fundamental building blocks of the collaborative relationship.

The process of organizational learning is spread throughout the life cycle of the IJV. Remember that this learning activity is a strategic objective of the organization rather then a series of small and disconnected tactical steps so it needs a bit of planning. The type of learning will change throughout the IJV life cycle but the need for it remains equally valid at all stages. Even in the final termination stage of an IJV there will still be room for mutual learning between the separating parties.

Given that organizational learning is an admissible objective of IJV management, what should it actually consist of? Figure 5.10 shows a general pattern taken from successful IJVs in several business sectors. The overall vehicle of the learning is rotation of management and operational staff (represented at the top of the figure). The subject of the learning is then divided into two classes: that relating to the organizational aspects and structure of the IJV and that to do with cultural aspects. A good system of objectives will always divide the content of the learning process into these two broad classes; there is a danger of confusion if they are linked too closely together.

In summary, organizational learning at group and individual level has an important place in the structure of objectives of an IJV. Within this principle, various types of learning will all have their place – some organizations concentrate on institutionalized arrangements such as courses and training days while others prefer to see learning as a freer exchange of experience and ideas. Management and staff rotation plays a useful part in both methods, and those in-between. It is true that organizational learning can lack the objectivity and clarity of, for instance, the commercial objectives of an IJV. It is best seen as a perhaps slightly 'background' member of the structure of objectives, which doesn't mean it is in any way relegated to second place, merely that it is more difficult to see at a first glance. The most dangerous thing you can do with organizational learning is to ignore it – many IJVs have failed because of poor understanding between the partners of either their ways and practices, or their business and technical skills. The purpose of organizational learning is to stop this happening.

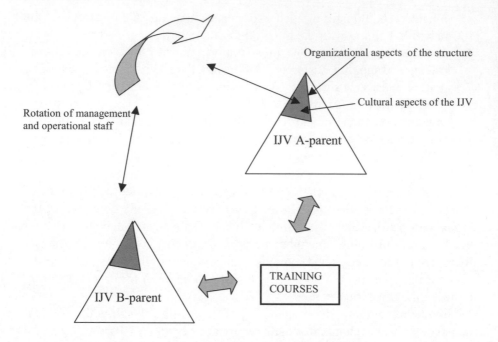

Figure 5.10 A suggested pattern for IJV organizational learning

TECHNOLOGY OBJECTIVES

The strategic behaviour of IJVs normally contains some aspects of technology objectives. Sitting alongside commercial and development objectives discussed earlier, technology objectives are instrumental in the technological positioning of an IJV organization. Technology plays a part in all sectors of businesses, not just for those that are involved in manufacturing. Pure service operations such as finance, communications or sales are often as dependent on technology for their competitive edge as ventures involved in the design and production of complex goods.

The driving force behind the formation of many IJVs is the desire of one party to gain access to technology owned by the other. An IJV can be a convenient vehicle by which to do this in the form of a structured operation that will provide business opportunities to both sets of participants, without the complication and commitment of a full merger. IJVs sometimes evolve from the formalized 'technology transfer agreement' commonplace in some business sectors. In developing countries, the practice of entering a joint venture with a more technologically-advanced partner has become something of a fashion – all have the common objective of getting access to something that could otherwise take them 20 years to develop.

Characteristics of technological objectives

The main point is: *technological objectives (like IJVs themselves) are transient and temporary.* Figure 5.11 shows what happens when two parent organizations combine to set up an IJV based on complementarity of technologies with the position at start-up being one of significant technology 'gap' between the two (or more) parts of the IJV organization. Analysis of the gap reveals that it is comprised mainly of a few large technological differences surrounded by a greater number of areas where the gap in understanding or ability is actually quite small. Once the joint organization starts to operate, the gap starts to close very quickly because the initial rate of learning between specialist partners is always high. The result is that the technology gap will soon eliminate itself, in some cases within the first stage of the IJV life cycle, and almost certainly before the joint organization has managed to achieve financial stability. There is nothing wrong with this (it could even be attributed to 'good management') except for the attendant rush of short-termism – remember that there are two stages of IJV life cycle still remaining.

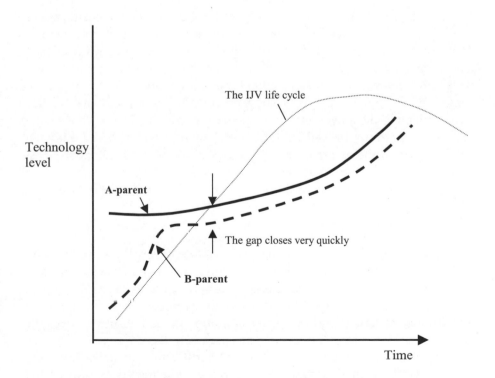

Figure 5.11 The quick closing technology gap between IJV parents

The technology level

There is nothing sacrosanct in the *level* of the technology objectives adopted by an IJV. Although some are centred on overtly high technology products and services, there are probably an equal number that deal in the lower technology end of the spectrum. IJVs based on consumer products, in particular, prefer to concentrate their combined corporate efforts on market access and economies of scale rather than necessarily more advanced product specifications. In contrast, those IJVs involving advanced communication, medical and engineering applications are undeniably high-tech – the heavy cost of R&D is often the driving force behind such collaborative ventures.

The important message is not to *confuse* the level of technology objectives adopted by an IJV. High technology companies do not respond well if pressured into collaboration with a partner whose skills lie in the marketing of low technology commodity goods and vice versa. The level of technology objectives has to be tailored to make it compatible with the partners' technical skills and aspirations, if it is to have any chance of success

Technological portfolios

One popular reason for initiating an IJV is the desire of the dominant partner (see Chapter 4) to diversify the portfolio of technologies under its control. The approach finds favour with consumer-goods based businesses which already have a range of products – the desire for these businesses to diversify fits in well with the developing global market for consumer goods. There have been some notable failures in this field. The problem is basically one of mismatched time-horizons – the longer-term strategic approach to product diversification does not necessarily fit well with the life cycle of a typical IJV. Additional confirmation of this is provided by the quality of the products themselves; products which have been developed to artificially tight timescales (to fit in with the IJV life cycle) can suffer from poor specification, quality or both.

Technical legitimacy

This is where the driving technological objective of an IJV is purely to do with getting a product 'legitimized' in a foreign market. Typical examples are products that have to be registered as compliant with overseas industry standards or directives. While the objective of legitimacy is a valid one, there is a danger in classifying this as a *technology* objective. In practice, the technological input from the host country partner of the IJV is generally very limited, their role becoming instead one of certification or rubber stamping an already developed design. This is better considered as one of the commercial objectives of the IJV, rather than confusing it with genuine technology transfer.

CASE STUDY 5.6

A question of objectives: IJVs vs global sourcing

Large corporations looking for the most cost-effective outsourcing of goods have the choice of either forming some sort of IJV or strategic alliance or following a strategy of straightforward global sourcing. Discussions with managers from global firms produced the following common list of objectives:

- cheaper price (and the chance of spot deals);
- consistent quality;
- lower taxes, duties etc;
- quicker, more responsive deliveries.

Some corporations have entered into IJVs to try to achieve these sourcing objectives while others have returned to the commercial buy–supply relationship but increased its efficiency. For example:

- *General Electric (USA)* uses an Internet trading post network (TPN) to specify components to potential suppliers world wide – a situation of near-perfect competition.
- *Unilever* prefers a limited number of strategic 'partnership' alliances with key suppliers but has not become involved in formal IJVs.
- *Boeing (USA)* has strategic IJVs with several aero-engine manufacturers. This has the effect of reducing risk and is also driven by technology objectives – the complex interaction between the engines and the airframe.

Less technically complex businesses such as clothes suppliers have followed the General Electric model of building a world-wide outsourcing network. One reason for this is the lack of a clear technology objective to drive the formation of an IJV. This adds weight to the argument that commercial development and technology objectives belong together as a set.

Rules for the decision?

There aren't any – at least none that are prescriptive in deciding the 'correct' objectives for all IJVs. In this chapter we have, however, looked at the scope of possible objectives, and seen the way in which they can be structured. The corporate wants of most IJVs can be divided broadly into the three categories of commercial, development and technology objectives. The important thing is to fit them all together in a coherent way and to make sure that they stay outward looking. Many IJVs have experienced the problems of internal conflict that result if corporate objectives are too internally focused, rather than being firmly referenced to the business world *outside* the organizational system. The end result is poor performance and a much-shortened IJV life cycle. This is so well proven as to be almost a business *law*.

SUMMARY

Many IJVs lack firm objectives. The best ones have objectives which are outward-looking. There are three generic types to consider: commercial objectives, development objectives and technology objectives.

Commercial objectives

These are:

- the search for legitimacy;
- value creation;
- risk sharing;
- economies of scale;
- pure financial targets (normally divided into three stages).

Financial objectives are the most complicated because of the links between funding and accountability to the IJV's parent organizations.

Development objectives

Developments objectives are often seen as the softer parts of IJV strategy. The main one is organizational learning; about the organizational aspects of the IJV structure, and cultural aspects of the IJV.

Technology objectives

These are an important influence on the technological positioning of the IJV organization. Technological objective (like IJVs themselves) are transient and temporary because organizations learn quickly which soon closes any technology 'gaps' between the IJV partners.

Chapter 6

Structure

ORGANIZATIONAL STRUCTURE: WHAT IS IT?

Try these quotes:

1. '"Structure" includes the allocation of formal responsibilities –
   the typical organization chart' (Handy, 1987).
2. 'Managers asked to describe their organizations usually respond
   by drawing an organization chart, thereby attempting to map
   out its structure' (Johnson and Scholes, 1984).

So, do they apply to IJVs?

It is easy to think that designing the structure of an IJV is simply a matter of
deciding the general form that it will take (from the options in chapter 4) and
then drawing up an organization chart or 'organogram' in an attempt to transfer
the ideas onto paper. The traditional notion is that this is sufficient to show
the form of an organization both to those that will work within it and those
whose role it is to view it from somewhere outside. This is fine – no doubt
thousands of IJVs have started like this, as a collection of boxes soaked in a
well-defined, but largely hidden, atmosphere of hierarchy. Figure 6.1 shows
a typical example, in this case for a single-location transplant IJV.

Consider what happens, however, when the various staff and resources are
in place and the IJV starts to operate. Questions arise about how the venture
should be operating, its values, and the solutions to its day-to-day management
problems. Disputes about strategy and direction get passed up the organization
tree, reverberating around the management levels. This is a common enough
occurrence in any organization, but its worst effects are seen when the
management is composed of a mixture of people from different parent
companies.

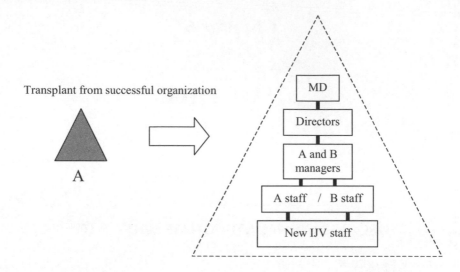

Figure 6.1 IJV structure: the traditional view

It should be clear by now that the traditional organogram is weak in describing the way that a complex organizational form such as an IJV actually works. It can often seem that its main function is to show where to apportion blame when something goes wrong – it can even be argued that this is its *only* function. The organization chart certainly contributes little of strategic significance, and not much in the way of operational help either. This does not mean that IJVs are destined to exist in a state of management anarchy, simply that the risk is always there, if the managers do not have a better way of understanding and visualizing what is going on. One way to help this understanding is by thinking of the structure of IJVs on a conceptual level, ie *thinking about the conceptual structure of an IJV can help you understand the real thing*. This may be a slightly different connotation of the word 'structure' than you have used before. By *structure*, it infers all the parts and linkage that make up the separate working organization that we have called 'IJV' – a far different concept from the parade of staff and managers assembled neatly into the organization chart. This is worth repeating, for the sake of good order: *the structure is not the organization chart*.

THE IDEA OF IJV STRUCTURE

The easiest way to assemble a conceptual structure that we can use to understand a complex IJV is to start with those things that we already know about IJVs. We have seen that they are:

- full of problems for managers (you);
- a transitional form of organization;
- unstable;
- always reaching for *viability* (from Chapter 4).

The key characteristic here is the final one – the quest of every IJV to attain a separate and continued existence of its own – to be viable. The nature of viability means that, to attain it, an organization (or a part of one) must itself possess all the bits and pieces that it needs to support itself because no-one outside the viability-seeking unit is likely to come along and provide them. This means that an IJV has to be a system. It also has to act like a system and regulate itself in system-like ways if it is to survive. Hence the structure (which is not represented by the organization chart, remember) is *the system* – the assembly of activities, responsibilities and communications which gives the organization its function.

So what does an IJV system look like? Figure 6.2 shows what it does *not* look like – a random collection of bits of structure. Interestingly, there is nothing wrong with the content of the various boxes and circles, it is the way in which they are linked together that is poor. A diagram like this has little practical use in helping you to understand the workings of an organization, and even less value when it comes to the job of managing it. Where do we go from here? The answer lies with the concept of 'systems thinking'. This is a way of representing the structure of a complex organization by a series of heavily simplified system diagrams. Its job is to attenuate the complexity that all organizations have to the point where it ceases to act as a barrier to comprehension. The act of thinking of an IJV in terms of system diagrams is not alone going to change its organization, but it can help you *understand* it. Changes come later; do you really think you can make desirable changes to an organization if you don't understand it?

All we have to do now is to decide what the system for an IJV looks like. The remainder of this chapter shows an approach to simplified systems thinking about IJVs. The method is not particularly new, but is one which has proved its effectiveness in many business situations since its inception in the late 1960s. It revolves around the central tenet of viability and the broad form of system diagram shown in Figure 6.3.

THE 'VIABLE' ORGANIZATION

We have set our standard that the organizational form to be called 'IJV' has to have the property of viability. To be viable it needs to be able to manage itself, solve its own internal problems and above all, survive the rigours of

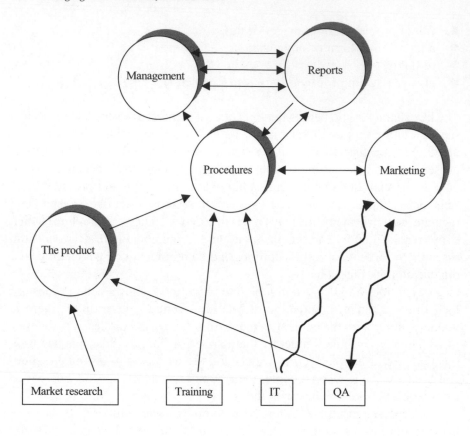

Figure 6.2 A poor attempt at an organizational system diagram

the business world. We have seen also (in Figure 6.3) the rough shape of the system that we will use to describe this organization, and help us to improve it. To be able to illustrate this properly it is necessary to look at a small group of basic concepts that underlie the construction of the viable organization system diagram. There are four of these: system levels, autonomy, control and the resource bargain (see Figure 6.4).

System levels

Systems do not stand alone in the world, even the conceptual world of systems thinking. The smallest and simplest business venture has links with its parent company and, in a wider sense, with the commercial market system that it serves. All organizations, everywhere, are like this. Think of the legal system, or transport system, or a supermarket, and you will find that they are all

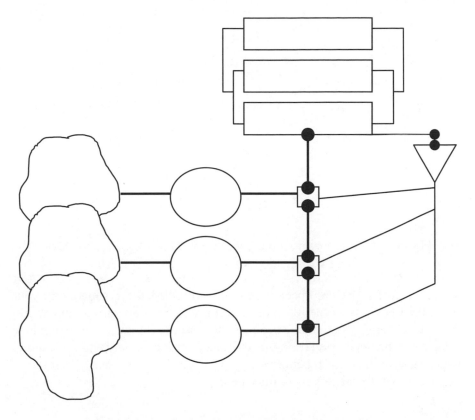

Figure 6.3 An IJV 'viable' system: a blank model

interlinked with other organizational systems around them. We can express this as a general rule: *all systems contain, and are contained within, other systems.*

Given that the business world (both conceptual and real) is full of all these nested systems, how is it possible to comprehend what is going on – are we not complicating things by the systems-thinking approach? The answer lies with the concept of the *system in focus*. This involves concentrating on a single level of system, working with and making observations within that level, while keeping clearly in mind where your system at this level ends, and the next nested level begins. Figure 6.5 shows a simplified example for a rail transport IJV and should hopefully clarify the situation. Be careful not to confuse the idea of system level with that of hierarchy in an organization – it is not always the same. Figure 6.5 shows this; look how the system in focus S_f (in this case the train operation) does not necessarily contain the ordered management hierarchy that its managers would probably tell you was a vital feature of that system. You can also see the need to identify separately each

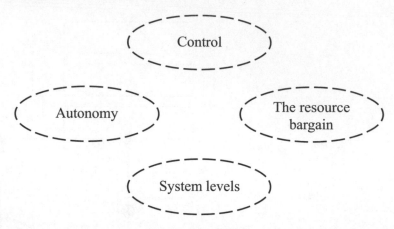

Figure 6.4 The four concepts behind the IJV viable system design

system-in-focus. It would become interminably difficult to separate in your mind the functions of the railtrack operator and train operating companies, from the general system that surrounds them whose purpose it is to organize things, sell the tickets and bank the revenue. Everyone would end up blaming everyone else. It is much better to keep a system-in-focus clearly in mind, if you want to understand how to manage it.

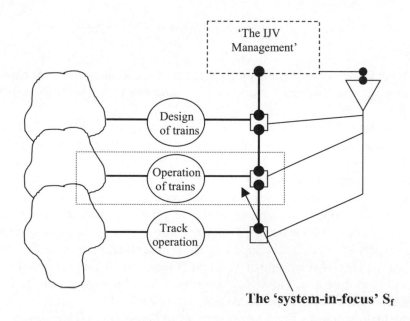

Figure 6.5 The idea of system levels for a railway transport IJV

Autonomy

Autonomy is a term which is used loosely in organizations. It is easy for almost any group, branch or department, given a bit of freedom in the way it does things, to proclaim itself as autonomous. The fashion for autonomy is an identifiable business trend, ranking along with those in Chapter 2. The result is that the real nature of autonomy is easily misunderstood. True autonomy is to do with the capability of a piece of an organization system to do two things:

- be the actual *producer* of one of the goods or services that is generated by the system;
- be capable of organising production *itself* without day-to-day help from other bits of the system.

The main criteria of these two is the first; this limits the property of autonomy to the parts of the system that 'produce the goods to sell'. Note how it does not include various other bits of the system such as support services, administration, IT departments and such like that are necessary to make the system work. This also includes management; this and the other support functions are *facilitators* rather than producers, and so cannot meet the requirements for being defined as purely autonomous. This doesn't mean that they can't think they are, or stop them wanting to be. Figure 6.6 picks out the autonomous parts of the railway business in Figure 6.5, and how they are separated (conceptually) from the other facilitator parts.

Control

You can think of control simply as control, or as control and co-ordination, but somewhere along the line it infers the activity of management of the system. Whereas the autonomous 'producing' parts of a system make it what it is, it is the task of the non-producing parts to help the producers work together. This overall role of facilitation can be conveniently lumped together under the general heading of control or, more specifically, control links (as yet unspecified) joining the parts of the system together, enabling them to have a relationship with each other. Don't infer anything yet from the large dotted box in Figures 6.5 and 6.6 called 'management', or even what might be inside it. Accept, for the moment, that there has to be a management function, of some sort, and that it has control (plus monitoring if you prefer) links with the autonomous producers and their facilitators.

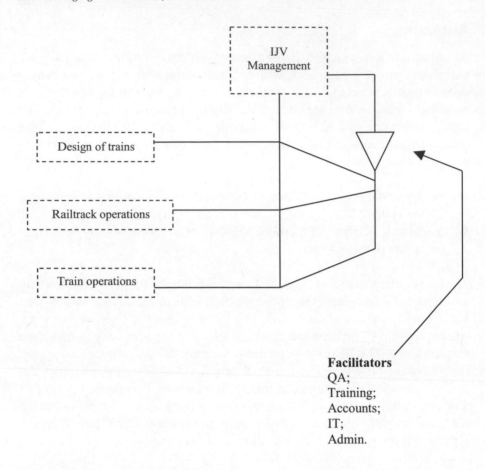

Figure 6.6 The autonomous parts of Figure 6.5 and their facilitators

The resource bargain

The idea of a resource bargain fits well into IJVs and similar system structures that have a high level of interdependency. The resource bargain is a systems thinking way of describing what happens along the control link between any two parts of the system. These links are present in all the system figures shown earlier in this chapter; Figure 6.7 shows the situation. Because all linked parts of a system are interdependent (or they wouldn't be there), all have an interest in helping each other to achieve their mutual aims within the system. The resulting co-operation takes the form of a *bargain*, with each trading its own resources (cash, time expertise, etc) for those it desires from the other party. You can think of this as a flow of resources along the link in both directions. This has the secondary effect of keeping the link stable (remember the ever-present quest for stability?) and hence squeezing the organizational system into a form of equilibrium. Now for the key question: *what happens if the linked parts disagree over the resource bargain?* The answer is this – the equilibrium forms anyway, but not in such an efficient or effective way. This means that the system-in-focus will not be so efficient; its producers will waste their time arguing between themselves, with their own system-level facilitators, and likely with other levels of the system as well. The result is a system which is full of internal conflict, which seems to expend most of its energies in fighting itself. For system read organization – how many times have you seen this? Designing good resource bargains is therefore a way of helping a system operate efficiently, making sure that its parts work well together; allowing the producers to produce and the facilitators to facilitate.

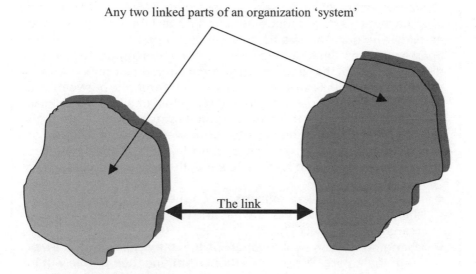

This link is a 'resource bargain' comprising a mutual transfer of resources, time, attention, commitment, responsibility and assistance in organizational tasks.

Figure 6.7 The resource bargain

These four concepts of system levels, autonomy, control and the resource bargain are the building blocks of the viable organization system diagram. It is easy to dismiss them as mere conceptual tools with little relevance to the real world of organizations but they have proved their usefulness time and time again in helping solve problems of IJV organization design. It is only necessary to look around at the IJVs that seem to be in perpetual conflict, or are mediocre financial performers, to conclude that maybe they weren't designed with any forethought at all. The conceptual tools of system thinking are powerful allies when it comes to sorting out structural problems in complex organizations. With this in mind the next step is to move on to apply these principles to the specific question of the structure and organization of IJVs. We need to start to *use* them.

CASE STUDY 6.1

Resource bargains in difficult relationships: R & D-based IJVs

IJVs between R & D-intensive businesses run the risk of being a structural victim of their own success. One US/Asian IJV in the pharmaceuticals sector made outstanding technical discoveries in its early life, only to have its success act to pull the IJV structure apart as each parent fought for their share of the 'rights' to the new discoveries. All of the senior management attention became focused on one or two links in the system of agreements between the partners while most of the 'resource bargains' of all the other links necessary to maintain the organizational system were left to their own devices. Some continued to work well but others grew, or shrank, to the point where the system became unbalanced. The situation was recovered by three clear actions:

- relieving several key managers completely of involvement in the discussions over who owned the new discoveries – to avoid management 'overkill';
- changing the physical location of the same discussions away from the A-parent's premises (hence limiting their profile within the organization);
- implementing the two actions above *by design*, rather than by default, before the situation became too serious.

THE VIABLE IJV

The viable form of IJV has been developed in several sectors of IJV activity over the past 15 years. The model is entirely general in that it applies to all types and structures. Its strength lies in the guiding principles involved, rather than compliance with the minutiae of every individual IJV deal. The prevailing corporate cultures (and indeed national cultures) of the parties involved will have some effect on the form the system takes but fortunately this does not have too much constraining effect at the systems-thinking level. A good viable system design can actually reduce the unsettling effects of corporate cultural differences – an indication of the power of the systems thinking approach. In developing the IJV model we will be approaching from the viewpoint that the system structure of an IJV can be *designed*, rather than have to happen by chance. This design is not somehow preconceived, it comes from those that commission and manage the venture whose interests and careers are entwined with it. This means: *the designer is YOU*. Try to develop an easy familiarity with that statement.

DEFINING THE SYSTEM LEVEL

This is easy for an IJV. Figure 6.8 shows the three main system levels of interest – these are nested and three-dimensional, not linear or necessarily hierarchical. The levels are:

- *The system-in-focus* is the IJV, ie the separately identified legal entity containing the parts that the parent organizations have handed over to provide exclusive input to the business activities of the new venture. It also includes the management of the IJV organization. Under the conditions set earlier this IJV system-in-focus contains all the autonomous and facilitation parts needed to enable the IJV to produce its commercial output. We will call this system S_f (f for focus).
- *System h (S_h)* is that system existing at the next level up from S_f; h means 'higher' because S_f is contained within S_h to fulfil the idea of nesting introduced earlier. The main constituents of S_h are the parent organizations that spawned the IJV. While not directly involved in the day-to-day management of the IJV they probably retain a role in monitoring its financial performance. They nearly always control the capital investment resources of the IJV and sometimes the revenue expenses as well.
- *System p (S_p)* are the 'doing' subsystems of our system-in-focus (S_f). Because of the co-operative ethos of IJV, any lower nested system is going to contain various bits of organization that come from the parent organizations – part of the reason why there is more than one sub-system at this level. At their own level, these S_p sub-systems also exhibit full system characteristics, ie they have the capability to manage and regulate themselves, albeit that their activities, being almost purely production-orientated contain less complexity than at higher system levels. The managers of S_p units would of course be unlikely to agree, because they see the full complexity of their activities and know less about what happens at higher levels in the organization.

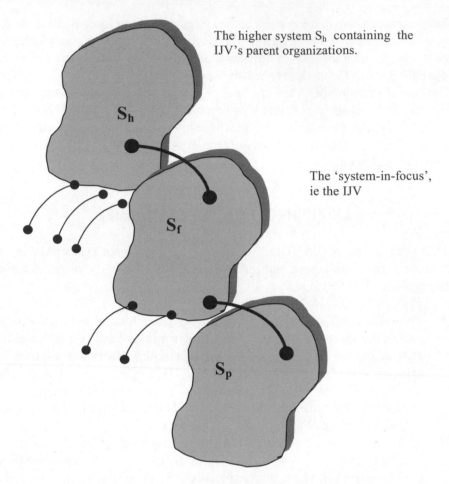

The higher system S_h containing the IJV's parent organizations.

The 'system-in-focus', ie the IJV

The 'autonomous producers' S_p that make up the S_f

Figure 6.8 The three system levels of interest

Identification of these three system levels is clear enough, but what about their character – what do they look like? Are they the same, or different? We can approach the answer by considering the hereditary nature of IJVs. It is in general only fairly successful parent organizations that can afford to spawn IJVs. You could also expect successful parents to want to transfer their skills to their IJV offspring systems – to try to replicate themselves in another organizational disguise. This leads to another key observation: *the character of an IJV system replicates itself 'down' the different system levels*. This is important enough to warrant classification as one of the key success criteria of IJVs. Good IJV management is about *helping* the system design to replicate itself between the levels rather then constraining it from doing so. Don't confuse this with transferring management styles, staff structures or bits of paper called procedures (or something similar). The subject is system design, a set of mental constructs at system level, not pieces of paper, however valuable they are perceived to be.

CASE STUDY 6.2

Replication of system character: automotive transplant IJVs

Transplant IJVs in the automotive industry provide a good example of system replication. The automotive industry is a complex, but predictable, system of vehicle assemblers and their first, second and third-tier suppliers of component parts. In successful IJVs such as Japanese/US ventures, the systemic character of the business transplants (into the United States) has been replicated in the tiers of suppliers to the point where all parts of the supply chain resemble smaller or larger versions of each other in areas such as personnel practices, quality assurance and customer service. Automotive IJVs from other parent countries that have not managed to match this natural tendency of systems to replicate themselves on different levels have had more business problems than those who have.

The autonomous producers (S_p)

The autonomous 'producing' parts can be harder to sort out in an IJV than in single-parent, more unitary companies. This is because of the always present potential for complexity, in all its forms, that results from joining organizations and their commercial output together. Put in simple terms, the system-in-focus (S_f) is big and complicated. A lot depends on the nature of the commercial product of the IJV. A combined organization with multiple products or services will have a larger number of naturally autonomous producers than, for instance an IJV commissioned to deal in a single or straightforward product. This also has implications for the identification of the autonomous parts of the system – there is no guarantee that they will be the same in different IJVs. It is common, for example, for the sales function in one IJV to exhibit natural autonomy while in another you would be correct in classifying it as a facilitator and a weak one at that. Don't worry too much about this possible crisis of identity: accurate identification of autonomy can become second nature, with a little practice.

There is one constant fact – the designation of truly autonomous areas is *independent* of the relative size or strengths of the IJV's parent organizations. It is the product that designates them, not the collection of people and practices that make it. It is a sad fact that many IJVs with a good product and strong management have failed because of the strength of that management being used to worst effect by designating the wrong bits of the venture as warranting autonomy. The result is confusion, followed closely by failure.

Figure 6.9 shows the designation of autonomy for two common IJV formats. Note the different numbers of autonomous areas in each and how 'sales' is a facilitator in example (a) but an autonomous sub-system in itself in example (b). The difference is in the nature of the IJV's product: in (a) the purpose of the IJV is to manufacture better products rather than introduce a new method of selling, while in (b) the act of selling a large infrastructure project is dependent upon the organization and technical competence of the IJV, hence it warrants its own 'system' within the IJV. This demonstrates how the nature of an IJV's product can affect the internal structure that it needs to be viable. Now attempt this question about Figure 6.9: what do you think would happen to any of the IJVs in the figure if you got the designation of autonomy *wrong*?

It is unlikely that the venture would crumble overnight, because, as we know from our system thinking earlier in this chapter, a certain amount of self-balancing would occur as the system tries to return to its natural form. Organization systems do try to repair themselves – they *want* to be viable, in order to survive. The answer is, of course: *INTERNAL CONFLICT*.

Get the autonomy wrong and all the sub-systems start to oscillate and argue with each other – almost any subject will do, as long as it is something remotely to do with the IJV's business operations. Welcome to the world of IJV internal arguments.

Now look at Figure 6.10 as we start to develop the IJV-specific detail for the rough viable organization system model started in Figure 6.3. The first stage of this development is shown using the 'International Technology Partners' case study example of 'simple design and manufacturing' IJV structure. This type is typical of many IJVs between mature industrialized and developing countries. Note the key points:

- Only the activities of design and manufacturing are designated the autonomous (S_p) parts of the system-in-focus (S_f). The design activity relies on the *application* of technology, so technology does not warrant an autonomous designation for itself.
- Design and manufacture possess equal status in the IJV. There is no suggestion that either is senior to the other, or somehow enjoys more attention or privileges within the hierarchy (in fact, there isn't a hierarchy yet).

Example (a) A technology transfer IJV for manufactured goods

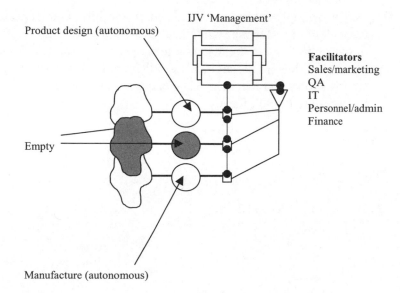

Example (b) An IJV consortium for the design and building of infrastructure projects (roads and airports)

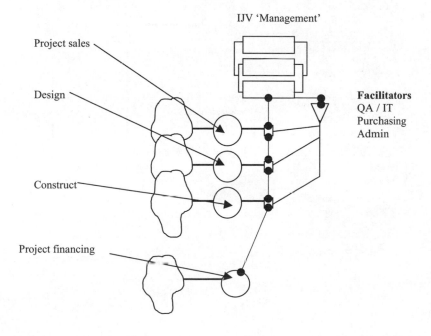

Figure 6.9 Typical designations of autonomous sub-systems S_p in IJVs

- The design and manufacturing subsystems operate on the *horizontal* 'autonomy' axis of the system-in-focus diagram.
- Design and manufacturing are joined by the link A–B, representing the technology transfer-type agreement as formal recognition of the transfer of the technology to the manufacturing partner of the IJV. The existence of this link has no hierarchical significance in this system diagram – it simply shows that there is a technical contract agreement in force, if you know where to look for it.

The IJV 'system-in-focus' S_f

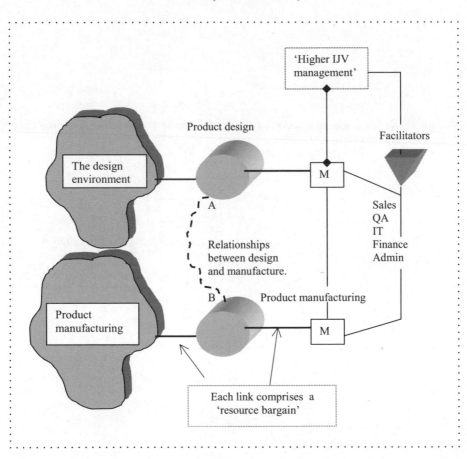

Figure 6.10 International Technology Partners IJV: developing the viable system diagram

The common feature of the autonomous (S_p) parts is their format. As well as being horizontal, each has its own 'management' (shown as the small square) separated from its producing 'operations', all of which are contained within the ellipse. Similarly, the operations are shown separate from the environment or market to which they provide those operations. Despite its conceptual nature, this system diagram takes account of the inherent problems of an IJV-type structure. A consequence of splitting the activities of design and manufacture is that they will disagree with each other as part of their day-to-day interaction within the larger system (S_f) of which they both form a part. This will happen even if they both deserve and want their autonomy – because they have to interact as each provides its own input towards the production of the finished product. This phenomenon is known in systems thinking terms as *oscillation* of the producing sub-systems.

Now we know that while the design and manufacturing sub-systems might work well in the developing system there is no guarantee that they will work well *together*. This simple statement is part of the reason why IJVs often prove to be unstable. There is no way to prevent these oscillations happening – the complexity of the interdependence between design and manufacturing will always produce more areas of conflict that can be counteracted by procedures, persuasion or managerial edict. The answer lies in the concept of *damping* – imposing constraint on the oscillations to keep them under control. The next question is: how?

Higher IJV management

Look at the large dotted box in Figure 6.10 identified only as 'higher IJV management'. Doesn't this represent the general idea of management – people and procedures that are seen to be in charge, and whose role is to organise and motivate the people and systems beneath them? There is only one thing wrong with this: *'HIGHER MANAGEMENT' ARE NOT VIABLE ON THEIR OWN*. We know this because, if they were, they would be shown as one of the autonomous horizontal areas in Figure 6.10. Nor can management control the sub-systems for which they are responsible, because of their complexity, and that of the interactions between them. These surprisingly simple conclusions place a huge burden on those that occupy that dotted box. Figure 6.11 shows the content, in systems thinking terms, of the IJV higher management dotted box. Note the three main functions:

- *Control function*: Its job is to pull the (weak) threads of control to stop the horizontal autonomous subsystems (S_p) oscillating with each other. It is concerned only with what is happening inside the IJV system. The purpose of the control function is to achieve as much stability as it can.

- *Change agent*: This is almost the opposite. The purpose of the change agent is to implement necessary changes within the IJV. It needs to do this, because the system has to change and develop in order to remain viable, and therefore survive. To fulfil its role, the change agent needs to draw information from what is happening *outside* its system-in-focus, feeding the resulting change ideas back into the system, down to the producing areas.
- *Policy*: The term 'policy' fits well with traditional management thinking, seeing the higher management as a function whose job it is to make policy and then somehow persuade those below to go and do it. Under systems thinking, the policy duty of higher management is an anti-oscillation role. Its job is to damp out the disagreements between its own change agent and control functions.

The 'higher IJV management' box in Figure 6.10

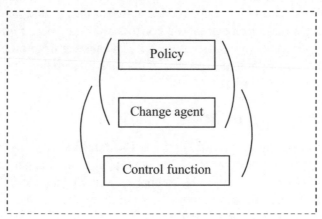

Figure 6.11 Higher IJV management – what is it?

A careful look at Figure 6.11 should suggest that all of the three functions of the higher management dotted box cannot be combined into a single role given to an 'IJV manager' or similar. The nature of the roles means that they can only be fulfilled if their responsibility is shared, with a mixture of representation from the IJV's existing parent organizations and the internal structure of the IJV operation itself. Oscillation between the autonomous (S_p) systems is damped by the existence of the higher management box, while the contents of this box are themselves subject to internal damping by the existence of the policy function contained as part of it. We have a built-in internally self-stabilizing mini-system – one which can reap the benefits of technical freedom for the autonomous design and manufacturing activities but without the risk of oscillating itself to death in the process. In a design and manufacturing IJV, the management issues covered by the contents of the dotted box are:

- resourcing of the IJV;
- monitoring customers' changing requirements;
- product variations;
- the production schedule;
- financial targets and investment criteria.

You can soon recognize these as issues which, left uncontrolled, have caused the downfall of many IJVs, merely because they were not addressed at the correct system level. This is a common problem; how many times have you seen these types of issue left to be solved down at the S_p level, or conversely, rebounding around at even higher system levels (IJV parent organizations' Board levels perhaps) causing all manner of interference and internal strife?

CASE STUDY 6.3

Warning: devolved IJV strategy

The desire to appear impressive in the eyes of investors and holding company management can lead senior managers to 'invent' profits. The pressures to show rising profits in the limited time frame of a mining IJV were so great for the managers of a silver mine in Russia that the IJV board apparently decided to invent them.

The A-parent had announced from its Dutch headquarters that its 10 year mining IJV had broken even in its second year of operation and showed an IRR of 12 per cent in its third, outstripping expectation. To avoid upsetting the previously agreed financial return structure, however, A announced that dividends would be maintained below the projected level, to allow extra revenue to be recycled into 'consolidation of the situation underground', thereby ensuring the longer-term viability of the mine.

Three months later a further announcement from Holland confirmed that two of the local B-parent and one A-parent member of the IJV board had been released for other duties following discovery that the mine had over-reported profits by $US 12 million. There were in fact, no profits at all; the retained dividend premium

---

being needed to fund escalating revenue costs to replace plant inherited from the (previously bankrupt) B-parent state mining company which was falling to pieces.

The message

Although an extreme case, this highlights a potential problem when an A-parent's IJV strategy includes devolving too much responsibility to a new entity IJV in a post-communist developing country. Reports on the state of B-parent assets at the IJV negotiation stage may not concur with the reality discovered later. Financial pressures then mount on the IJV board to convince the A-parent investor that 'they are doing well'. The absence of a good financial control system allows local A-parent IJV management to continue the self-delusion until pressure for further cash injection brings the real lack of profitability into focus. It is almost never in the B-parent's interest to destroy illusions like this – remember that much of their corporate strategy before the IJV was probably *based* on illusion.

And the systems viewpoint?

This is basically a problem of the capability of a sub-system to accept autonomy that is handed to it. To be able to survive within the IJV system, each autonomous (S_p) sub-system must be capable of regulating *itself* (one of the definitions of true autonomy). In this case the historical central planning ethos of the B-parent part of the mine management encouraged this part of the system to delude itself that it was operating correctly. The higher system of IJV management left the control channel a little too weak, allowing the financial problem to grow. From a systems design viewpoint, the solution would have been to reinforce the early warning financial monitoring on the mine's management so the problem could be resolved sooner.

REGULATION

Having agreed the existence of the control function of IJV management, how is this control exercised? We are beginning to move outside the pure world of systems thinking here, starting to home in on the more traditional concept of management *style*. IJVs, by definition, involve people and systems that can be culturally very different, so the question of a suitable style with which to manage the combined organization is important. Despite the wide variety of styles that could be adopted, the issue of management style can be reduced neatly to the situation depicted in Figure 6.12 with the straight question about the amount of command that will be exercised (on the vertical axis of our system diagram). Figure 6.12 (a) shows strong command, involving lots of procedures, quality targets and deadlines – the managers of such an arrangement probably consider themselves 'firm but fair'. Figure 6.12 (b) reflects a more democratic and relaxed approach – terms such as 'hands off management' or 'minimum intervention' abound in such cases. It may even look as if there is a certain amount of *vertical* autonomy in the system, trying to match that which exists in the horizontal direction. Which of these gives the best results? Here is one view of the answer: *NEITHER OF THESE WORK WELL* because *BOTH CAUSE MORE PROBLEMS THAN THEY SOLVE*.

The reason for this is that both the approaches miss the point of the role of the dotted higher management box. They see it as *part of* the 'producing' system rather than as an anti-oscillation service to it. Any attempt to *control* the activities of the autonomous design and manufacturing sub-systems will erode their autonomy, and so start to dismantle the very structure that the whole system needs to maintain its viability. The system will start to fall apart.

A better alternative is to think of the action of the control function as a mechanism of *regulation*. It is by regulating the behaviour of the sub-systems that the IJV higher management can damp out the destructive oscillations, thereby helping the system to survive. The ideas of regulation provide a convenient home for those organizational functions that have not already been lodged in either the autonomous producing areas or the higher management box. They have to *have* a home, because it is clear that they exist, and so have to fit in somewhere. The ones common to most organizations are:

- technical specialisms;
- the personnel function;
- quality assurance;
- health and safety;
- budgeting and accounting;
- general administration.

The main plea heard from these functions is that they feel important enough to be autonomous in themselves. This is little more than an attempt to gain more organizational freedom. With this in mind, you can see that to grant full autonomy to any of these functions will upset the viable system structure; its effect will be to introduce organizational conflict centred around who is

Example (a) Strong and direct management control

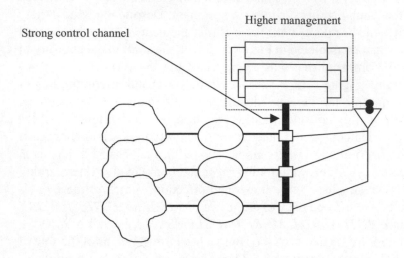

Strong control channel

Higher management

Example (b) Weak management control

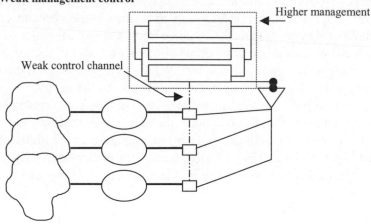

Weak control channel

Higher management

Figure 6.12 Strong vs weak management control

allowed to have autonomy, and why, and who is not. Welcome again to the spectre of oscillation and conflict, and the crumbling of the system's viability. The binding energy of any IJV system lies in the differentiation between those parts of the assembled system that are properly autonomous and those that are naturally facilitators and regulators. You have to *design* the system that way, to fit in with the pattern that will make it work, rather than encourage it to dissolve into internal conflict. This can save you (as a manager) lots of trouble. The facilitator (or regulator) functions fit neatly into the inverted triangles of the previous system diagrams. They are 'owned' by the control part of the higher management box but only implemented outside of the direct management control links with the autonomous sub-systems. It is this *indirect* application of the regulators' power that is the key to their success – it enables them to regulate without threatening the autonomy of the sub-systems and the attendant conflict and disputes. We will look at the mechanism of indirect control in more detail in the next chapter.

CASE STUDY 6.4

Banking IJVs: the slow matrix

To control their portfolio of complex cross-border financial activities, some Western–Eastern European IJVs in banking and financial services sectors adopted a matrix structure. This allowed for joint responsibility: the Western Europe A-parent bank provided the financial systems and hardware and the Eastern European B-parent small branch network and local borrower/investor contacts. The idea was to maintain 'local' investment while capitalizing on corporate strengths. For example, if a manager of a local branch wanted to develop an interest structure for agriculture loans the matrix required him to do this in consultation with loan sector advisers in the A-parent partner in London. The rationale was that while the local manager might know the local market, only the A-parent's management would see whether agricultural loans fitted into the model of loan portfolio that the accounting and recovery systems were being installed to handle.

Initially this structure worked well, but a drop in loan income soon caused the IJV board to question the suitability of the structure. A strategic review report stated that while the matrix structure was useful in providing constructive criticism it was causing operational inefficiencies in that management became slow in responding to problems. Various control systems were installed, but the basic matrix structure remained. Corporate planning benefited from the matrix because it brought the strategies of the two IJV partners together. Marketing and lending decisions however, were the opposite – the division of responsibility between the A and B parents was continually unclear and cultural differences and misinter-pretation came along to fill in the gaps in mutual understanding about who was in charge. The situation was illustrated by one newly appointed regional manager in Bulgaria:

We see the problems associated with lack of direction on loan decisions here. We feel at a disadvantage not being responsible for our own lending decisions above $US 2000 – we have people trying to sell these loans which get continually delayed or vetoed by a manager in London who has only been to Bulgaria once. We keep losing potential customers, but are still expected to contribute the agreed percentage of the IJV profits.

She continued: 'The problem is that the matrix is slow – we need quick decisions to be able to respond in a competitive and turbulent market. At the moment we're having to spend an extra 25 per cent on advertising, just to keep up the flow of loan enquiries to replace the potential customers that get tired of waiting and go elsewhere!'

The messages

- Matrix management is *slow*.
- IJVs do not suit slow decisions because of the type of emerging, competitive market in which they operate.
- Good IJV management is about constructing a careful balance between speed and thoroughness in the joint management system.

And the systems viewpoint?

In systems thinking terms, matrix management does little to encourage the property of *viability* in an organizational system. In this case study there is confusion over which parts of the business warrant autonomy and which parts are there to act as regulators. The design of the system has been clouded by the overplayed importance of the A-parent 'corporate planning' department. The mistake is in allowing corporate planning to attain the status of an autonomous 'producer' sub-system, exercising the various relationships with higher levels of the system that accompany this status. In this type of IJV, corporate planning is better considered as a facilitator, with its strengths in exercising indirect control over the B-parent network. This way it adds to the viability of the system by preventing oscillations and conflict, rather than causing them.

SUMMARY

This chapter started with the broad statement that decisions relating to the structure of an IJV are basically about the organizational form that the IJV will take. From our initial assertion that the traditional 'organization chart' approach is ineffective in describing the way in which an organization actually works we have progressed through simple elements of systems thinking to the assembled viable IJV model shown in Figure 6.13. So what? For companies and managers steeped in the practice of straight hierarchical thinking this systems approach can be difficult to grasp. There is little doubt that, while it does not exclude the relevance of hierarchy in a joint organization, it subordinates it to a lower level of importance, preferring the terminology of autonomy, facilitation and regulation to try to describe what is happening in the dynamics of a complex IJV.

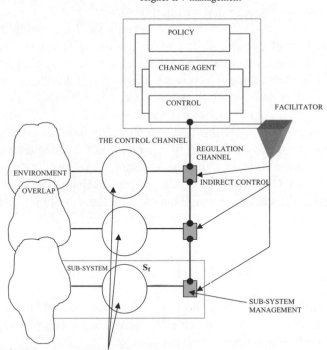

'Higher IJV management'

POLICY

CHANGE AGENT

CONTROL

FACILITATOR

THE CONTROL CHANNEL

REGULATION CHANNEL

ENVIRONMENT

OVERLAP

INDIRECT CONTROL

SUB-SYSTEM S_f

SUB-SYSTEM MANAGEMENT

AUTONOMOUS 'PRODUCING' PARTS OF THE ORGANIZATION

Notes: *All links are really 'resource bargains'*
There is no hierarchy inferred within the system – it needs all its component parts equally in order to be viable and survive

Figure 6.13 The assembled IJV viable system model

Ideological differences apart, there can be little doubt that organizations *do* work as systems. Casual observation of the smallest, or the largest, business organization will show the self-division into autonomous sub-systems, and the existence of functions that facilitate and regulate parts of the larger system of which they are a part. It is unlikely that they will be named in such system terms, but their actions will fit the general systems pattern. You can think of the system operation as being the limiting case of what a viable organization actually does – an idealized picture of the business in its dynamic state.

Systems thinking represents a change of plane from the usual micro-politics of management interaction within an IJV. Too many IJVs have allowed their strategic direction and hard cash to drift away while preoccupied with minor internal battles between the partners' management, polarized as they always are in IJVs by differences in management culture and style. This is why they fail. Systems thinking is one way to help solve this kind of problem. Its only purpose is to be useful in understanding how an IJV organization works, and so enable you to have discussions about it, make changes, and generally design the organization in the way that will help it to work well.

As managers of an IJV (and that is the standpoint from which this book is written) you have the responsibility to *design the structure* of that IJV. For this you need a mental picture of how an organizational system works. How can you manage something if you don't know how it works, or even what it looks like? Systems thinking is on your side. Don't make the mistake of thinking that it is a stand-alone, overly conceptual way of thinking about organizations. It is not – it is absolutely in harmony with the other chapters in this book and the kind of tricky problems that you will encounter in the day-to-day IJV management. Relying on organizational politics to define the structure of your IJV is one approach but, on balance, you will get better results by using the soft architectural hands of systems thinking. So: *SYSTEMS THINKING CAN HELP YOU (BUT ONLY IF YOU LET IT)*.

STRUCTURE: KEY POINTS

1. The traditional 'organization chart' is a poor way of representing the structure of an IJV. *Systems thinking* is a better way of describing how things work in practice.
2. Key concepts of systems thinking are:
    (a) *viability*: the ability to maintain a separate existence through time;
    (b) *system nesting*: the idea that each system contains, and is contained within, other systems;
    (c) *autonomous producers*: the sub-systems that produce the output of the system;

    (d) *higher management*: part of a system level that prevents oscillation of its sub-systems (and itself);

    (e) *control*: a better term is *regulation*; management action that stops oscillation, and thereby internal conflict.

3.   The viable IJV system model is a conceptual way to address real problems of IJV structure. It has general application to all IJV variants.

4.   The only purpose of the systems thinking approach is to be useful. It can help you design the structure of an IJV but don't expect it to solve all your management problems.

Chapter 7

Control

International joint venture businesses are not easy to control. We saw in Chapters 3 and 4 that the IJV organizational form is characterized by instability, with a life cycle comprising a series of sequential but finite chronological stages. Control is a wide-ranging problem which is not restricted to any single part or function of the organization. The problem also has depth – the basic make-up of an IJV, consisting of a technologically and commercially mature A-parent and a less well-developed but committed and enthusiastic B-parent means, that control is always going to be a difficult issue. This is a high-energy organizational situation.

CASE STUDY 7.1

International Technology Partners: the question of control

Some high-level thought had obviously gone into the discussions about which partner would be in charge of the market research studies. The geographical area of the study was easy to agree – it would cover the developing markets of the Pacific Rim and Far East tiger economies. The A-parent marketing director (recently self-appointed as in charge of humour) commented that no tiger would be left untamed in the quest for profit for the International Technology Partners IJV. The management of the market research study wouldn't cause a problem – one of the monthly alliance meetings (they used the wrong term) would sort that out.

The market research studies

The A-parent directors were, as they put it, disappointed when the $50,000 invoice was presented for their approval at the next IJV senior management meeting, fully two months after the studies were known to have finished. 'Where', they asked, 'were the conclusions?' Glowing with pride, the B-parent delegation explained that not only were the studies finished, but the findings had already been analysed and implemented. There hadn't been too many changes needed, only to the document package to get rid of a few words that meant something quite different in the Philippines.

On studying the survey, the A-parent decided they didn't like the scope of survey after all – where were the results from Japan and Korea? The resulting discussion eventually distilled itself down to the issue of control: the A-parent had agreed to pay for the survey by a respected Hong Kong company but the B-parent had been trusted with preparing the terms of reference. It was felt that because the A-parent was paying for the survey it was they who should be in control – didn't this make good business sense?

The market research studies; rewind

Where are the following considerations in the above scenario?

- an understanding that control is about preventing conflict between the IJV partners? (see Chapter 6, Figure 6.13);
- the commitment to an IJV as a 'learning organization'? (see Chapter 5, Figure 5.10);
- the anticipation of the resulting difficulties of splitting the management of, and payment for, an activity across intra-IJV boundaries?

IJV CONTROL: GENERAL PRINCIPLES

The purpose of this chapter is to provide you with guidelines that will help you control the instability inherent in an IJV organization. These guidelines have general applicability – they apply to all the IJV organizational forms, large or small, however fluid their business environment. Another fixed point is the link between the control of an IJV and its performance – difficulties with IJVs that produce mediocre financial performance can usually be traced back to problems with the mechanisms of their management control. In extreme cases, the internal tensions and conflict that result from bad control will cause the downfall of the business, irrespective of any other underlying competitive edge or market strengths.

Setting the scene: the extent of control

Well-proven management guidelines exist about the 'span' of control that managers in any organization are able to exert on the individuals that work alongside or, subordinate to, their position in the organizational structure. The underlying inference is one of hierarchy, delineated within flexible but well-defined organizational boundaries. Traditional concepts of line management and matrix management are used to describe the way that control is supposed to be exercised over staff and resources. In an IJV the concept of extent of control is different – it is the control of the corporate IJV organization complete with its links with its A- and B-parent organizations that is the area under study. This is a much larger task than the one referred to as the span of control of individual managers. Another difference is in the *direction* of the control. Traditional management science perceives control as a vertical mechanism in the organization but the task inside an IJV structure is more horizontal – the challenge is in controlling parts of each parent organization that have nominally equal hierarchical status within the IJV, as shown in Figure 7.1. These observations of the character of organizational control are helpful in understanding the task of exercising it within the IJV.

REALITY: DIRECT OR INDIRECT CONTROL?

Now that we have identified the necessary extent and direction of IJV control, the next step is to find *how* it is best exercised. The quickest solution is normally that of direct control. This uses directives, rules, regulations and procedures gathered together within a collective atmosphere of firmness; some IJV managers take pride in their style of 'firm management direction'. IJVs that work like this normally have some success in replicating their working

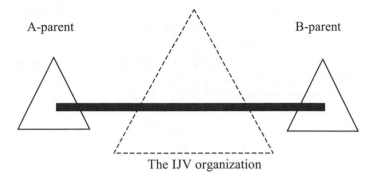

A-parent   B-parent

The IJV organization

The mechanism of control is in a horizontal rather
than the traditional vertical 'hierarchy' direction.

Figure 7.1 The task of IJV control

atmosphere across the cultural and geographical boundary (look back at Figure
4.4), from the A-parent to the B-parent. Global IJVs in the automotive and
food industries traditionally work like this but the method is not without its
problems. Direct control results in:

- Difficulties in its interpretation – it has different effects on different
  people, because they receive it in a variety of ways;
- Surprisingly, different rates of organizational change between the A- and
  B-parent 'parts' of the IJV. Direct control helps to knock them out of
  step;
- Shortening of the overall IJV life cycle;
- Good old-fashioned bad feeling.

This does not mean that IJVs have to be a model of democracy – there are
successful ones world-wide that are almost the opposite, but simply that the
mechanism of control is better and more efficient if it is applied indirectly. In
short, it works better like this.

INDIRECT CONTROL

The principles of indirect control arc ccntred on a set of management measures
that are used to do the controlling. They have four 'lowest common denominator' characteristics.

1. They have a conscious *monitoring* action (to find out what is happening).
2. The monitoring is linked to the controlling action (to actually make things happen).
3. The recipient of the control feels it as a gentle, almost groundswell action rather than control, as such.
4. All of this is *designed*, rather than being left to happen by chance.

The management measures possessing these characteristics need to be installed within the IJV organization so they can perform their task. In most cases they will only be formed by direct intervention from the IJV management – it is rare for them to carry over from the A- or B-parent organization, even if they use them themselves.

Figure 7.2 shows the five main measures of indirect control: quality assurance, strategic review, timescale planning, Information Technology (IT) and training – shown as boxes. Note how they are all linked in turn to the controlling and controlled parts of the IJV structure and how they differ in size – meant as a crude representation of their effectiveness. Looking at each in turn, we can see the difference between them:

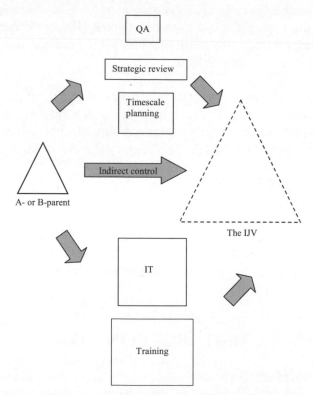

Figure 7.2 The mechanisms of indirect control

Quality Assurance (QA)

Widely heralded as a way to help organizations pull together, as well as improve their product, QA has, in reality, more links to the practices of direct control than indirect control. One reason is that the implementation of ISO 9000-based quality management systems is rapidly reaching maturity in both developed (A-parent) and developing (B-parent) countries. The effect has been to remove the QA function of an organization from a quasi-external role, to one which is established deeper in the norms and processes by which the organization operates. The result is that QA procedures are being increasingly seen as simply another mechanism of hierarchy, adding to those that are already present. QA is no longer new. There is evidence for this in the way that businesses, large and small, have added the 'QA Director' position into their senior management structure. Witness also the increased inter-departmental tensions that result.

QA has a more positive role to play in implementing indirect control in service IJVs rather than those involved in the manufacture of products. Service businesses have a softer, more outward-looking character which complements the ability of QA systems and procedures to gently control the workings of the organization. As a mechanism of indirect control, QA belongs here. The main parts of a QA system that affect control are:

- the (optional) requirement for certification of the system by an external body;
- internal (inside the IJV) system audits;
- quality plans and procedures.

External certification of the system (involving rigorous audits), has a sensitive character – it is easily seen as a mechanism of direct control if handled badly, with an emphasis on fault-finding rather than a carefully managed search for possible areas of improvement.

Strategic review

The traditional model of a strategic review is the wide-ranging examination of all the business pressures and options open to an organization, ending with an agreed action plan. Strategic review processes are a sign of maturity; an indication that the organization has attained a level of stability and isn't going to fall apart tomorrow. Similarly, well-developed strategic review mechanisms are rarely found in new organizations – they can take years to develop.

The challenge is to install a good strategic review programme in the transitional organization form that is the IJV, then develop it into a mechanism of indirect management control. There are broadly two fields to this, neither of which is well delineated – you can think of them as 'fuzzy' areas of review which will eventually sort themselves into the hard lines of a meeting agenda or business plan. Figure 7.3 is an attempt to show the difference.

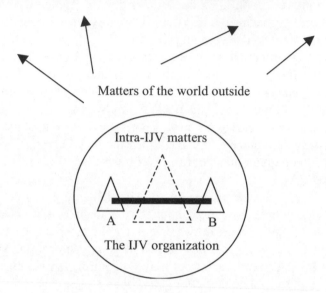

Figure 7.3 The two 'fields' of strategic review

Exclusions

In order to maintain the *indirect* control effect of strategic review it is essential to exclude anything to do with the internal structure of the IJV. This also applies to its relationships with its parent organizations. The reason for this is necessity rather than organizational logic: the main enemy of strategic review meetings is the long and often circular discussions about internal inter-partner matters that have little effect on what the IJV actually does. Even the introduction of seemingly minor points will cause problems – they soon grow into inter-partner disputes out of all proportion to their real importance. If allowed to progress, internal issues have proved their ability to hijack the strategic review process, leaving the more externally focused strategic issues unaddressed. Figure 7.4 shows a typical checklist of the two fields of IJV strategic review. Note how the points concentrate heavily on the issues that cross the boundary of the IJV out into the business environment – it is these issues that make the organization *live*. Chronologically, the activity of strategic review starts at the stage when the IJV is first initiated, continuing to act as a control mechanism almost up to the end of the useful life cycle. Correctly managed, it provides the IJV manager (you) with a ready-made tool for implementing indirect control.

Intra-IJV issues	Issues of the world outside
• project management;	• selling and pricing;
• management opportunities;	• customer service;
• transfer pricing;	• market intelligence;
• intra-IJV structures and the IJV life cycle;	• business trends;
	• opportunities for expansion;
• staff recruitment.	• threats from competitors;
	• product development;
	• product (or service) life cycles.

Figure 7.4 Strategic review: typical checklists

Timescale planning

You can expect to find some kind of timescale planning in most business organizations. It is in common use in IJVs in the form of various bar charts, line diagrams or Gantt charts, showing the development of products or services over the next few months or years. It is notable that the timescale is rarely referred to as the predicted life cycle of the IJV – the inferred assumption is that the venture is permanent. Four points are particularly relevant to the use of timescale planning for indirect control (horizontal remember) within an IJV structure:

● *Time as the motivator*: the most efficient planning processes play on the value of time pressures rather than 'manager pressure' as the best motivator for controlling bits of the IJV structure. People will respond better if it is felt that the time pressure is independent of the managers or department that are responsible for implementing the timescale plan.

● *External time constraints*: this means constraints which are set by activities and pressures outside the IJV and are therefore outside the control of managers within the IJV's structure (either the A- or B-parent parts). Time constraints which are set *in*ternally, while valid, are frequently seen as being arbitrary, with undertones of management attempts at direct control.

● *Communication*: it is essential to distribute the timescale targets widely within both the IJV and related parts of its A- and B-parent organizations.

This is a common fault in IJVs that grow from older, traditional parent businesses – the distribution is kept too narrow, encouraging negative feelings and distrust. Problems then arise and manifest themselves, once again, as tensions and conflict between the parts of the IJV. Welcome to the beginning of the end of the line.

- *Keeping a sense of perspective*: effective use of time-planning needs a clear focus on what is time-critical within the IJV and what is not. If every departmental memo is designated as 'urgent', the advantages of using timescale planning as an indirect control measure soon recede, to be replaced by a disorganized system of direct control as imaginary deadlines are missed, extended and eventually forgotten altogether.

The final test of any system of timescale planning is its acceptability in the face of an IJV's cultural variety. The nature of the parent organizations involved in IJVs is almost a guarantee that they are likely to have differing impressions of the role of time in any business strategy. As a general rule, the developing-country B-parent can be expected to give less priority to time, preferring that a business activity be 'done properly' rather than rushed through to meet some arbitrary deadline. A-parent organizations, in contrast, are probably well adapted to working to tight deadlines, real or otherwise, and are apt to see their partner's approach as a problem of attitude, and a business weakness. The antidote to these cultural differences is, fortunately, in harmony with the view that the best management control measures are indirect ones – the valuable side-effect is that it helps to avoid intra-IJV cultural problems as well.

Information Technology

Information Technology (IT) is management control by stealth, but it fits well with the ideal of indirect pressure needed to mould the actions of an inherently unstable IJV. The power of IT is its ability to move large amounts of high-quality information around inside an organization. Multiple sites or offices and geographical separation does not cause a problem and IT networks are easily adaptable to cope with complex structures of procedures and people. Seemingly unstoppable technological progress continues to reduce the cost and increase the quality and ease of use of IT systems – they have now spread almost everywhere in the business world. In the context of IJVs, IT systems are a practical way of managing the three-way information flow between the IJV entity and its A- and B-parent organizations. Figure 7.5 shows the elements of a typical system – note the comments on the positive and negative points of each.

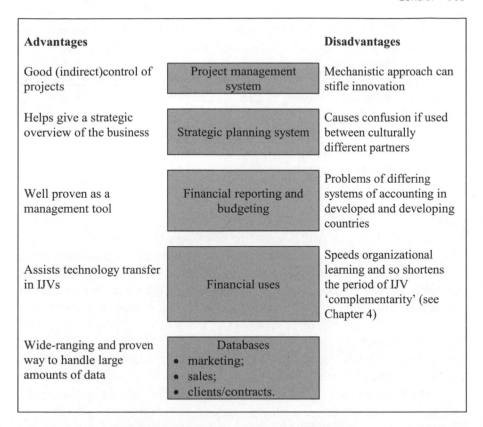

Advantages		Disadvantages
Good (indirect)control of projects	Project management system	Mechanistic approach can stifle innovation
Helps give a strategic overview of the business	Strategic planning system	Causes confusion if used between culturally different partners
Well proven as a management tool	Financial reporting and budgeting	Problems of differing systems of accounting in developed and developing countries
Assists technology transfer in IJVs	Financial uses	Speeds organizational learning and so shortens the period of IJV 'complementarity' (see Chapter 4)
Wide-ranging and proven way to handle large amounts of data	Databases • marketing; • sales; • clients/contracts.	

Figure 7.5 Elements of an IJV IT system

IT systems – a warning

There is one inherent danger of IT systems that has particular relevance for their use in IJVs. This is: *IT IS ONLY A TOOL – NOT A BUSINESS ACTIVITY IN ITSELF*. The danger associated with forgetting this is that the introduction of IT systems will complicate the organizational system that they are supposed to simplify. The result is additional IT directors, IT managers (on both sides of the IJV) and a complete mini-structure in itself. This causes imbalance in the system of the IJV, reduces its viability and creates a whole raft of further problems. The end result is a reduction in the stability of the joint organization. This is an example of how the positive aspects of a service function can be unwittingly turned negative. Sadly, it is not an uncommon phenomenon.

Training

Most IJVs express an interest in staff training at some point in their life cycle but do they make the best use of it? The conventional view of training is that it is a way of increasing the knowledge of an organization's staff in areas relevant to their business. It is seen, therefore, as a tool for development, perhaps even innovation. This approach neglects one of the greatest strengths of training – its capability to act as a *moderator* within complex organizational forms. Such a view of training is finding increasing use in global IJVs in which it is necessary to try to establish common understandings and norms amongst staff from different cultural backgrounds. It can achieve this by fostering two things: common expertise; and common thoughts.

The first, common expertise, is mainly a result of technically based training programmes, ie about the nature of the IJV's business. The second, common thoughts, is the more powerful of the pair – this is about the structure and nature of the IJV organization itself, rather than the business environment in which it is involved. A strong programme of training in this area is an effective way of exerting gentle management control across the international boundaries of the IJV, without having to resort to too much 'executive' authority. It is especially effective when combined with some of the other instruments of indirect control such as QA or strategic review. Such training programmes don't have to be excessive or over-elaborate but they must be directed. Remember that the IJV itself provides the most productive source of training. This is better than yet another job-specific training course, which staff on both sides of the IJV have probably done already.

Try to grasp this view of training as a mechanism of indirect control, as an instrument which can help reduce the trend of the people and systems of an IJV to slide towards instability. In extreme cases, staff training can be the saviour of an IJV that is in the grip of self destructive internal conflict. Training is a moderator, as well as an innovator.

MANAGEMENT STYLE (THE IJV MINDSET)

The problem

Any discussion involving the control of a business organization would not be complete without a look at the issue of management style. The style of people-management is a crucial factor in any organization – the people *are* the organization. The traditional debate about management style in a joint organization usually centres around the amount of staff democracy and freedom that is to be allowed or encouraged. This manifests itself initially in the form of a spate of discussions about the way that 'things will be done', sliding rapidly (in the early phase of the IJV's life) into a series of increasingly ethnocentric disagreements about who is best suited to be in charge of various bits of the IJV's business. This is a well-worn path in the world of IJVs. It is as if the original issues of management style exist only to disguise the range of organizational tensions that lie beneath the surface.

The reasons are easy to see by looking at Figure 7.6. The 'difficulties' side shows four factors (all of which are inherent to IJVs) that act together to impede the implementation of a single 'instant solution' form of management style. Although there are corresponding opportunities (the right hand side of Figure 7.6), they are no match for the distorting influences on the left hand

Difficulties	**Opportunities**
a collection of individuals with cultural differences;	a high-level portfolio of technical and business skills;
different geographical locations;	opportunity to hand-pick staff from the IJV's parent organizations;
the natural transience of the IJV organizational form;	organizational learning as one of the IJV's objectives.
organization politics of joint-working.	

Figure 7.6 IJV management style: difficulties and opportunities

side. The natural end to this is that the traditional management style debate often founders on these differences. This wastes everyone's time and effort.

Solution: a different approach

An alternative approach is to think of the management style of an IJV as the guiding force behind the mindset of its people, refreshingly free of any reference to the authority vs democracy arguments. Mindset can help IJV staff to:

- shape their perceptions of their IJV;
- decide who their customers are, and how best to serve them;
- understand the strategy and tactics of the IJV business.

The key criteria is, of course, the nature of the mindset that results from the amalgamation of A- and B-parent management styles. The two extremes are shown in Figure 7.7. The two mindset models: global and ethnocentric, do not easily mix, so IJVs bend strongly towards one or the other. It is a feature of past experience of the automobile and consumer goods industries that IJV business success is closely correlated with the existence of a strongly global mindset within the joint organization. Conversely, those IJVs retaining predominantly ethnocentric values have proven to be less in tune with their business and its marketplace. They are also slow to adapt to enforced changes, and suffer from periods of panic and over-reaction – classical signs of a business that has poor internal control.

A global mindset results in:	An ethnocentric mindset results in:
a mixture of management attitudes and practices;	concentration on the management style of one of the IJV parents;
openness;	narrow-mindedness;
understanding of cultural differences;	continual inter-parent criticism;
different assumptions of business reality;	parochialism.
acceptance of diversity.	

Figure 7.7 IJV management styles: global vs ethnocentric

A good IJV management style is one which encourages the formation of a global mindset amongst the staff originating from both parent organizations. One objective of style is to encourage cultural understanding and the acceptance of diversity – attributes shown on the left hand side of Figure 7.7. This encourages an environment in which the other aspects of indirect control can work successfully, producing an IJV which has the property of self regulation, and is not trying to shake itself to pieces.

CASE STUDY 7.2

Process licensing: management style

IJVs involving licensing of chemical processes have been around for nearly one hundred years. The early days of petroleum processing, coal/mineral production, agrochemicals and pharmaceutical products were characterized by joint ventures between technologists and manufacturers, formed to exploit commercial opportunities.

These early ventures, while initially successful, had short life cycles. Their management styles were authoritarian with a strongly ethnocentric mindset. The 'clustering' of competitors around the opportunities of new technological developments produced a highly competitive situation, placing the structure and resolve of all the competing organizations under stress. One of the best examples is the situation that existed in the catalytic cracking of petroleum: a rapid rise in similar processes managed by multiple IJVs was followed by the equally rapid crash of 85 per cent of them within their first two years of business. Those that survived had developed a more global mindset, promoted by their choice of an open management style with an understanding and acceptance of diversity. The skeletons of some of these early IJVs still survive today within the structure of the global petroleum corporations. The others have disappeared, martyrs to their own ethnocentric approach.

Modern IJVs in business sectors with a long and traditional history still have difficulty in adopting a global mindset. The cross-border exploitation of useful technologies from Eastern Europe is an example of a field whose business potential remains capped by residual ethnocentricity. Western–Eastern European IJVs formed to try to capture the business potential experience difficulty in controlling the venture. Many become unstable, write off their investment and disappear.

CASE STUDY 7.3

Forestry: multiple IJVs: centralization vs decentralization

Following the success of several forestry IJVs in the Far East and Africa a Swedish forestry company tried both centralization and decentralization in an attempt to link them all together. By 1996 the

Swedish-based forestry group (the A-parent) had completed its programme of expansion by investing in six separate IJVs in distant countries. The increased size of the group meant that the existing head office board was unable to maintain close personal control, leaving many of the separate entity IJVs under the full control of their local management teams. A sudden slump in the value of hardwood led the company to seek tighter control through a policy of centralization.

The centralization phase

Centralization of the management of the IJVs included the appointment of an 'overseas operations' executive at head office, the grouping of the IJVs into divisions (the sequence of Figure 3.4), each with a divisional director, and the formation of task forces to undertake cost-cutting assignments in each host country. Stocks of all woods were built up while management tried to decide on the best strategy to adopt. Problems started to occur during the period of re-absorbing the IJVs back into a divisionalized structure; local management teams saw enormous delays in getting decisions made and reported; 'There are a lot of people not taking responsibility for discussing things with the B-parent, who feel their country owns the trees before they are cut.' Recession in Far Eastern furniture markets reduced the price of wood further, so head office instructed all divisions (as they were now called) to reduce their stocks by 80 per cent. This flooded the market and the price dropped further.
  The messages are:

● IJVs do not react well to recentralization into a company structure. In this case they rejected the central instruction to consolidate stocks, causing resentment and demotivation.
● Trying to manage too many IJVs with limited A-parent monitoring capabilities is full of risk. Too much IJV autonomy can be as dangerous as too little.

The decentralization phase

Following the market slump, having written down stock and carrying $US5m bank overdraft, the Swedish parent company was in a crisis situation. The solution was to pass control of each overseas 'division' to its managing director, with a reduced head office staff retained to undertake mainly financial functions. The decentralization allowed each overseas location (still formally configured as IJVs) to organize its own response to local market demand, choosing its own stock levels to suit. When local furniture makers changed some of their ranges from hardwood to softwood the relevant IJVs were able to respond quickly. The previous expensive time-wasting disputes with head office soon subsided, leading to increases in efficiency in almost all areas of the business operation.

The messages are:

- Separate-entity IJVs behave like divisions in a group structure. They benefit from just the right amount of autonomy.
- It is possible to decentralize IJVs once they are operating successfully. The overseas B-parent influences will help the process of decentralization if you let it.

CONTROL: KEY POINTS

Control is about getting the IJV to do what you want, without internal tensions and conflict. The main points are:

1. *Control problems*: IJVs have these in breadth and depth. The main objective is to design the control system to minimize conflict between the IJV partners.
2. *The span of control*: the span of control is horizontal (between the IJV partners) rather than the traditional vertical convention.
3. *Direct vs indirect control*: indirect control is a gentler, more effective way to manage an IJV. The main instruments of indirect control are (from Figure 7.2):
   (a) quality assurance;
   (b) strategic review;
   (c) timescale planning;
   (d) information technology;
   (e) training.
4. *Management style*: the management style of an IJV provides the environment necessary to support all the other instruments of indirect control. The best style is that which promotes a global mindset, rather than trying to solve the rhetorical arguments of organizational hierarchy vs freedom and democracy.

Chapter 8

Finance

This chapter is about money. More specifically it is about the financial techniques and practicalities that accompany the life cycle of an international joint venture from its genesis to its end. We will refer to this throughout the chapter as the IJV investment process.

THE FINANCIAL SCENERY

The territory of IJVs is one of risk, tinged with the expectation of reward. An IJV is an entrepreneurial venture with roller-coaster promises and problems rather than the comfort of a slow corporate crawl from one decade to the next. For this reason, the financial scenery that surrounds IJVs is wide and varied – it contains many of the standard financial techniques found in other areas of business but with two main differences.

- *timescale*: the contracted timescale of the IJV life cycle means that financial events are accelerated;
- *distortions*: the international aspect of IJVs can cause distortions in traditional areas of investment criteria and accounting practice.

To see how these distortions modify the financial engineering of an IJV we need to consider a model of the financial scenery of an IJV over its life cycle. Figure 8.1 shows this divided into three stages, each containing the relevant financial techniques as they appear in the life cycle (take a look back at Figure 4.5 in Chapter 4 if you need a reminder of the form the life cycle takes). The process starts from the early stages of raising the finance for the initial capital structure through to the endgame of changes of ownership and resultant buy-out or buy-in options. The purpose of this model is to provide *insight* – an IJV is potentially a high-risk venture and has to be well structured in terms of its financial engineering if it is to succeed. Financial structure is one of the few areas of IJV business that is wholly under the direct control of its management. You must get it right.

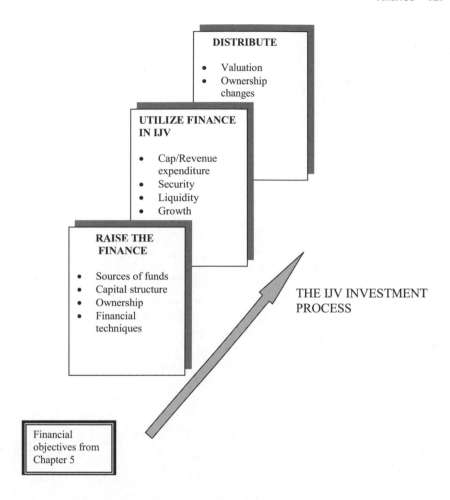

Figure 8.1 The financial scenery of an IJV

THE IJV AS AN INVESTMENT MODEL

Exactly what kind of an investment model does an IJV represent? Figure 8.2 shows a simple model; note the features that form the basis of the IJV structure:

● parent organization (A) in a highly developed country;
● parent organization (B) in the less well developed 'host' country;
● a geographical (and cultural) divide between the two.

Compare this with the accepted model of business investment shown in Figure 8.3. The key difference is that our IJV model is actually two separate but adjoining models, one each side of the international boundary. The A-parent's model is fairly simple while that of B is more complex, containing the core of the host-country IJV business activities. Analysing this situation a little further we can look at the characteristics of each side's investment model:

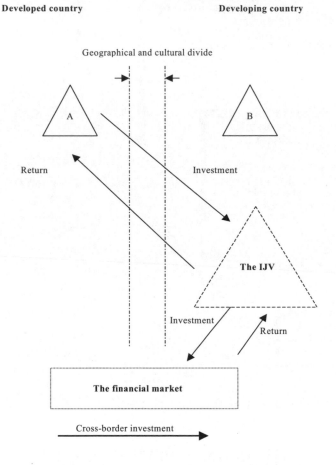

Figure 8.2 The IJV investment model

The definition of A's investment environment is:

- biased towards a single investment/revenue path;
- this path will always cross the international boundary;
- the investment/revenue path is characterized by high uncertainty, almost as soon as it leaves the direct control of the A-parent;
- the investment activity is strategic in nature, because of the practical difficulties in making quick secure returns from a distant market.

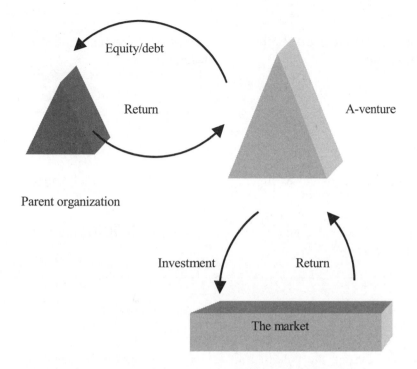

Figure 8.3 The traditional model of business investment

In contrast, B's environment is:

- in intimate contact with the market for the sales of the IJV's goods or services (it is in the same country);
- a cash generator, via sales commissions and general support of the IJV's output;
- capable of rapid growth.

We are starting to see now why the financial structuring of an IJV is so important. Any financial structure that would suit both these investment environments would be little more than a shabby compromise. It would lack direction and cutting edge – almost a guarantee of failure. One way to prevent this is to have a dual financial structure to the IJV, mirroring the different environments (see Figure 8.4).

This is a neat fit with the situation in which IJV partners commonly find themselves. The A-Parent can afford the long-termism of a low dividend-return equity investment while the B-parent, in its less-well-developed economy, needs to maintain its cash level to protect its liquidity. Both parents can still consider themselves part of the wealth creation process – in global

Parent A's investment model is based on:	Parent B's investment model is based on:
● capital growth;	● vigorous revenue-earning activity;
● limited dividend return;	● quick dividend returns;
● IRR as the main investment criterion.	● the problems of maintaining liquidity.
Hence it is suited to equity investment	Hence it is suited to debt finance

Figure 8.4 The dual financial structure of an IJV

economic terms, the wealth transfer would probably be seen as being transferred across the international boundary from A to B rather than B to A. Draw your own conclusions on this one.

IJV FUNDS

There are two aspects to this: *sources* of funds and the *cost* of them. Things are made more complicated in an IJV structure because there is more than one country involved.

The A-Parent: sources of funds

Equity is normally more easily available to the A-parent. Successful businesses in economically advanced countries can have tangible assets in the form of cash or capital items that are available for transfer into a new IJV. The assets will often be under the total control of the parent, which makes things easier. Such organizations are often comfortable with a passive investment as part of their business portfolio. Access to debt finance is also straightforward because the A-parent country will have its own banks and financial system well accustomed to the idea of long- and short-term debt finance. There will likely be government protection systems available to act as assurance for specific cross-border transactions. In general, you can expect such countries to exhibit a market-driven financial economy with multiple possible sources of debt and equity funds. There are exceptions – South Korea for example, which although well developed economically, has a financial market which is dominated by state influence.

The B-Parent: sources of funds

In contrast to their partners in well-developed countries, B-parent organizations traditionally have difficulties in obtaining funds. The reasons can be:

- a previous history of central planning by the state (ex-communist countries);
- a poorly developed (or non-existent) banking system;
- poor credit rating (for external borrowing);
- liquidity problems (no cash).

These problems are a daily part of life for millions of business organizations in developing countries. Many have a good product, educated staff and commendably big ambitions but are technically insolvent. The net result is that any type of funding for these organizations is difficult. It is necessary to accept that B-parents may have little cash equity to contribute to the formation of the IJV – their contribution being limited to fixed assets (manufacturing/R&D facilities, etc) and local management and workforce.

The availability of debt finance is easier. Debt in the form of fixed term loans in local currency is possible in about 80 per cent of developing countries. The finance has a tendency to be short-term, with a practical time horizon limit of 5–7 years. This places pressure on the B-parent organization to have access to regular cash payments from the IJV operation so it can service its debts.

The cost of funds

The cost of debt or equity funds to parent organizations (either A or B) is set by the market rating of the parent and its business activities. Under normal financial management principles it is the status and past history of the parent alone that governs the cost of funds rather than its future plans, ie to start an IJV. In practice, there is normally a premium to be paid somewhere when the funds are channelled into an IJV because of the higher risk category of this type of investment. The result is something like Figure 8.5. Treat these data as comparative only – the actual percentage margins vary depending on the sector of business and particular countries involved. Figure 8.6 shows a typical example from the manufacturing sector showing the link to projected IRR.

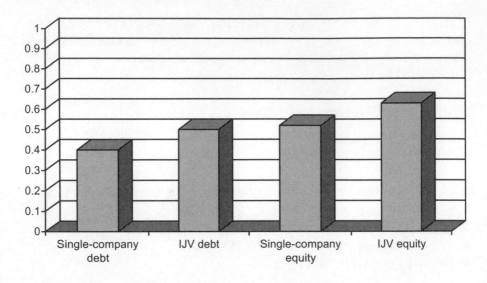

Figure 8.5 Comparative costs of IJV capital

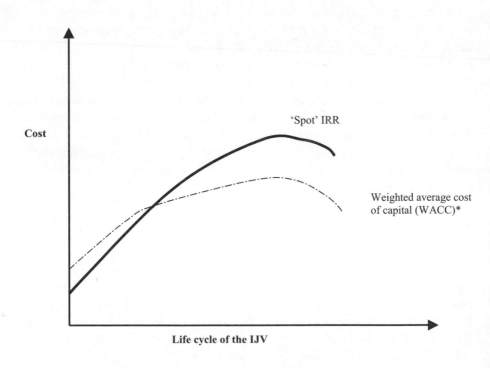

*Note: *Data based on colloquial evidence from manufacturing sector IJVs (1992–96)*

Figure 8.6 WACC vs IRR in manufacturing IJVs

Equity costs

The main point of concern here is the true cost of equity capital to the IJV organization. The true cost of IJV equity is different from its nominal cost, as shown in Figure 8.7. The difference arises mainly because of the finite form of the IJV life cycle, ie provision has to be made for the costs of realizing the capital value of the investment, known loosely as the 'cost of conversion'. All these costs arc seen by the investing parent over the term of the investment, causing the true cost of equity to be several percentage points higher than the nominal cost.

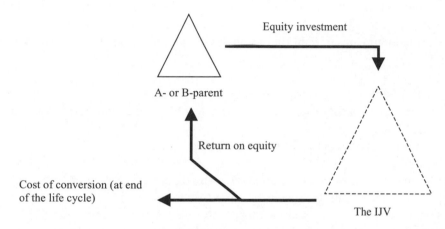

The true cost of equity to the IJV has to incorporate the final cost of conversion.

Figure 8.7 The true cost of IJV equity

Another influential factor is equity *risk*. IJV investment is not excluded from the general principle of investment that the more risky the nature of the investment, the higher the investor's required rate of return. In theory, provided that an IJV's parent organization holds an efficiently diversified risk portfolio elsewhere in its business dealings, there is no reason why the inclusion of one high-risk IJV should make too much difference to its overall risk exposure. In practice, it rarely happens like this – joint ventures with developing countries are now accepted as being high risk activities with the result that IJVs now have a type of notoriety in certain sectors of business. It follows that you can expect any mention of an IJV to attract a lot of higher management attention, much of it devoted to talking about risk. Corporate risk assessments inevitably increase the level of risk apportioned to an IJV project and they are frankly, often correct. This risk premium adds to the true cost of equity capital to the IJV because the investing parent wants a higher return from its investment in the new IJV company.

Debt costs

The costs of debt finance are most relevant to the B-parent in its attempt to raise the money to fund entry into the IJV. You can expect a direct financial linking between the B-parent and the IJV organization itself, because they are both located in the 'B' host country. There tends to be a close comparison between the cost of debt finance to the B-parent and of that to the separate IJV organization – they will be seen (and act) almost as a single body. It is possible therefore to assume the same cost of debt finance for both.

The characteristics of debt finance in developing countries follow common trends:

- debt has to be secured in some way;
- short-term floating rate debt is easier to obtain than longer-term fixed rate debt;
- the concept of debentures is not well developed.

Not all this is helpful. An emerging IJV is better served by longer-term debt at a fixed interest rate to match the time horizon of its life cycle. Security may also be difficult – existing manufacturing facilities cannot readily be called in as security if the IJV borrower is unable to service the debt and IJVs in general operate with low levels of 'interest cover' in their early years. All of this paints a bleak picture for the cost of host-country debt to the emerging IJV. Fortunately, this doesn't always happen and the actual cost of debt finance in developing countries often owes more to macroeconomic influences in the region than the individual credit-worthiness of the host-country organization. This provides an emerging IJV with a lifeline for financial survival.

The availability of debt finance is much easier for the A-parent (if it needs it). There is still a risk premium to be paid of course, and in practice the difference between the theoretical risk-free 'government' borrower rate and the cost of debt to the IJV parent (known loosely as the 'yield spread') varies between about 5 and 12 per cent.

CAPITAL STRUCTURE

Capital structure is simple in concept but complex in practice. For every IJV, there exists somewhere, a suitable capital structure – the one which will provide the most appropriate mix of risk, reward and organizational freedom. It will also produce the WACC that is most suitable for the venture, given the market and business environment in which it operates.

The capital structure of an IJV is not predetermined – you can expect it to change suddenly in response to organizational developments within the business, and more predictably with the progression of the venture's natural lifecycle. The general principles, however, are basically about allocating degrees of risk and reward, and have universal application. The financial structure of any IJV owes more to the concepts of venture capital than to the world of precisely calculated portfolio risk. The basic model reflects the need of the parent company 'investors' to obtain return on their investment in three possible ways:

● capital gain over the operational life of the IJV investment;
● through-life revenue stream;
● profitable exit route (to increase the overall capital gain).

This is achieved by the apportionment of the various types of equity and debt in a way that will satisfy the requirements of all investors in the venture. An interesting characteristic of an IJV is the different investment expectations of the two parents, the existence of differing economic conditions across the international boundary having clear effect on investment expectations. Paradoxically, this makes a suitable capital structure *easier* to define than if the two sets of investing parents were in the same geographical region.

The best way to understand the nature and effects of IJV capital structure is to look at an example. We will start by looking in further detail at the on-going case study used as a 'model' throughout the chapters of the book.

CASE STUDY 8.1

International Technology Partners Ltd: introduction

The concept behind International Technology Partners (ITP Ltd) is simple enough – a plan to build a range of advanced consumer goods in an already existing factory in a developing country. These products (according to their designers, at least) are of very advanced specification: new high strength polymer materials, smooth aesthetic design and manufactured to the highest standards of safety and reliability. These products (if you listen to their manufacturers) are almost too good to be true.

And the prize? A blossoming market of perhaps one quarter of the world's population, with ever-increasing spending power. In the words of one founder director of International Technology Partners: 'With local manufacture to our closely controlled technical specification we can provide these new products at an attractive price to all who want them.' This was reinforced by ITP's quality director who reiterated the overriding need for quality in all aspects of the products' manufacture: 'Quality', he had been heard to recite, 'is a journey, not a destination.'

As the publicity ebbed away the structure of the planned IJV business emerged, broadly as shown in Figure 8.8. The technology licensor has already successfully manufactured and sold the range of products in the mature industrialized markets of Europe and the United States. The same licensor (designated as the A-parent) is facing steep competition from cheaper but, in their own view, technically inferior product ranges manufactured in a developing country by an existing manufacturer (designated the B-parent). International Technology Partners (ITP) will be an IJV, commissioned with the objective of building A's products in B's manufacturing works, for sale to B's existing large and rapidly expanding market. Figure 8.9 shows the initial financing requirements for the IJV. These features are common to many IJVs operating in batch manufacturing, consumer goods and similar technology based markets.

There are two main questions about the capital structure:

- What is the overall debt/equity structure of the IJV company?
- How much of the equity portion of the capital structure is funded by each parent?

These two questions arise during the formation stage of most IJVs and large amounts of management time and effort are wasted looking for the correct answer to the second question. The reason for this is simple: the A-parent feels that, as technology licensor and arguably the driving force behind the IJV's formation, it should get the lion's share of the IJV equity, but at a cheaper unit price than that paid by B. Conversely, the B-parent sees itself as the vital link in the chain, because without its indigenous manufacturing capability near the developing market, the A-parent would remain uncompetitive in, or even excluded from, this lucrative opportunity. Both arguments are right (and wrong) but are a poor basis on which to base critical decision about the apportionment of equity with its wider implications of the financial architecture of the IJV.

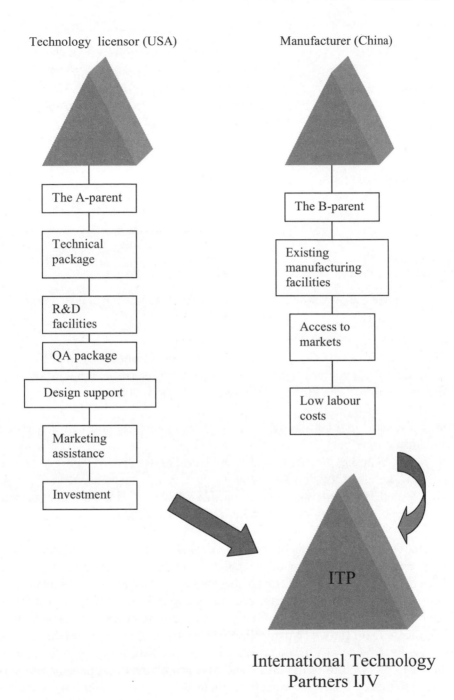

Figure 8.8 International Technology Partners: the IJV structure

From A-parent	Machinery / capital equipment	£8.0m
	Technology transfer package	£1.0m
	QA support package	£0.3m
	Design support package	£0.4m
	Management assistance	£0.4m
From B-parent	Capital equipment	£1.0m
	Staff training	£0.3m
	Stock at valuation	£0.5m
	Total requirement	**£11.9m**

Figure 8.9 International Technology Partners IJV: initial financing requirements

The accepted way of organizing the financial structure is to follow the methodology of venture finance. This gives a degree of financial rationale to the proceedings. The three basic tenets of this method are:

● IJV 'start-up' equity is treated as a rational commercial investment rather than a sunk cost;
● both A- and B-parents want a return based on the risk of their investment and the effort they put in;
● A- and B-parents understand that IJVs have a finite time horizon and accept the validity of 'exit route' realization of their equity.

There is nothing unreasonable or theoretical about any of these three points – they are a simple statement of the reality of any business investment, be it in IJVs or not. Their only restriction is that they apply best to large and financially sound businesses, rather than those that are small, technically insolvent or have permanent cash flow problems. The requirement for financial stability is a prerequisite for any organization that wants to enter into an IJV.

The final piece of information needed before we can develop the capital structure of ITP Ltd is the profit and loss projections. Despite the obvious uncertainties of financial projections there is, sadly, no better way to start – IJVs and uncertainty are, without doubt, co-partners in the world of business. Table 8.1 shows the P&L projections, for ITP Ltd over its projected life cycle. The choice of time horizon is crucial; we know from Chapter 4 that the venture is going to possess a life cycle, the question is: how long? In a real business situation there is little chance of being able to predict this with any degree of accuracy, a fact which has important implications for strategic planning of the IJV. The knock-on effect of this uncertainty should now be clear: the only way to maintain any semblance of certainty in IJV investment planning is to see the initial capital funding as a *fixed term* investment. Yes, this is artificial – it raises the scenario of 'snapping-off' the investment in your IJV brainchild after a predetermined fixed time horizon. It does, however, have the beneficial effect of bringing one element of certainty to the IJV planning process. The P&L projections are in standard format, ending with the annual post-tax profit of the IJV. These projections apply only to the separate joint organization – totally independent from the financial fortunes of A- and B-parents. Note the four year finite time horizon.

Table 8.1 International Technology Partners IJV: P&L projections

P & L projections years 1 to 4 (£m)				
	Yr 1	Yr 2	Yr 3	Yr 4
Sales	23.50	28.20	33.93	40.61
Profit before interest and tax	2.89	4.02	5.13	6.49
Interest	1.52	1.57	1.27	0.80
Profit before tax	1.37	2.45	3.86	5.69
Tax	0.48	0.86	1.35	1.99
Net profit	0.89	1.59	2.51	3.70

The debt/equity split

The example of ITP Ltd shows:

Total 'start-up' cost of IJV:	£11.9m including:
Cost of fixed assets: (parent A)	£ 8.0m
Cost of fixed assets: (parent B)	£ 1.0m

Under conventional company financing arrangements the total debt available would be about 60 per cent of the securable assets purchased by the A-parent, ie £4.8m. It is unlikely that the £1m of assets from the B-parent would be considered discrete enough to provide valid security. When the funding required is part of a large-scale IJV, however, the situation is different. Most A-parent organizations have enough financial stability to secure borrowings in the assets or shares of the parent, giving, in theory, the possibility of near-100 per cent debt funding, so avoiding the prohibitively high cost of equity. Some notable IJVs have started their life like this, accompanied by a sharing of the nominal equity ownership between the parents.

Problems soon arise, however; the high cost of debt servicing is a danger to all but the most financially sound IJVs, and the lack of real 'sweat' equity from the parents is a sure sign that the parents are not as committed to the joint venture as they could be. A lot of apparently well-financed IJVs deteriorate quickly due to these peripheral reasons. A better idea is to structure the debt:equity ratio along the more conventional guidelines mentioned earlier (ie 60 per cent maximum debt) but with an artificially structured equity distribution. This extra distribution is there for strategic reasons – to increase the amount of participation felt by the parent organizations in the IJV. The lower debt servicing requirements can be seen as a secondary benefit. This points towards the ideal debt/equity split for an IJV being somewhere in the range of 60:40 to 50:50, not, in itself, a startling conclusion. There is general evidence that IJVs that structure themselves along these lines get the best compromise between an acceptable weighted average cost of capital (WACC) and a large enough equity component to make sure the IJV parents maintain their interest and commitment to its success.

Equity distribution

This is a fertile source of internal conflict within IJVs. You can expect both A and B parent organizations to produce mildly convincing arguments why they should have more equity than the other, irrespective of the funds that they actually invest. The dichotomy is not difficult to understand: both organizations naturally feel that they are the core part of the IJV with the other merely providing 'support' to enable the venture to go ahead, not a situation conducive to quick and amicable agreements on how to divide up the shares of the new joint organization. Arguments relating the number of shares directly to the amount of equity funds injected are equally unproductive – it is not easy to draw direct comparison between the 'value' of a currency contribution in a mature industrialized country and the same amount in a developing country.

A first attempt to apportion the equity of our case study ITP Ltd is shown in Table 8.2. This is a simple prorata share based on the initial monetary contributions of each parent, with a small percentage left set aside as an incentive for the IJV management team themselves. Looks good, but will it work? Given the B-parent's significant role in actually producing ITP Ltd's goods in their factory, it is almost unthinkable that the B-parent would be satisfied with less than a 15 per cent share of the IJV equity. The return, whether taken as dividend or capital growth, would be small compared to A's and the whole venture would exist in an atmosphere of imbalance. Such unequal distribution of profits owes more to looser 'licence agreement' ways of working rather than ones which infer a fairer, more co-operative way of doing things. This simplistic solution also does not take into account the influence of any debt in the financial structure. Fortunately, the character of the parent organizations that form IJVs allows a better solution. The reasoning, similar to that we developed in Figure 8.4 goes like this:

- The B-parent, as a member of a developing economy, will benefit more from taking a *regular revenue stream* from the IJV's business operation;
- The A-parent is probably not cash-starved, and can afford to see its participation in the IJV as more of an *investment exercise*. It will be more likely to welcome a high IRR on its investment, realizing its capitalization value at the end of the IJV life cycle.

Neither of these positions are absolute; there are always examples of B-parents in developing countries that do have cash resources. On balance, however, the two points hold true for the majority of IJVs between organizations in mature industrialized and developing countries.

Table 8.2 ITP: initial 'pro rata' equity split

	Amount invested	'Pro-rata' shareholding
Parent A	£10.0m	84.0%
Parent B	£ 1.7m	14.3%
Allocated as incentives	£ 0.2m	1.7%
Totals	£11.9m	100%

The first step is to make provision for a typical amount of debt in the IJV structure. Table 8.3 shows a slightly more equal split of equity, amended to take into account a financial leverage of approximately 38 per cent (ie 38 per cent of the initial finance requirement being provided by commercial debt). This still suffers, however, from the same type of equity imbalance as in Table 8.2.

Table 8.3 ITP: equity split after debt provision

	Amount invested	'Pro rata' shareholding
A-parent	£6.0m	81%
B-parent	£1.4m	19%
Totals	£7.4m	100%

Notes: Initial financing requirement: £11.9m
Debt provision @ 50% of fixed asset value: £4.5m
Amount to be financed as equity: £7.4m

To develop the structure further, we apply the investment criteria of the A-parent. Figure 8.10 shows the situation upon sale of the IJV at its 4 year time horizon, assuming a typical price/earnings ratio (PER) of five. This shows that if it is to realize its required IRR, parent A needs 60.2 per cent of the equity, leaving 39.8 per cent for the host-country B-parent. The corresponding share structure is given in Tables 8.4 and 8.5, including the effect of the share premium paid by parent A in excess of the nominal price. There is still a problem with this structure; note how, if the IJV fails and has to be sold for its asset value shortly after formation, parent A would make a substantial loss while the B-parent makes an instant profit – clearly an impractical 'break-up' situation.

Pre-tax earnings at year 4 = £5.69 m

Valuation = £5.69m × 5 (assumed PER) = £28.45m

The A-parent's target IRR = 30 per cent

On sale of the IJV, the A-parent requires a return of
£6.0m × $(1.30)^4$ = £17.14m (using compound investment formula)

Hence to realize its IRR, the A-parent requires $\dfrac{17.14}{28.45}$ = 60.2 per cent
of the equity

Figure 8.10 ITP: looking forward to sale of the IJV

Table 8.4 Share structure

	Share price	No. Shares	Total cost	Percentage
Parent A	£10.91*	550,000	£6.0m	60.2
Parent B	£ 3.85 (par)	363,621	£1.4m	39.8
Totals		**913,621**	**£7.4m**	**100**

*Note: *Share premium of £7.06*

Table 8.5 The problem of IJV break-up value

	On sale of IJV after 4 years	On early break-up of IJV
Parent A receives	60.2% of £28.45m = £17.14m	60.2% of fixed asset value – debt repayment = 60.2% × (9 – 4.5) £m = £2.7m (a £3.3m loss)
Parent B receives	39.8% of £28.45m = £11.32m	39.8% of (9 – 4.5) £m = £1.79m (a £0.39m profit)

Note: This structure has poor break-up consequence for parent A

An answer: preference shares

The problems of break-up loss for the A-parent can be solved by the use of preference shares in the financial structure. These have a preferential claim on the equity (after repayment of debt) on break-up or final sale of IJV. Table 8.6 shows how the structure develops and Table 8.7 shows the influence of preference shares. This type of financial model forms a sound basis for IJVs – the A-parent can plan its strategy around IRR with the B-parent taking its return as a stream of divided payments. Also, both parents have sufficient equity interest to repay their initial commitment to the venture, and to hold them into their relationship with their IJV partner.

Table 8.8 shows the result on break-up of the IJV. Other refinements normally involve the use of shorter-term financial instruments such as mezzanine debt.

Table 8.6 The structure with ordinary shares

	Share price	No. Shares	Total cost	Percentage
Parent A	£3.85	550,000	£2.12m	60.2
Parent B	£3.85	363,621	£1.40m	39.8
Totals		913,621	**£3.52m**	**100**

Note: This has a financing shortfall of 7.4 – 3.52 = £3.88m which is corrected by preference shares issued to the A-parent as shown in Table 8.7.

Table 8.7 The influence of IJV preference shares

	Share type	Share price	No. shares	Total cost	Percentage
Parent A	Ordinary	£3.85	550,000	£2.12m	60.2
Parent A	Preference	£3.85	1,007,792	£3.88m	
Parent B	Ordinary	£3.85	363,621	£1.40m	39.8
Totals			**1,921,413**	**£7.40m**	**100**

Table 8.8 The result on break-up

	On sale of IJV after 4 years	On early break-up of IJV
Sale price	£28.45m	£9m
Bank debt	Taken over by purchaser	£4.5m
Preference shares	£3.88m	£3.88m
Available to ordinary shareholders	£24.57m	£0.62m
Parent A gets	£14.79m + £3.88m = £18.67m	£0.37m + £3.88m = £4.25m
Parent B gets	£9.78m	£0.25m
The end results	Parent A exceeds its 30% IRR target.	Parent A loses £1.75m
	Parent B achieves 60% + IRR available as divided stream.	Parent B loses £1.15m

Use of mezzanine debt in IJVs

The normal debt provision to a venture is known as senior debt. Mezzanine debt is, basically, debt which does not have first charge over the borrower's assets. It carries a higher interest rate and so reduces the level of interest cover. Some IJVs have used mezzanine finance as a substitute for proper equity investment by the parents with bad results. As a rule, unquoted IJVs in the early stages of their life cycle do not generally enjoy the stable levels of cash flow that are needed to service mezzanine debt.

EXIT ROUTES

The financial plan of any IJV needs to include consideration of the exit route. There are four possibilities:

1. *Sale to a third party*. This may be in the form of a flotation or, more commonly, the sale of either A's shares, B's shares, or both, to an external purchaser.
2. *Buyout by the A-parent*. This tends to occur if the IJV has been successful, fitting well into the business environment of the developing country. It coincides with the A-parent's ongoing plans for further expansion into local markets, accompanied by perhaps more joint ventures or acquisitions.
3. *Buyout by the B-parent*. There are two forms; either the venture has been so successful that local B-parent managers want to buy it (ie a Management buyout [MBO] scenario) or its performance has been mediocre or downright bad. In the second situation it is not uncommon for the A-parent licensor to want to 'disinvest' from the IJV, leaving the local B-parent to make the best of anything that remains.
4. *Restructuring and expansion*. Again, this is a feature of IJVs that have been successful, to the point where both parent organizations wish not only to maintain their investment but to increase its scale. This normally triggers a new round of funding negotiation and, more often than not, a rethink of the overall capital structure and equity distribution.

The choice of which of these four routes is taken depends on the details of each individual case. The common denominator of them all, however, is the subject of valuation – at some point in the negotiation surrounding all IJV financial exit routes, the question arises as to the value, or lack of it, of everyone's equity holding.

IJV valuation

There isn't a single unequivocal way of valuing an IJV, or any other business for that matter, it would be nice if there were. IJVs raise the added complication of having two parent organizations who exist in business environments with very different market practices, financial procedures, and probably accounting practices as well. The reality can be a very confusing picture. Figure 8.11 shows the main classes of valuation techniques used for unquoted IJVs. We can look at them briefly in turn.

Discounted PE ratio;

The basic share valuation model;

Earnings valuation models;

Pure negotiation.

Figure 8.11 Possible IJV valuation techniques

Discounted price/earnings (PE) ratio

This is a financial technique in which the last year's post-tax IJV earnings are multiplied by a ratio to provide an overall capitalization value of the shares. The ratio is obtained from comparison with similar business and varies from 2 to about 15, depending on the business sector. This is undeniably a nice idea but not much use for unquoted business. While the PE method can be used for 'guidance', it rarely bears any resemblance to the real capitalization value of the IJV. There are three reasons for this:

- Most true IJVs are not quoted companies and never will be.
- They often don't have maintainable profit levels – they are a transitional form of organization, remember.
- It is well-nigh impossible to fit many IJVs into the formal risk categories used by the financial world in deciding 'how risky' a business is (an esoteric topic known as beta-risk).

Despite these disadvantages, the PE ratio method is used as the basis of some IJV exit route negotiation. Use it as a benchmark, by all means, but don't be misled as to its real character.

The basic share valuation model

This is a traditional method of valuation based on a combination of the future expected price of a share and the expected dividend. There are various special cases assuming constant dividends, consistent growth dividends or permutations of the two. All fit into little boxes of calculation providing a neat, if unimaginative, way of valuing a company's shares. In the context of an IJV, such methods are at best misleading. Few IJVs ever attain a level of stability where dividends are predictable, with the result that they rarely come close to the precise assumptions of the basic share valuation model. Treat these models as an interesting financial convention, but don't expect them to be much use in valuing your IJV.

Earnings valuation models

These are almost as bad. The earnings valuation model is a way of valuing a company based on its earnings, rather than its dividends or capital gain potential. Again, there are various adaptations of the basic model, each claiming to provide more realistic results than the last. One of the best is sufficiently refined to take into account reinvestment of previous annual retained earnings – itself a fair assessment of the confidence felt by the IJV management in its future IRR potential. The end result, however, still owes more to financial convention than to reality. It is not unknown for such techniques to overestimate (or, less often underestimate) the capitalization value of a moderately successful IJV by a factor of two or three. Draw your own conclusions.

Pure negotiation

Ultimately, the exit 'sale' valuation of IJVs (successful and unsuccessful) is arrived at by a process of unfettered negotiation. It often uses some of the previous theoretical valuation methods as benchmarks but soon discounts them while the parties get down to serious negotiation about 'the real value' of the IJV. There are a few commonly found constraints or distortions to the financial negotiations:

- *The A-parent lacks enthusiasm* If the IJV has been a mediocre performer, the A-parent is likely to lack the will to prolong negotiation. Its main objective is often simply to disinvest from the IJV to pursue other strategies.
- *The B-parent has no cash*. This is an all-too-common end to IJVs. Initial optimism and commitment can be soon swept away if promised product

quality, manufacturing value or sales markets fail to materialize. The final chapter of most failed IJVs reads much the same: 'bills to pay but no cash left'.

● *Buy-in optimism.* This has the opposite effect. Successful IJVs often form lucrative MBO/MBI (management buy-in) opportunities for managers in the developing market of the B-parent country. The result may be an increase in the valuation over and above what either of the original IJV parents would consider its true value.

Once these constraints are absorbed into the picture, everything that is left is open to negotiation. Sometimes the negotiations are quick and decisive and other times slow and inconclusive. Most reach an end eventually, because they have to. It is difficult to find a firm pattern with exit route valuations of IJVs; published information about those that are sold rarely includes any background information about how the final sale price was arrived at.

A CAUTIONARY NOTE: FINANCIAL ACCOUNTING STANDARDS

The transnational nature of IJVs brings with it the problem of differing financial accounting standards. It is easy, in the early enthusiastic days of an IJV, to relegate the question of accounting standards to almost administrative significance – one of those things that will be 'sorted out' when the need arises. Nothing could be further from the truth – problems with accounting standards have been the root cause of failures of many IJVs, small and large. Sadly, it is so often a hidden enemy, waiting until a less stable part of an IJVs life cycle before revealing its true form.

The basic problem is that different countries have different ways of financial accounting. They differ not only in their methodology but also the in fundamental assumptions that underlie the accounting process. The traditional UK tenet that accounts should provide a 'true and fair view' of an organization's financial affairs is not mirrored in all developed countries. Some Northern European countries' systems, for instance, are biased clearly towards protection of creditor interests rather than the ethics of disclosure. There are also differences between Europe and the United States, mainly in methods of accounting for assets, development costs and goodwill. In recent years the work of two European organizations – the International Organization of Securities Commissions (IOSC) and the International Accounting Standards Committee (IASC) – has resulted in the formation of a set of International Accounting Standards, known throughout the profession as 'the IAS'.

While it is a valid attempt at harmonisation, the IAS have not met with universal acceptance. The United States prefers its own Generally Accepted Accounting Practice (GAAP) methods and even some European countries such as Switzerland add amendments or claim exemptions on some points. Outside Europe and the United States, the situation is even more divergent. Japan does not accept the IAS and many of its established industry groupings have a rather rarified system of accounting. Korea and China are shrouded in difficult conventions and secrecy and do not accept the IAS (nor probably the US GAAP) either. This pales into insignificance when compared to Eastern Europe where the systems are either totally fragmented or non-existent. Accounting is a novelty to ex-communist-bloc countries and they are only slowly adapting to the idea. Hungary and Poland are making attempts to introduce the IAS but the others are struggling.

How does this affect IJVs? The obvious point is that accounting information cannot be assumed to be comparable across international boundaries. For ventures between mature industrialized and developing countries, only an optimist would assume that there is any meaningful comparison possible at all. This affects the management of the IJV in two ways:

- It is difficult to assess an IJV partner before committing to an IJV with them;
- Apportioning 'profits' is fraught with difficulty and the potential for misunderstandings.

These are fundamental points which are at the core of the financial fortunes of an IJV. Notice how they operate at different ends of the venture's timescale – the assessment problem exists to trap you into selecting a financially unsound IJV partner with the conflict over distributing the profit (or loss) waiting to weaken what is, by the later stages, an already strained relationship. As the final consideration, think about what happens when you add a legal dispute, with both sides working under different legal procedures and understandings as well. Welcome to the IJV party.

No-one looks for this type of end to an IJV. Sadly, many go this way, let down by blind reliance on shaky accounting conventions and fuelled by the cultural differences between the partners. The answer, of course, is to make sure you apply, and rely on, your own proven set of financial methods, not the neat illusion of published accounting standards.

CASE STUDY 8.2

The fifty-fifty food consortium

It wasn't a consortium really, it was just called that – it was more of an IJV, of similar structure to one of the forms of Figure 4.3 in Chapter 4. It was made up of two companies: a large food distribution corporation from the United States (the A-parent) and an even larger market owner from Eastern Europe (the B-parent). The market premises were huge, taking over a large part of the main shopping square in one of the major provincial towns. The problem was with its content – without any kind of refrigerated storage facilities it was frequently half full of fruit and vegetables of doubtful freshness. More than half of the produce had to be thrown away at the end of every week.

The concept was simple enough: the A-parent would fund and build a complex of refrigerated warehouses on the market site and the B-parent would operate it as part of its traditional market business. In return, the A-parent would become a joint equity owner of the new venture and the two parties would share the profits. The A-parent would also bring some of its flair for sales and marketing to the venture, helping to sell more of the fresh new produce to traditional customers who, it was felt, could not fail to be suitably impressed.

From the beginning, goodwill between the two parents was maintained at all times. It was decided that, while each of the two parties would carry out the responsibilities that 'it knew best', profits would be apportioned equally, everybody getting their fair share of the cake. Everything would be split fifty-fifty and equality (it was heralded) would be the watchword. The agreements were signed with a flourish, pleasantries exchanged and the IJV was formed.

Day 1 didn't go well. Further investigation of the financial assets of the B-parent produced a few surprises – it soon became doubtful whether they actually owned the freehold of part of the market, and the first contact with local banks was enlightening – they wanted the A-parent to secure any debt finance, preferring not to rely on the assets of the B-parent. An urgent meeting was convened to discuss the situation of B's fixed assets – A's request to see B's audited financial accounts was met with the well-meaning response: 'what audited accounts?' Tension was soon released when it was revealed that the accounts did exist *and* they showed healthy fixed assets, including the market premises. They also showed steadily increasing profits for at least the past ten years and a lively, it not a little optimistic, liquidity position.

With some embarrassment, B's director explained that their 'accounts' always looked like that, in fact, so did everybody else's – it was simply the done thing in this part of the world. 'Sorry, but there never was any debt security available and maybe somebody else does own a bit of the market premises,' he explained, when pressed.

The problem got worse when the question of profit distribution was discussed. How, asked the A-parent, could the equal split in profits be worked out if there was no way to agree on the amount to be shown in the P&L account for depreciation of assets? The B-parent didn't really see the problem with this; they would simply split the cash left at the end of the year, after paying all the expenses – including those of the new party that now owned that other bit of the market premises of course!

FINANCE: THE ORGANIZATIONAL IMPLICATIONS

In this chapter we have considered the IJV as effectively an investment activity of its parent organizations, looking at the broad effects of equity and debt finance and the way that finance has an effect on the structure of an IJV's activities. You would not be alone in concluding that IJV finance is a complex area, with many possible combinations of financial techniques to keep the aficionados happy. The financial positions of the parent companies follow a certain pattern, as we saw in Figure 8.4, with the formation of an IJV often being an exercise in complementarity between two very different organizations. We have also looked, with perhaps a little controversy, at the inevitability of the financial exit route at the end of an IJV's life cycle.

One of the dangers of IJV finance is the effect that it can have on the way that the venture organizes itself in other areas. Finance is often seen by senior management as the guiding force of a business venture, with implications well outside its own field. This can cause problems: there are many examples where the financial structure of a parent organization, replicated into other areas of activity, has resulted in a management structure which is unwieldy or lacks coherence. Such organizations often complain that they feel 'run' by accountants, or that the status of the producing parts of the business are relegated to second place behind those that hold the purse strings. Emotions can run high in situations like this.

There is a useful way of thinking about such dilemmas in Chapter 6. Remember how the IJV was conceived as a 'system' model, put together with the objective of obtaining viability of the business and other functions which act a facilitators – essential parts of the business in themselves, but better classed as a support function than as parts which warrant true autonomy? Finance fits neatly into this category – its true role is as a *facilitator*, which should be allowed to influence unnecessarily the other parts of IJV strategy.

CASE STUDY 8.3

Food distribution sector

From experiences in Western–Eastern European large-scale IJVs in the food distribution sector there is evidence that the type of IJV structure and financial performance are related.

IJVs which have grown big enough to become divisionalized in the Eastern Europe (B-parent) country have been seen to consistently out-perform other types. They perform better than 'functional' IJVs on measures of percentage growth than on, for example, internal rate of return (IRR). There is not much difference between the two types using return on equity (ROE) or return on investment (ROI) as assessment criteria. In these cases, high growth figures can be a little misleading, because IJVs which divisionalize generally do so because they are expanding, and so might be expected to produce high growth figures.

For mature-stage IJVs in the food distribution sector, divisionalized IJVs again show higher growth, but functional IJVs perform better on measures of return. A few IJVs that have retained a holding company structure have performed poorly in both respects, due to insufficient control at a strategic level, of the individual distribution activities in the Eastern Europe country.

SUMMARY

The financial scenery

IJVs are risky business, with lots of potential for financial problems. The two IJV parents have different financial priorities which doesn't help things.

The investment model

IJVs can be thought of as an investment for the two parents in the JV company. The model follows the conventional rules of finance, but with a few distortions:

- IJV funds: equity is usually more easily available, but more expensive, than debt.
- The A-parent normally ends up funding most of the initial equity injection.
- The B-parent, from the developing country, is often short of cash.
- The A-parent's objective is often linked to the IRR of the project. The B-parent is more likely to be interested in dividends and regular liquid payments.
- Capital structure, ie debt/equity ratio is of key importance for IJVs.
- All IJV financial projections should have a planned exit route.

A cautionary note

Accounting standards and practices differ dramatically between countries and continents. Even the mature industrialized countries cannot agree on a single set of standards. Many developing countries have a flawed illogical system or none at all. Misunderstandings in the financial position of IJV partners, and disagreements over the apportionment of profit are a common feature of IJVs that underestimate the problems these can cause.

Chapter 9

People

RETHINK: MERGING COMPANY CULTURES

For many managers, their vision of the international joint venture (IJV) company is one of merging of company cultures to a state where its people adopt a new set of expectations, values and ways of behaving, somewhere between those existing in the IJV's parent companies. Managers in one or other of the parent organizations may feel, quite naturally, that they alone can design a system of personnel practices that is best for the new joint organization.

The opposing view is that two different groups can only be successfully configured for co-operative working by creating a new group in which managers from both groups have an input into the system under which the joint group's people will work. This is a more sensitive and softer way of doing it.

INTRODUCTION: THE PROBLEM OF INDIVIDUALITY

The big dilemma of IJV personnel management is whether the system of personal practices used in an IJV is formulaic or bespoke. Historical precedent is split: many of the early transplant IJVs commissioned from Western European and Japanese A-parents used a formulaic system of personnel management based entirely on proven staff practices exported into the IJV host-country. In contrast, modern management practices in global organizations are swinging towards the idea of integration – carefully tailoring the system and practices to the precise needs and sensitivities, however fickle, of culturally different participants. Because of the variety of organizations, this requires that every IJV's personnel system is unique, or bespoke.

At the level of managers within the structure of an IJV, some individuality in the design of personnel systems is inevitable. Few modern, successful IJVs retain the ideal of a formulaic solution for very long – it soon becomes eroded by the practicalities of day-to-day people-management in the IJV host country. The implication here is that IJV personnel management is about flexibility and compromise rather than imposition. This requirement for flexibility extends throughout the hierarchy of an IJV structure. There are five main parts to it as shown in Figure 9.1. Note how these are 'nested' levels, rather than sequential, or complementary in the traditional business sense. Don't even start to confuse them as anything to do with a matrix management structure or the traditional routes of line management. We will take them in turn; remember that the common tenet of all five is *flexibility*, not management imperialism.

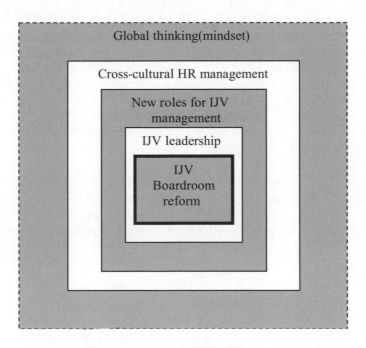

Figure 9.1 The five levels of IJV personnel management thinking

GLOBAL THINKING

A better term for this is the global mindset. Once any form of business organization extends outside its national boundary, it faces the challenge of internationalization. With IJVs, the nature of the business and location, places them firmly in the bracket of 'global' businesses. Globalization brings with it the difficulty of designing the organization and holding it to its viable organizational form against all the pressures that it faces. Personnel issues are at the centre of this because people-management is the *champion* of the art of globalizing a business. A central theme of this people-management is, in turn, the idea of a global mindset.

An IJV global mindset: what is it?

It is the mental filters through which the people in the IJV see their organization and to a lesser extent, the world outside. Employers (managers included) who possess a clear global mindset can make sense of the international form of their IJV, rather than seeing it as a desperate assembly of parts located in different countries. At a personal level a global mindset is linked to people's abilities to accept the fact that different parts of the joint organization will have different value systems and so place different levels of importance on features of day-to-day business life such as timescale, cost and quality. At a higher level, it also influences people's views on qualities such as reliability, honesty and integrity.

CASE STUDY 9.1

Creating a global mindset

Three organizations with extensive global IJV-type activity are Unilever, ABB and Dow Chemical. All place value on attaining a global mindset at senior level in the organization either by having different nationalities in the Board of Directors/Executive Committee or by ensuring high regard is given to foreign experience and language knowledge when selecting people for high level executive positions.

Why is mindset important?

A global mindset is important because of its strengths in shaping the way that an international organization works. It has three main effects:

1. It encourages the IJV's ability to take advantage of business opportunities.
2. It reduces much of the driving force behind inter-IJV tensions and conflict.
3. It helps to make the joint organization stable and viable (remember Chapter 4?).

Not all IJVs find a global mindset easy to achieve. Of those that do, many succeed in spite of significant cultural and ideological differences between the parent organizations. Investors in ventures between the United States, Japan, China and Arab countries can provide supporting evidence that 'different' does not necessarily mean 'incompatible'.

Implications for personnel management

Irrespective of the form or area of business of an IJV, one of the key roles of personnel management is to encourage the formation of a global mindset in the IJV. This cannot be added as a bolt-on extra somewhere during the life cycle of the business – by then it is too late – it has to form the bedrock of the venture at its formation stage. IJVs have shown incredible growth of mindset 'inertia', with personnel practices being decided during the final draft of the initial partner agreements, before the joint organization has even been conceived. Prejudices formed at this stage soon become ingrained and virtually impossible to change.

Figure 9.2 shows some of the ways in which personnel practices can be biased to encourage the growth of a global mindset amongst IJV staff. Note the implied training requirement contained in all the points. Several generations of IJV managers at the most senior level have discovered that it is rare for a global mindset to suddenly descend on their managers and staff – you have to train them. An IJV planned without a well-funded and culture-based training programme is likely to be restricting the chances of its own business success.

Start by encouraging individuals amongst other managers and staff from *both* IJV partner organizations.

Spread the encouragement from individuals to groups and intra-IJV collectives (eg design groups, quality committees etc).

Don't expect people to naturally adapt to differences in value systems and norms. *Teach* them.

Treat cultural differences as a chance to learn, rather than a reason for conflict. Start this from the very earliest stage of IJV formation.

Figure 9.2 Encouraging a global mindset – practical levers

CROSS-CULTURAL HR MANAGEMENT

It is useful to think of cross-cultural human resource (HR) management as a practical sub-activity of the global mindset. Its qualities make it difficult to apply in isolation to an organization, but if successful, it provides an excellent foundation for the wide task of managing staff across international boundaries.

The principles

Figure 9.3 is an adaptation of the model developed in earlier chapters concerning the IJV as a system of management interaction between different cultural groups. An important characteristic of the model is that the main route of management control lies horizontally 'across' between the practices of the different IJV parent organizations rather than vertically within each parent (which already have their own well-established ways of working). The message here is that the predominant HR issues within an IJV are cross-cultural ones, ie it is the intra-IJV personnel skills and attitudes that are the main lever for success or failure of the HR management system. This is a slightly different angle from the traditional view that HR management is about developing skills in production, finance, quality, marketing or whatever. These are undoubtedly useful skills but are not at the edge of the issue of whether an IJV will prosper or fail – it is the intra-IJV HR skills and attitudes that do that.

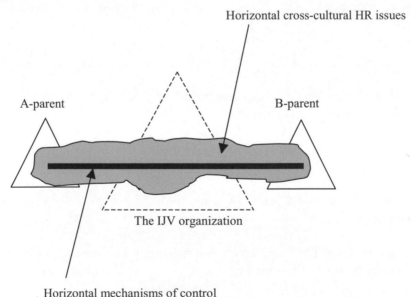

Figure 9.3 The principle of cross-cultural 'horizontal' HR issues

Cross-communication infers direct and expansive discussions between managers and staff from both IJV parent organizations. It is clear from successful IJVs that they have installed a carefully thought-out programme of meetings, seminars and job rotation to encourage this communication to grow. There is an easily observed contrast with poor or failed IJVs that have tried to avoid (unsuccessfully) the cross-cultural situation altogether, preferring to try and 'manage' each other at arm's length – by memo.

The cross-cultural skillset

If the root task of IJV HR management is to develop personnel who have an inherent sensitivity to intra-IJV cultural differences there has to be a target 'skillset' that goes with it. Figure 9.4 shows a typical one, in this case adapted from a successful European–Asian IJV in the consumer product sector. This skillset formed the basis of the IJV policy documents at the highest level of the HR function of the organization and was instrumental in bringing the two sides of the organization together, in spite of their obvious cultural differences and diversity. Note again how the general skills of business management are not excluded, but *are* relegated to lower down the list of priorities.

* *understanding* basic cultural differences;

* *appreciation* of variety in business practices and norms;

* *seeing* the IJV as a single business (rather than two halves);

* *developing* flexibility in approach;

* *avoiding* communication misunderstandings;

* business skills such as sales, marketing, customer service etc;

* discipline skills in production, contract management, quality etc.

Figure 9.4 A typical cross-cultural skillset

CASE STUDY 9.2

International Technology Partners: a question of cross-cultural commitment

It was the committee structure of International Technology Partners' Shanghai manufacturing facility that was causing the problem. Whenever a minor question about quality, design or production schedules arose, the B-parent committee structure took the issue, injected a lot of misunderstandings and spent the next seven days discussing a problem that didn't really exist.

The A-parent's view

The situation frustrated the US licensor A-parent to the point where even the most senior managers concurred on the following accusation about their IJV partner: 'first, they won't work to the structure we agreed; and, second, they tell lies (or at least not the truth).'

Senior A-parent directors back in the United States convinced themselves that the only explanation of the above report was that their Chinese partner lacked commitment to the IJV, were unprofessional, and just about impossible to work with. 'The only way to get this project moving,' reported the personnel director, 'is to cut through all of this committee stuff and replace them with our own people...'

The B-parent's view

The Chinese B-parent committee had just about had enough of the way the local US staff tried to bypass their structured way of making decisions. The committee continued to invite them to attend the morning meetings but they had only come once and had left half-way through to make some telephone calls. It was felt that the committee had made real efforts to accommodate the staff structures and way of working set out in the IJV operating agreements but their US partner didn't seem to be interested, preferring to implement their own, unilateral solutions to subjects like design and quality. Several times now there had been the need to remind this partner that the whole philosophy of the IJV was supposed to be about joint decision-making and complementarity. The situation had frustrated the committee's six directors to the point where the following accusations were thought (but not spoken): 'first, our partner won't work to the real-world implications of the content of the IJV operating agreement; and, second, our partner is losing commitment to this IJV.'

It was difficult to know how to improve the situation – suggestions to their US partner that 'further discussions are required on a number of points' were answered rather brusquely – the Americans were even insisting on an agenda, and a list of people who would attend the meetings. One of the more junior members of the design department had the nerve to suggest that maybe all Western licensors were as bad-mannered and insensitive as this one.

Is there a solution to this?

Yes. These arguments have nothing to do with lack of commitment of either side. They are almost purely culture-based – the problem is simply that the structure and working arrangements set out in the IJV agreements were not well adapted to the cultural behaviour of either IJV partner. They were a weak compromise, a solution which ultimately benefits no-one. The cultural implication must be understood and built in to the personnel practices and protocol at an early stage if the above questions of commitment are to be avoided. Cultural acceptance (and a bit of corporate humility) is the answer.

IJV LEADERSHIP

Viewed as a temporary marriage of convenience of two or more companies, it is easy to set the leadership qualities required of IJV managers as the same as those in any other business: vision, drive and determination, tempered with a bit of understanding. Take a more incisive view, however, of the IJV as a different form of globalization and the requirements increase: leadership of truly globalized IJVs needs genuine industry foresight.

Styles

IJV leadership styles in past years have tended towards the 'programming' (top down) type of approach, reflected in the practices (and problems) of early automotive industry and manufacturing-sector IJVs. Contemporary practice now favours a wider, consensual approach, sympathetic to the issues of cultural differences and interdependence between the A- and B-parent organizations of the IJV. It is this acceptance of the consensual approach to leadership which is the core of the 'new vision' of IJV management, replacing traditionally business orientated visionary concepts such as quality, design or customer service. The essence of this newer consensual approach is given in Figure 9.5.

IJV leadership is about:

- stimulating a free flow of cross-boundary ideas;

- building networks of flexible relationships between culturally different parts of the IJV;

- creating an open and empowered organizational climate;

- keeping a methodical approach to quality and cost issues.

Figure 9.5 Consensual style of IJV leadership

Leadership responsibilities

There are no hard-and-fast rules which say that IJV leadership has to come from either the A- or B-parent organization alone. In technology-based IJVs it is commonplace for the licensor organization A-parent to *want* to provide the leadership – it often sees itself as the founder of the IJV. Conversely, for ventures in the communication or infrastructure sectors, where the joint organization's main assets are to be based in the developing B-parent country, the B-parent's position is stronger, and it may see itself as the leader of the enterprise.

Both of these arrangements have proved successful and unsuccessful in individual cases. The greatest opportunity of developing good IJV leadership, however, seems to be that related to the use of the consensual approach mentioned earlier. This is not the same as leadership *by* consensus. The idea is that both parent organizations commit to discussing with each other what the leadership issues of their IJV are, and the actual leaders evolve from the process of this discussion. This type of approach has found use in pharmaceutical and food-product-based IJVs – newer industries with fewer historical geographical prejudices.

Leadership actions

The suggested 'actions' of managers who strive to provide leadership for a business has been covered in many management books. Most will tell you about the virtues of having a vision, listening to staff, defining clear strategic objectives and so on. It is fair to say that these wholesome principles apply also to IJVs. Fine – so is there anything new?

Not all recent IJVs have done well using these standard techniques. For every venture that has thrived under the influence of a leader with incisive vision of the market opportunity, there are others that have become inward-looking to the point where they have been unable to react to these opportunities, despite their transparency. There are also those that have failed to perform because of conflicting leadership visions and strategies between the parent organizations. In these cases, two leaders have proved worse than one.

Some of the best research information comes from the automotive sector, from IJVs set up between 1984 and 1992 and still in operation in 1997. These are above average performing businesses which have proved their resilience. The core leadership actions in these businesses were summarized as:

- *initiating* a global mindset – mainly at higher management levels (it then cascades downwards);
- *encouraging* the parts of the IJV to communicate with each other;
- *pulling* the joint organization into shape rather than trying to push it;
- *dissolving* intra-conflict across the cultural divide.

While not exactly traditional in origin, these are good IJV-specific leadership actions that will help the venture to develop and survive. You can think of them as an essential supplement to other well-documented, but more generic, types of leadership actions – not a substitute for them. Use them all together.

CASE STUDY 9.3

IJV ambassadors in the minerals sector

IJVs in the rapidly expanding minerals sector in Eastern Europe and Central Asia exhibit particular forms of leadership action. Those IJVs that have developed quickly and successfully have had easily identifiable leaders who relinquish the reins of direct control for a role as ambassador to people and groups within the joint organization. They convey the impression of a joint organization that is responsible, keen and effective – one in which the A- and B-parents trust each other. Internally, their ambassadorial role is directed towards filtering out intra-IJV stresses and strains.

NEW ROLES FOR IJV MANAGERS

The role of managers within an operating IJV is wider than their equivalent role in a unitary business organization. This widening of the role is present at all levels – not just those generally attributed as being 'senior' management positions. As well as possessing a global mindset as a higher-level ideal, IJV managers' roles involve four particular aspects and it is the expansion of managers' roles to encompass these that makes the job so challenging, and occasionally difficult. They are:

- understanding the IJV model;
- sensitivity to the IJV life cycle;
- cross-border information ability;
- capabilities within the control mechanism.

Understanding the IJV model

It is perfectly feasible for managers working within a single culture business not to understand the real form of their organization. Many rely on their quasi-technical skills laced with political behaviour to fulfil their management role within the company structure. IJVs are not so easy. The cultural and political complexity, coupled with the unstable organizational character means that managers need to work towards a detailed understanding of the *form* of their joint organization, before they can hope to manage within it. It is this understanding of the structure of a joint organization (rather than merely its organization chart) that provides the key to making things happen, particularly across international boundaries. Many managers find this difficult.

CASE STUDY 9.4

Understanding the IJV model: virtual teams

Large businesses in the petroleum sector are involved in IJVs based mainly on achieving economies of scale (scale alliances) or technical complementarity. The industry is noted for its competence in HR polices that promote organizational learning between global partners. One company has enrolled nearly 1,000 of its managers onto 'virtual' teams (nothing to do with matrix management) with the objective of sharing knowledge on best practices in their industry. The high corporate commitment to the IJV model is demonstrated by the fact that this occurred at the same time as a company-wide delayering plan for middle management.

Sensitivity to the IJV life cycle

As well as having the correct picture of the joint organization, managers need to understand the life cycle of the IJV. You can think of this as appreciating the dynamic position of the joint organization, as well as recognizing it in its static state. The nature of many of the day-to-day management problems, and their solution, depends on the position of the IJV in its life cycle (see Chapter 4). This is a key message for managers – that the result of their actions and decisions are time-dependent – which means that the nature of their management role will change as the IJV ages. The effects are important enough to make this sensitivity to the effects of life cycle almost a management discipline in itself. It is also easily neglected, because it can involve uncomfortable changes in stance and opinion – not always popular things to do.

Cross-border information ability

This is about pure information-handling skills, but applied in a cross-border context. The difference is that an IJV manager's role is more to do with information *processing* than the mechanics of the communication process. Figure 9.6 shows the difference: note how it is the processing activity that adds value to the role of IJV managers. Large volumes of communications are unavoidable in IJVs but it is the processing ability of its managers that helps slash the variety of this communication down to a level that the organization can handle. The alternative is information overload – an all-too-common occurrence in manufacturing-based IJVs whose information processing abilities are traditionally poor.

Capabilities within the control mechanism

Experienced managers would see nothing new in being required to exercise control as part of their management role. This is particularly the case in heavily divisionalized or project-orientated businesses with a matrix management structure where it is necessary to exercise control and co-ordination across various organizational boundaries. The challenge for IJV managers, centres around the two characteristics of this control that we saw in Chapter 7, ie:

1. IJVs respond better to indirect control mechanisms than direct hierarchical ones.
2. The key span of control in an IJV is horizontal (between the partners).

Managers generally find the first of these easiest to adopt. It is within the repertoire of most competent man-managers to alter their style to suit the

Information processing skills (valuable)	Communication skills (desirable but not so valuable)
Interpretation of the meaning of communication between different nationalities.	Getting the parts of the IJV to communicate with each other.
Attenuating large amounts of information into a concise summary.	Cascading faxes to other IJV managers (big deal!).
Balancing written and verbal communication across cultural boundaries.	Confirming verbal discussions in writing to other managers.

Figure 9.6 Management roles: the difference between information processing and communication

situation – even adapting this to work across the international boundary of the IJV. The second is more difficult. The idea of replacing well-established mental models of hierarchy and vertical spans of control with the softer, horizontal mechanisms of indirect control can be difficult. The natural tendency of having to manage across geographical and cultural boundaries is to want to increase the level of hierarchical control, rather than relax it. Expect to see (and feel) the pressure of this dilemma in the role of IJV management. The greatest organizational reward, however, results from resisting the pressure to rely on hierarchical methods, rather than succumbing to it.

CASE STUDY 9.5

A rethink: the Board

The board of any business, chosen largely by itself, normally turns out to be a bit of a mixture. A careful balance of traditional skill and experience, edged with a touch of acquisitiveness works well. The carefully crafted Board acts as a focus for decisions concerning 'the business' and provides the mechanism by which the organization is run.

Boards are self-referential, and so exert close control of their own membership. Value is placed on members' time spent as member of that particular board, and their still-current legacy of decisions made and proposals debated and accepted. Boards have precious little time for attractive novelty, even if it does not hurt.

BOARDROOM REFORM

The traditional comfort of the boardroom situation rarely extends to IJVs. The nature of the venture is such that the business environment is loose and transient – it may even have an uncomfortable feel to it. On a positive note, the role of IJV boards is stimulated by the newness of the business challenges ahead – there is often a feeling of opportunism, tinged with only a little apprehension. The international character, and the co-operative nature of joint venture activities places the coherence of the most closely knit boards under stress. Coupled with the change of management structures, to include the other partner, senior IJV managers and directors can be excused for seeing the situation as a threat to the status quo. This situation is not restricted to traditional or inward-looking businesses – those that consider themselves modern, market-orientated and entrepreneurial are equally at risk.

The challenge of IJV management provides a useful chance to obtain a new impression on what 'the Board' actually does – or at least what it is supposed to be doing. You can think of this as an exercise in IJV thinking rather than the promotion of any particular management theory or ideology. Figure 9.7 shows one way to illustrate it. Figure 9.7 (a) is the traditional view of management board: a balance of internal control responsibilities and external views, keeping a running brief on developments outside the organization, watchful for new opportunities. Within those parts of the board charged with the duties of internal control of the organization are various parts (directors) with responsibilities for production, personnel, design, IT and so on. The marketing and externally-looking functions bring to the board a system of checks and balances, working to help the organization adapt to the changing external environment of its business.

Part (b) of Figure 9.7 shows a more IJV-orientated approach. This conceives the role of the board as a clear bilateral group (with A- and B-parent members) with the traditional responsibility 'blocks' replaced instead by an assembly of accountability loops. The three main loops extend between each parent's board members and its operations, and between the parents' board members themselves. The idea of the accountability loop is that each party is accountable to its partner for its actions, and vice versa. Instead of causing

(a) A traditional view

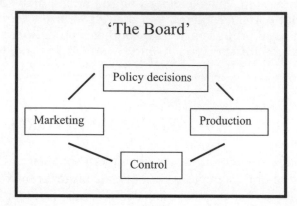

(b) An IJV-specific view

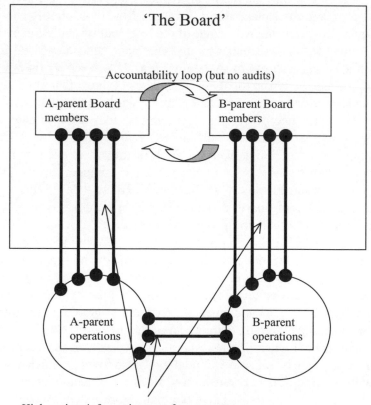

Figure 9.7 A model of Board responsibility

divisions within the board, this has the effect of encouraging bilateral decision-making and actions – as long as the accountability applies to everything within the board's role, not just selected parts from it chosen to suit one partner or the other.

To many non-IJV managers, this approach constitutes boardroom reform. Look at the four main characteristics of the model:

- *Equality*. The rules of the new boardroom are that the A- and B-parent organizations both have representation – in physical number and influence. The partners to the IJV are organizational equals, irrespective of their level of share-holding. This new board sees itself as an instrument of organizational power, not a servant of some earlier financial allocation.
- *Absolute trust*. Each partner in a loop relinquishes its legitimate right to audit the other on what it is doing. This is done on the understanding that each partner's interests on the board are allowed to be thoughtfully represented.
- *Rich information transfer*. The accountability loops have to be filled with high-variety information transfer for the loop to work properly at all. At this senior level, the information is about the rules and regulations of the IJV's organizational system (Chapter 6 again), and subject to continual review between the partners. This helps iron out cultural and procedural differences. It also helps to diffuse any potential authoritarian atmosphere that is (always) in danger of developing.
- *Internally focused*. This is about the board's ability to be concerned with its cultural balance. It is *not* the same as having a board (and therefore its IJV organization) which is inward looking and parochial – the internal focus is kept in perspective, while leaving the organization free to pursue aggressive marketing, technology development, or whatever, as it thinks fit. The main purpose of this focus is to stop the board itself becoming biased towards one parent or the other. Uncontrolled bias at this high level can be detrimental to an IJV's life cycle and its business prospects.

These four steps lie firmly at the centre of the problems and challenges that face the board level manager in an IJV. While there is no guarantee that they are *success* criteria (it is the IJV organization that decides its success or failure, not just its board), they do seem to have an effect. Coupled with the overall organizational objective of the global mindset, IJVs with this type of board reform suffer fewer and less serious management problems than those with the traditional 'blocks of responsibility' structure.

CASE STUDY 9.6

International Technology Partners: boardmanship

Phase 1: The early life cycle

After the first twelve months of operation of the International Technology Partners (ITP) IJV it was widely known that the current Board arrangements were 'not working'. Almost everyone above middle management level knew this except, that is, for the board themselves. The structure was as shown in Figure 9.8 (a) – a board constructed along traditional lines with a split of directors from the A- and B-parents, chosen to match their suitability to the role and strategy of the IJV organization. Design and quality directors were drawn from the technology-licensor A-parent, a natural move, given that design and quality formed the core of the technology packages that was being transplanted into the overseas IJV. As a concession to the local culture and employment practices of the developing country, B part of the venture, the personnel director role had been agreed to be shared between A and B. Directors remained based in their country of origin, with monthly board meetings being alternated between Cincinnati, Shanghai and a neutral location (Frankfurt Airport business centre).

The sources of the discontent in the ITP board were not difficult to find (or even *foresee*). The hierarchical precedence of 'design' above 'manufacturing' caused problems from day one with the design and manufacturing directors (communicating through interpreters) unable to agree on almost anything. Design changes, once initiated, were implemented with a disdain clear to middle management and technical staff. It felt sometimes as if the manufacturing staff *wanted* to find problems with manufacturing new designs. The same type of arguments arose over quality. To avoid too much high level conflict, each ITP board member soon retreated back to the emotional security of their own parent organization. By the end of the fourth month of the IJV there were two clearly identifiable 'camps' to the board, cleaved precisely along the geographical plane. Increasingly elaborate excuses were used by board members to excuse themselves from attending board meetings in each others' location. The only consensus was that everyone disliked the meetings in Frankfurt Airport business centre. All of this had to change.

Phase 2: Evaluation

Figure 9.8 (b) shows the evolved form of the ITP board as it moved uncomfortably into the second year of IJV operation. The structure had drifted away from its hierarchical origins into more democratic arrangement. Each director's role maintained its relative importance to the success of the business, but they related to each other in a less restrictive way. Note the other changes:

- The board are now all located at the manufacturing works in the B-parent developing country (China).
- The technology licensor A-parent (from the United States) has relinquished its ambition to be 'in control' of the IJV. Control is now exercised less directly (as discussed in chapter 7).
- Quality, design and manufacturing directors have undergone a role-reversal. Local Chinese B-parent directors now play a bigger role having learnt quickly to almost close the early technology gap.
- Personnel function remains locally managed (as before). Language training has taken over as the most important training requirement (not design or marketing).

This revised structure may look less directed in its approach but it is much better at handling the organizational and cultural complexity that lives in IJVs. It involves less boardmanship and internal bickering and a balanced approach to the challenge of international business management.

PEOPLE: KEY POINTS

IJV personnel management is about merging the skills and requirements of diverse cultural and organizational groups. There are no simple formulaic answers about what an IJV personnel system should look like. Expect them all to be different.

Successful IJVs have generally introduced a global mindset into the thinking repertoires of their managers and staff.

The important aspects of personnel management in IJVs are:

1. *Global thinking*: understanding (and accepting) the international character of the IJV form.
2. *Cross-cultural HR management*: seeing HR management as the 'horizontal' control of diverse cultural groups within the organization (see Figure 9.3).
3. *IJV leadership*: appreciating that consensus is better than conflict.

(a) Phase 1 – the initial Board 'structure'

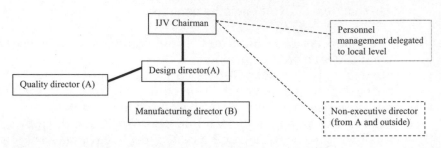

(A or B shows origin and location of each Board member)

(b) Phase 2 – how it developed

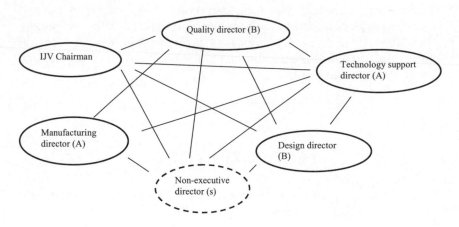

All directors located on the B-parent's site

Figure 9.8 International Technology Partners IJV: development of the Board

4. *New roles for IJV managers*: four 'new' roles are:
    (a) understanding the IJV model (properly);
    (b) sensitivity to the IJV life cycle;
    (c) cross-border information ability;
    (d) capabilities within the control mechanism.
5. *IJV Boardroom reform*.

Chapter 10

Agreements

While it is true that some IJVs seem to operate quite successfully without a lot of formal licences and agreements, some get themselves into awful problems. The concept of a joint venture between two or more parties infers, in the Western world at least, that there is some kind of binding agreement between them, setting out who is responsible for what. We have seen in previous chapters the ever-present potential for internal conflict within the structure of an IJV – the international character alone is sufficient to produce problems of misunderstanding and misinterpretation if there is no proper written agreement to which the parties can refer.

An IJV is, in effect, a three-way contract between businesses. The two parent organizations and the new jointly-owned IJV company all have responsibilities to each other – responsibilities that need to be fulfilled if the new business is to be able to work successfully. In contrast to buy-supply contracts, the IJV commitment contains not only formal legal responsibilities but also softer, often unwritten, organizational aspects about how the joint venture will work in practice. This places IJV agreements in a difficult position; they have to be instruments that both decide the allocation of resources and responsibilities, and set the framework for the culture and shared values of a complex (and transient) organizational form. In addition, they must be careful not to stray too far into the field of the strategic operation of the IJV – they are not a handy way to persuade the IJV partners to follow a 'mission statement' put together by enterprising IJV managers.

This chapter looks at the scope and extent of the agreements that are used in IJVs. We will look at them mainly in their role as a 'fall-back position' for the IJV parties rather than in their context as a tool for defining organizational culture, which is a separate story. You will not find advice in this chapter on the detailed wording of the IJV agreements themselves because that is the role of the lawyers. Instead, emphasis is placed on the scope and content of the agreements – information that needs to be presented to the lawyers anyway before they can add the detailed legal wording. We will also look at some short case studies illustrating major points. Again, there is nothing contrived about these case studies – they are all taken from the real commercial world.

CASE STUDY 10.1

Agreements: a rethink

Agreements do not have the same meaning in all cultures. A parent organization from the United States or Northern Europe may enter into an agreement on the understanding that it represents a single, unique way that things will happen and that no changes are either desirable or possible. The same agreement, interpreted by a Southern European or Latin American parent, will more likely be seen as a statement of general intent – as a basis of negotiation for what really happens when the business activity starts. A few other cultures in the world will see it as something that has to be signed merely as an item of protocol because that is what everyone else does, and that the whole idea is for it to be replaced with another agreement (which will also have to be changed as things progress). These types of misunderstanding can be expensive.

THE SCOPE OF IJV AGREEMENTS

Agreements apply to all phases of an IJV's life so their scope is very wide. It is of little use having detailed agreements covering some parts of an IJV's business operation with other parts left to chance. With the overall complexity of a venture extending across different countries it becomes inevitable that the agreements themselves are going to be complex, with some areas that are overlapping, or incomplete. In a well-organized IJV the agreements are divided into five sets covering the way the business is to be structured and operated (see Figure 10.1).

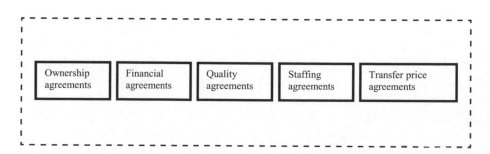

Figure 10.1 The scope of IJV agreements

OWNERSHIP

This is the simplest, but arguably the most important, part of the agreement structure. Traditionally, the apportionment of shares in a joint business is set by the Memoranda and Articles of Association. The same procedure applies to IJVs but with additional complicating factors. The main one is the influence of the IJV life cycle. We saw in previous chapters how this life cycle influences the behaviour of an IJV business in several areas. This manifests itself in the need to build provisions for *change* into the IJV agreement, to enable the apportionment and responsibilities of ownership to match the challenges faced by the business at the various stages in its life cycle. To do this, the ownership agreement is configured into two parts: initial share structure and share options.

Initial share structure

The initial share structure is apportioned using the general methodology shown in Chapter 8. While you will see other, less complex ways of doing it, the use of venture-capital based techniques fits well into most IJV situations. One of the main purposes of the ownership agreement is to set out the initial types and structures of shares in a way that satisfies both parents' investment criteria.

Options

IJV agreements must contain the provision for changes in the ownership structure. Over, say, a five-year time horizon of an IJV agreement it is not uncommon to have two or three review points at which the apportionment of the number and types of shares can be changed. It is fundamentally the effect of the life cycle that brings the need for such changes.

GUIDELINES ON IJV OPTION AGREEMENTS

IJV share ownership options clauses should:

- specify *specific times* for the options (normally annually);
- be constrained to *specific options* rather than encourage free-for-all discussion;
- link the take-up of options to the financial performance of the complete IJV business, not that of its component parts, or its parent organizations.

This last point carries an important message for IJV managers. Its objective is to reinforce the idea of the IJV as a true separate business entity, rather than a convenient arm's-length liaison between selected groups of managers from the parent organizations. It is important that it is the financial performance of the *complete* IJV that is the trigger for any lucrative share options clauses, rather than the performance of any individual management groups within it. The alternative is to encourage parochialism of management groups that 'originated' from either parent A or parent B with the inevitable conflict and in-fighting that follows. The emphasis of clauses in even high-level agreements should therefore be biased towards recognizing the IJV as a separate entity rather than a marriage of convenience.

CASE STUDY 10.1

International Technology Partners: share options

'The problem with new designs in an old factory is getting the quality right.' The managing director continued, 'and if you don't get the quality right that new market is nothing but illusion – it may as well not exist.' Not surprisingly, the new combined board of directors of International Technology Partners nodded in approval – or at least no-one seemed to have any better ideas.

It was decided that the share option structure of the new IJV would be based not just on profitability but also on the quality levels that the (ex-Parent B's) manufacturing facility could achieve. This would work in three ways:

- At the end of year 2 of the IJV, the B-parent would be given the option to purchase 200,000 preference shares if the reject rate of consumer goods produced was less than 1 per cent of production volume for the second year. This would increase B's overall rate of return from its IJV investment.
- Further incentive for the B-parent would be given in the form of a 'management ratchet'. At an agreed level of aggregated pre-tax profit, B would be given the option of converting half of its A-ordinary shares into ordinary shares.
- Under a reciprocal agreement based on the aggregated pre-tax profit, parent A would be able to realize 10 per cent of its cumulative growth to the end of year 2 as a dividend.

This is an example of a balanced share option scheme, with performance-related incentives for both partners.

FINANCIAL AGREEMENTS

Formal agreements setting out the financial arrangements of the IJV are often the first priority of the IJV parent organizations. They are generally seen as the 'core' part of the business agreement. In practice, there is no fixed format for these agreements, some are long and exhaustive while others end up as little more than a framework, leaving room for the detail to be filled in later as the business progresses. Figure 10.2 shows the breakdown of a typical set of financial agreements.

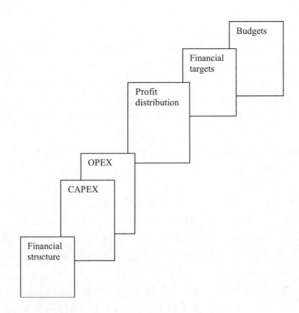

Figure 10.2 The IJV financial agreements 'set'

Financial structure

This covers the distribution of shares and other financial factors, including debt/equity leverage, as discussed in Chapter 8. The characteristics of this part of the agreement are:

1. It is *prescriptive* with little room for statements of principle or generality.
2. It makes provision for changes anticipated during the life cycle of the IJV.
3. It is legally binding on both parent organizations and the new joint venture organization.

Notice how Figure 10.2 infers that the financial structure agreement is separate from the others. This is commonplace in large highly-structured businesses which tend to place emphasis more on the formal and legalistic agreements than on those that deal with the operation of the business. In smaller businesses you should find that all parts of the financial agreements are given a more balanced status.

CAPEX/OPEX agreements

In the language of IJVs, CAPEX and OPEX are the names given to the agreements that apportion the capital and revenue expenditure of the parent organizations. They apply both to the formation of the joint venture business and the initial period of its operation, normally the first year. There is a link, of sorts, between the CAPEX agreement and the financial structure agreement. For a simple IJV structure the apportionment of capital expenditure (on fixed assets) frequently just mirrors the equity split between the A- and the B-parent raised in the financial structure agreement. Be warned that this is not a hard-and-fast rule – CAPEX and OPEX expenditure is sometimes amalgamated, only to be brought together in the end of year IJV accounts. There are a few well-worn guidelines in this area.

1. The parent (A or B) 'nearest' the expenditure (in an organizational as well as physical sense) is best equipped to manage that expenditure. This is one factor that can distort the practical CAPEX vs OPEX expenditure pattern from the idealized split inferred by the content of the financial structure agreement.
2. The OPEX agreement needs some flexibility because of unforeseen changes that always occur during the first year of IJV operation. It is wise to assume that both A- and B-parents will have such changes to contend with. The B-parent in its developing country is normally in the position of greatest business uncertainty and it is usual for local operating costs to be subject to several rounds of renegotiation immediately the IJV starts trading.
3. The worst things that an OPEX agreement can try to do is to attempt to manage all the aspects of the IJV. Its correct role is a financial one only – there is no firm link to any elements of hierarchy or strategic direction of the IJV.

All three features can be difficult to achieve in practice. CAPEX and OPEX agreements can be notoriously tricky to control: some attaining a too-powerful position while others lack decision and firm direction. Perhaps the best way to think of them is as one of the *facilitators* of effective management of the IJV, rather then as a set of inflexible rules which cannot be broken.

Profit distribution

The issue of profit distribution is responsible for the deterioration of many otherwise well-managed IJVs. Despite the apparent robustness of most financial structure agreements (which outline the agreed principles of profit distribution) there is still a surprising amount of interpretation that can be read into such agreements. Differences in cultural understandings between the IJV's parent organizations do not help the situation. The issue generally centres on how profit (or loss) is distributed as conditions *change* through the life of the IJV. Frankly, this is just about inevitable, which means that agreements about profit distribution need to be contingent on what is happening in the business at the time. The best way to do this is to have three or four different scenarios (about profit level, sales volume etc), each with its separate matched profit distribution agreement. This helps avoid internal arguments between the IJV partners.

There are interesting empirical findings for what happens when profit levels change in an IJV business:

- When profit out-turn figures are lower than projected, this is frequently attributed to the poor performance of the IJV's developing country (B-parent) managers and staff. This results in serious management pressure on the validity of the B-parent's financial return (mostly taken as dividend cash payments under the financial model introduced in Chapter 8).
- If profit exceeds expectation, the credit for the good performance paradoxically swings in favour of the A-parent. This is particularly prevalent in technology-based IJVs where the A-parent is the technology licensor.

These findings hold good for IJVs across various spheres of business. They point towards one of the fundamental characteristics of developed/developing country IJVs – that of the developed-country A-parent organization having a belief in its fundamental right to preferential profits from the IJV business but wishing to limit its exposure in the event of the venture producing a serious loss. The message here is that the profit distribution agreement does fulfil a role in defining the fundamental hierarchy of the joint organization. Furthermore, it does this in a way which is not immediately obvious, and slightly dangerous – the concept of the 'dominant' parent organization, introduced briefly in Chapter 4.

Budgets and targets

Financial budgets and targets form the binding energy of a business organization. The transient nature of IJVs increases the need for such mechanisms of financial control and regulation. Without them it is doubtful whether an IJV business could work at all; the instability that lives in most jointly-managed enterprises would soon take over, leading to a state of disarray, if not confusion.

Despite their importance, it is rare for financial budgets and targets to form part of the formal agreements between IJV parents. The result is that many suffer from budget-related problems during their first year of trading. The main culprit is nearly always insufficient working capital caused by slow sales growth or high revenue costs, rather than business volume-related factors such as over-trading. Only about 10 or 15 per cent of IJVs ever get into an over-trading situation; it is more common for them to suffer from lack of sales or poor supply-side cost control.

Given that we can expect new IJVs to experience working capital problems the next step is hardly surprising – the parent organizations are approached for more cash. In reality, this normally means the A-parent, who is likely to be in the best position to respond. There is nothing inherently *wrong* with this scenario – it is common, being played out in IJVs across all business sectors. The danger, however, is when it is unexpected – the sudden realization of working capital problems can place stress on the most carefully tailored IJV management structure. This is another root cause of lack of management confidence and its partner, internal tension – factors which lead to IJV failure. There is an easy way around this problem: proper agreement on funds flow control.

Funds flow control

The most stable early-life IJVs are those that have made well developed agreements between A- and B-parents on the control of funds flow. The process starts with properly-itemised funds flow monthly projections. This shows how funds are apportioned during the first year of a newly commissioned IJV, with emphasis on not only the traditional source and application of funds, but also the relative responsibilities of both the A- and B-parents for each piece of financial activity. The idea is to inject an extra financial control mechanism into the IJV management system (look back at Chapters 6 and 7 if you are still confused over this definition) at just the right place. The objective is better control – to help the venture through the tension-filled periods of its early life. The advantages of this funds flow mechanism are:

1. It introduces *detailed planning*.
2. It provides a better real-time analysis of the position of the fledgling business than the annual published balance sheets, which are often little more than a senior management placebo.

3. It is an early indicator of changes necessary in the IJV's capital structure (eg an increase in debt finance or a change in equity distribution in return for a further cash injection from one of the parents).

The main IJV businesses that are likely to suffer from not building funds flow control into the structure of formal agreements are those containing independent A-parents which themselves have a shaky working capital situation. Larger multi-company A-parents are better able to withstand early working capital problems by providing extra cash injection to their IJV. The downside, however, is that the decline of the IJV, if or when it comes, can be faster and more dramatic. Big companies can mean big losses.

QUALITY AGREEMENTS

Businesses in economically developed countries have made huge steps over the past 15 years in improving the quality of their goods and services. Standards such as ISO 9000 have gained wide acceptance as a workable model of quality management. This, in turn, has led to the development of more esoteric variants such as Total Quality Management (TQM), Taguchi techniques, and others. While these systems have not proved to be formulae for overnight business success, they have undeniably improved the quality of goods and services across many business sectors.

Although the adoption of quality management systems has not been limited to economically mature business cultures it is in these countries that it has had the most effect. Despite the almost feverish spread of ISO9000 accreditation systems in developing countries, the process has not been sufficient to overcome the cultural resilience to adopting practices that are necessary for these systems to be a success. Contrary to public relations-type announcements, it seems that quality management systems do not travel well across cultural divides – even if they *should*. Further evidence for this is provided by IJVs that have been formed with the prime objective of improving quality levels of developing-country businesses – consumer goods, food, and clothing manufacture are good examples. It is clearly not easy for developing countries to lay aside their long cultural traditions and replace them with the overnight implementation of a quality management system, no matter how well proven its success in other countries.

Against this background, quality problems in IJVs fall neatly into two areas:

1. *A-parent problems* are most often caused by management difficulties in transplanting a successful quality management regime into a new joint business with a local developing-country culture. Some A-parents expect

this to be easy, or are too arrogant and self-centred to understand the cultural problems.

2. *B-parent problems* are based more on a lack of global experience than poor business acumen or understanding. A high proportion of developing countries (particularly those with a history of communist or socialist thinking) labour under the debilitating effect of a philosophy of business governed by central planning, illusory production levels and a staff motivation level approaching zero. It is not difficult to understand why suddenly implementing a wondrous new quality management system in their part of a new IJV is going to be difficult.

These two categories of quality problems have the unpleasant habit of appearing together in a new IJV situation just, so it seems, to make things as difficult as possible for its management (you).

CASE STUDY 10.2

Quality (mis)management: International Technology Partners IJV

'Just how many quality control managers do they have?' The newly-appointed quality director (hot from his A-parent desk in Cincinnati) continued, 'And if they've got so much quality control, then why do they need to form an IJV to build our new designs properly in the first place, they could simply have done it under licence, couldn't they?'

The first quality management system (QMS) meeting of the new International Technology Partners IJV produced a few surprises. Held on-site at B's existing manufacturing plant in Shanghai, China it was attended by the new A-parent QMS director, his assistant, and 15 staff from the B-parent's manufacturing works, all of whom claimed to have something to do with product quality.

The QMS director's well-intentioned diplomacy hardly hid his increasing irritation as the morning progressed – claims of 'high quality goods' were made by almost everyone present. As if to prove the point an example of the B-parent's existing (pre-IJV) product range was produced for examination – proudly displaying no less than 10 QC inspection stamps – added at various stages of their manufacture and testing. 'So, exactly what is it', one of the (presumably) more senior B-staff quality people asked, 'that you would like to teach us about quality?'

This question was shelved until after lunch, the afternoon quorum consisting of the original three A-parent staff but only six of the original 15 B-parent staff, accompanied by two unannounced others who claimed to be 'directors of quality' for the existing production line. Discussions centred on quality plans, sampling techniques, statistical process control and bits of jargon such as 'quality is a journey, not a destination', 'right first time', and suchlike. Every question that the QMS director asked received an answer which indicated that the existing production line had a perfectly good quality system and, what's more it was workable, and the existing staff liked it.

Discussion went on for three days. Eventually, the only acceptable solution seemed to be to agree that perhaps the only time that quality could be assessed properly (rather than sitting talking about it) was after the new IJV production line had started producing the new range of products – 'then we'll see...', was heard to be muttered by somebody.

The solution: quality agreements

The pivotal role of quality in most types of business suggests that the whole issue of quality needs to be given formal treatment within the structure of an IJV. This means that there needs to be written agreement. The inherent difficulty with quality management (call it what you like) is its intangibility – it is open to interpretation and subjective opinion from all sides. This makes it a fertile breeding ground for problems in the volatile cross-cultural situation that exists in an IJV. The transplant types of IJV have proved particularly susceptible to problems caused by the informality of quality agreements. General statements of intent soon evaporate when faced with the realities and cost constraints of operating the business. In order to fulfil the JV objectives we saw in Chapter 5, quality has to be treated as a major issue of technology transfer, with a clear management focus on what is to be achieved, and how.

The role of quality 'techniques'

A mass of quality management techniques have evolved over the past 20 years or so. Structured methods based on the ISO 9000 published standards have been followed by a flurry of more esoteric techniques such as Total Quality Management (TQM), Taguchi methods, quality circles and others, each claiming to be better or easier to use than the last. Unfortunately (whether or not they are of any practical use), the more advanced of these techniques are just about impossible to incorporate into formal agreements between IJV partners. The agreement would soon be defeated by the absolute subjectivity of whether the A-parent or the B-parent had complied with, for instance, the 'total quality commitment' required by a TQM-based agreement, or, if not which bit had not been properly complied with. The situation is slightly better with the ISO 9000-based standards. In its basic form some of its content is capable of being grafted into agreements that can be used to agree and control some of the important quality management aspects of an IJV business but it can still prove difficult to implement.

Mission statements

It is best not to confuse corporate 'mission statements' with the real operational workings of an IJV. IJV mission statements (they all seem to have one) generally make reference to quality management in some way – expressing the organization's desire to excel at quality management, or something similar. Expect these mission statements to sound good. Opinions vary as to whether they actually produce any influence on the way that an IJV behaves – it is a fact that those IJVs that fail badly generally have equally impressive-sounding corporate mission statements. Draw your own conclusions. What is clear, however, is that mission statements are not part of the formal agreements that bind the organizations of an IJV together.

The quality-related agreements that *have* proved their merit in successful IJVs are:

1. supply chain quality agreements;
2. sales-side quality agreements;
3. customer service agreements.

It is the discreteness of these three agreements that helps with their *effectiveness* in the context of IJVs. The existence of separate agreements, each of which can be viewed independently of the cultural or political differences of the IJV's parent organizations, is useful in helping to bring a sense of direction to a complex organizational form.

Supply chain quality agreements

Figure 10.3 shows the objectives of the supply chain quality agreements. These agreements are needed because:

- IJV parent organizations will have differing philosophies and ideas about their purchasing practices;
- approximately 30 per cent of perceived 'quality problems' of an IJV can usually be attributed to its suppliers, rather than its own systems;

● it is difficult to influence suppliers' quality if the purchaser does not present a united front.

The objectives of supply-chain quality agreements are to agree:

● the way that the IJV specifies its input goods and services;

● the expected quality level of these purchased goods and services;

● what to do when things go wrong.

Figure 10.3 Supply-chain quality agreements

In fairness, it is normally the non-existence of a formal agreement on supply chain quality that causes the problems for IJVs, not a lack of understanding or perception by its managers. The agreements need to cover the relationship with suppliers in both the A-parent's and the B-parent's home country, as well as from third party countries' suppliers. The essence of supply-chain quality management is provided in published standards such as ISO 9000.

Remember that published standards provide guidelines only – they are little more than a skeleton on which to hang the clauses of a full agreement. Figure 10.4 shows a checklist for a typical supply chain quality agreement between IJV parents. Note that this applies only to goods or services purchased externally on a commercial basis by the IJV, it is not relevant in this form to goods or services provided by either of the parent organizations themselves. The content of this checklist needs to be defined and agreed *before* the IJV starts its initial purchasing (either capital- or revenue-based). By doing this it is possible to circumvent up to about 70 per cent of intra-IJV misunderstandings that will result from the inevitable occurrences of supply chain quality problems.

Sales-side quality agreements

These control the quality of the output goods or services of the IJV. The requirements are twofold: those of the IJV itself, and those set by the IJV's customers. Sales-side quality agreements are not simply mirror images of the supply chain agreements, because they have greater organizational implications. This is best illustrated by considering the management implications

---

Supply chain quality agreements checklist

- approved suppliers list;
- supplier approval procedure;
- supplier audits;
- requirements for single source purchasing;
- technical standards for purchased goods;
- qualifications/standards for purchased services;
- purchase schedules (timescales);
- commercial terms of purchase;
- compliance checking of purchased goods/services;
- sampling procedures;
- reject/return supplies;
- procedure for purchase orders;
- guarantees required from suppliers;
- purchase documentation;
- the costs of supply chain quality management;
- staff responsibilities for supply chain quality;
- what to do when things go wrong.

Figure 10.4 Supply-chain quality agreements: a checklist

of controlling the output quality of an IJV organization recently formed from parent organizations with different business cultures. The concept of making a value judgement on the quality of your own organization's output is almost unknown in some developing-country cultures – it is almost as if self-criticism is seen as a no-go area, even for senior management. Some ex-communist countries' businesses work like this, with the objective of inspection or assessment of product quality being to *confirm* that 'everything is acceptable', rather then to find non-compliance. Quality management, in circumstances like this, is relegated to little more than wishful thinking. Not surprisingly, it doesn't result in good quality of output goods or services. The basic objectives of a good sales-side quality agreement are shown in Figure 10.5.

As with the supply-chain quality agreements, published standards such as ISO 9000 will only help you by providing guidelines to work to – don't expect them to work wonders by themselves. The most prescriptive ones are those covering Statistical Process Control (SPC), but these are only relevant if the IJV is involved in mass production of goods; they have little or no relevance to service businesses. Figure 10.6 shows a typical checklist for a sales-side quality agreement between IJV parents.

The objectives of sales-side quality agreements are to agree:

- a single set of 'output' quality standards;

- procedures for inspection/assessment of the IJV's output;

- what to do when the IJV fails to meet its own quality standards.

Figure 10.5 Sales-side quality agreements

Sales-side quality agreements checklist

- technical standards for IJV output goods and services;
- sampling procedures;
- assessment/compliance checking procedures;
- qualification/standard for IJV-supplied services;
- guarantees provided to customers;
- sales documentation;
- the costs of sales-side quality;
- internal audits;
- procedure for dealing with non-conformances;
- what to do when things go wrong.

Figure 10.6 Sales-side quality agreements: a checklist

Customer service agreements

Complex organizational forms rarely have a good pedigree of providing high levels of customer service. Despite the understanding by IJV managers that customer service is important (and probably a corporate mission statement to suit), it is easy for an IJV to become too embroiled in its own structure and problems rather than concentrating on maintaining good relationships with its customers. The cross-cultural aspects of the IJV do not help much because the different cultural approaches tend to blur the focus of customer relations, rather than making it clearer.

In many large-company IJVs the issue of customer service quality has traditionally taken a subsidiary role to supply chain and sales-side quality. Such IJVs have preferred to see themselves as having been commissioned more to produce goods or services in a better or cheaper way rather than to act as a different form of 'sales agent' operating from the B-parent's host country. Consequently, only a small percentage of IJVs have actually used customer service quality agreements, preferring (so it would seem) to leave it to chance. The results have been poor, with few IJVs obtaining international recognition purely on the basis of an exemplary customer service record. Most have simply produced an average result, finding a mid-line customer service performance somewhere between the extremes of the pre-IJV performance of the two parent organizations.

The legitimate objectives of an IJV customer service quality agreement are less tangible than those of the other two types of quality agreement. The central theme is the product (or service) guarantee that the IJV provides to its customers – customers are more likely to be impressed by firm guarantees than by slick mission statements that promise everything but offer nothing. International quality standards are not much help; those that do address the quality of customer service tend to be esoteric and based on ideology rather than business practicality. For these reasons customer service quality agreements are difficult to implement in the IJV context. The alternative, however, is poor customer service performance, as some IJV customers have found out.

Figure 10.7 shows a basic checklist for a customer service quality agreement between the A and B parents of an IJV. The simplified content is commonplace – an agreement in this field which tries to be too prescriptive will soon become locked-up by the inevitable cultural differences about customer service quality that exist inside the management structure of any IJV. Once again, don't expect this aspect of IJV management to be easy.

Customer service quality agreements checklist

- commercial guarantees for the IJV's goods or services;

- the extent of customer sampling and feedback;

- customer ratings and segmentation;

- procedure for dealing with customer complaints;

- what to do if things go badly wrong.

Figure 10.7 Customer service quality agreements: a checklist

CASE STUDY 10.3

International Technology Partners IJV: quality (dis)agreements

The B-parent 'No 1 production line manager of quality' instantly got most of the boardroom blame. He was adjudged not to have followed the sales-side quality guidelines laid down in the memo from the new International Technology Partners IJV management – the result being that over 70 items from the first batch of 200 products had defective plastic casings. The hairline cracks, dents and discolouring were clear for all to see (including by their customer who had rejected the whole batch).

The resulting enquiry started (and ended) with discussions about what, exactly, the production line quality control staff were supposed to be doing – the defective items had been stamped with the now-famous 10 QC inspection marks, but were still found to be defective.

The 'manager of quality's' explanation was disarmingly simple, 'Of course we spotted the defective casings – so we stamped them with extra care, just to ensure that our valued customers would know that they were all right.' The IJV parents' service managers received this explanation in different ways: the B-parent treated it as a valid explanation, seamless in its logic. The A-parent representation were astounded and couldn't understand how any such activity could be condoned – it was a clear violation of the B-parent's agreement to meet the requirements of the agreed quality policy.

A dispute loomed inside International Technology Partners IJV – nothing like this had been expected, or even imagined – just how big was this difference in QC philosophy and when would it stop? – and where, indeed, was the quality manual? True to form, in stepped 'top' IJV management, oozing diplomacy (but not uncracked plastic casings unfortunately). It was agreed that the problem was based on misunderstanding and not unsolvable – a task force would be created which would get to the bottom of the problem and solve it.

Postscript: the problem was dutifully solved in four months. A further ten months later, however, discussions were still going on to try to decide who should pay for the task force. Strangely, each IJV parent thought the other should pay because it was obviously 'their' fault.

Question: does this sound like good IJV management?

STAFFING AGREEMENTS

CASE STUDY 10.4

International Technology Partners IJV: staff responsibilities

' I want to talk about these design changes, Tony. As design director of this IJV, I'm responsible for everything to do with design...'

'And I'm responsible for a liaison with the manufacturing plant, so let's look at this problem together – what's wrong, don't tell me they've fiddled with our Z1 model design again?...'

'Worse than that, they're accusing me of leaving all detail design change decisions to them, when it's *they* who are slow in sending in the design concession requests... half of them are incomprehensible anyway...'

'Who's in charge of design over there, isn't it that local "director of quality" character? ... I knew we should have sent one of our old ex-pats to keep an eye on them – make sure they didn't change our designs – old George would've been the man, look how he sorted out that job in Mexico...'

'This will need to go to high level – it's a question of apportionment of staff responsibility, we simply can't let them run it all, you'd think it was their factory.'

'The only small problem is, is that it..., er,... well, *is* their factory, at least before the IJV was formed it was; I suppose we own a bit of it now, so to speak ... Oh, and about the need to raise this issue at high level, well, we... actually,... are...'

'Are what?'

'The high level; here we are, it's us.'

'But we only signed the IJV staffing agreements – who put in the clauses about who is responsible for in-works design changes?'

'It wasn't me, thank goodness, it must have been them.'

This is not a book about the mechanics of personnel management. There are hundreds of (other) books on the market that will promise to improve your ability to select, organize and dismiss people of all nationalities in the most efficient way. I am not sure whether any of them will help you in managing the staffing aspects of IJVs. We have seen that in their purest form, IJVs are a breeding ground for a wide selection of personnel-related organizational tensions. Look how the short case study dialogue contains, in its few snatched lines, all of the following inferences:

- ownership;
- the IJV's structure (and who is 'in charge');
- management responsibilities (in both parent organizations);
- directors' commitment to the whole concept of IJVs;
- the deferring of responsibility for day-to-day problems.

The more sinister side of the dialogue is the undertone of a developing 'us and them' situation between the two founding parents of the IJV. The issue of staff responsibilities has turned into a vehicle for widening the organizational distance between the two sides. You are watching the beginning of the one-way slide from parochialism to divisiveness.

The purpose of staffing agreements is to marshal the personnel responsibilities within the IJV into some kind of order. It is wrong to think of them as being purely a mechanism of administration – they have much wider implications for the structure and cohesiveness of the joint organization. World-wide, IJV staffing agreements fall into the two distinct types shown in Figure 10.8. Those in older, established sectors such as engineering and agriculture tend to centre around a staff-based choice. The people are chosen first, for their apparent suitability, and they are apportioned a range of cross-functional responsibilities (along the horizontal axis in Figure 10.8 (a)). Newer, less traditional sectors such as high technology service industries generally favour a function-based approach (Figure 10.8 (b)). Here, staff are chosen with more specific functional responsibilities in mind, and so have higher levels of specialism in particular business disciplines.

The two models naturally produce different apportionment of staff between the A- and B-parents' sides of an IJV. The staff-based model is the best at producing narrow strategic views with its attendant parochialism, particularly by the A-parent, who like to think they are in total control. The function-based model produces a younger, more dynamic staff structure but sometimes at the expense of over-staffing. It is capable of swinging more IJV control over to the developing-country B-parent and encouraging a more co-operative approach. Teamwork aficionados like this method.

Within the scope of the two models the staffing issue divides into three neat categories: directors, managers and staff. These categories are valid for our analysis of IJVs in a general sense – they are not restricted to any particular country, culture or way of working. We will look at each in turn.

Directors' agreements

Directors' agreements in any organization owe more to the rules of corporate responsibility than to what is necessarily best for the business. In most commercially mature countries, the roles and responsibilities of the appointed

(a) A staff-based (horizontal) approach

	Production	Sales	Marketing	Quality	Commercial
Directors	A			B	
Managers	A	B		B	
Staff	B		A		B

(b) A function-based (vertical) approach

	Production	Sales	Marketing	Quality	Commercial
Directors	B		A		
Managers	A		B	B	
Staff		B			

Notes: *A = Appointment from A-parent*
  B = Appointment from B-parent

Figure 10.8 IJV staffing: staff-based vs a function-based approach

directors provide a corporate organization with its legal identity and personality. The situation in IJVs is complicated by the residence of the IJV in the B-parent's developing country. It is wise to expect stringent requirements on the appointment of IJV directors in these countries. Most are beset by the requirement for government approvals and bureaucratic compliance; some sensible and logical, and some not. As a general principle, each parent can normally appoint its own IJV directors with some tailoring to the requirements of the host country. The exact role and responsibility of each director are then open to negotiation between the parties. Again, don't expect the content of government compliance requirements or the Memorandum and Articles of Association to do this for you – they are only a framework.

Managers' agreements

These are the agreements about the roles and responsibilities of the managers that will actually 'run' the IJV business. Unlike directors' agreements they are likely to be unregulated by bureaucratic requirements of the B-parent host country and are therefore free to be negotiated and manipulated to the mutual benefit of the partners. Unfortunately, this flexibility brings with it the old danger of tension and conflict between the two sides of the organization. Some IJVs have developed this to such a fine degree that on the back of every management job description should be printed the words: *WARNING: MANAGEMENT AGREEMENT: IJV FRAGMENTATION STARTS HERE.*

The issues are similar in most IJVs: management roles and responsibilities become seen as the root cause for the type of internal problems that cause joint venture business to slide, wander, or simply waste their energy fighting within themselves. The solution lies with apportioning management responsibilities between A- and B-parent managers in a way that fits in with the greater plan of the organizational 'system' of the IJV – a concept we saw in Chapter 6. Such an approach can go a long way towards balancing out the organizational tensions that result from misunderstandings and conflict about what individual managers, or groups of managers, are supposed to be doing. The advantages of this kind of systemic view of IJV organizational responsibilities only become properly apparent when the business is subjected to stress. Under such conditions of missed production deadlines, quality problems, customer complaints, or whatever, disagreements about management responsibilities soon appear. It doesn't take long before divisiveness arrives in the structure, nominally between the A- and B-parent parts of the IJV, fuelled by the cultural difference and geographical separation between the two. This is when you need the help of Chapter 6 to decide what the role of each management player *really* is. There is a gulf of difference between this approach, implemented properly, and the often-used placebo of making the management agreements so general that they lack decisiveness, in the vain hope that they will, at least, hopefully not annoy anyone.

Staff agreements

You can think of IJV staff agreements as being organizationally neutral. The apportionment of operational staff from the resources of the A- and B-parents is governed mainly by geographical and cost constraints rather than by organizational theory – systemic or not. Most IJVs operate with a majority of indigenous staff from the B-parent host country. Staff recruitment in many developing countries is often controlled by national labour laws and practices. These are becoming fewer, however, and there is an increasing trend for foreign-funded IJVs to be given partial exemption from some of the more restrictive practices, notably of ex-communist-bloc countries.

You still have to expect a cultural mix of staff at the sharp end of the IJV's business operation. It is usual for the A-parent to second specialist staff to work alongside the established B-parent workforce. This is rarely such a potential flashpoint as might be expected – there is fair evidence that operational staff adapt to each other's cultures and working practices better than do their managers. The common experience of solving tangible problems at the working level acts more to dissolve differences than exacerbate them. Put in systemic terms, it is as if their level of the IJV is almost 'self-balancing'. This means that you shouldn't need to worry too much about orchestrating complex intra-partner operational staffing agreements. They will work themselves out.

The agreements themselves

IJVs need written agreements for the three levels of personnel we have considered: directors, managers and operational staff . You cannot run the business on theories alone. It is well proven by IJVs that have found themselves in a situation of business-threatening staff conflict that it is the ideas behind staffing agreements that are the root of the trouble, rather than the minutiae of the agreements themselves. The relative emphasis placed on bits of managers' job descriptions are a famous flash point – the cultural differences are just *waiting* for an opportunity like this to come in and join the argument. You have to get the staffing plan in your head with some precision before commissioning the IJV, then you have to be careful.

TRANSFER PRICING AGREEMENTS

Transfer pricing agreements are part of the commercial reality of IJV businesses. The most common transfer model is for both parent organizations to provide goods or services to the separate entity IJV in its host (B-parent) country. The transfers most often occur at the beginning of the 'value-adding' process of the business, although there are also cases where it occurs more towards the end, ie in the marketing and customer service disciplines. Unfortunately, transfer pricing structures are rarely as straightforward as a straight commercial agreement – they contain tangible (eg fixed/current asset) transfers and intangibles such as brand names, expertise and business goodwill.

In common with the cyclic nature of the business world, transfer pricing agreements also exhibit a life cycle. This life cycle adds its own set of management problems to those already present in an IJV. The four sequential phases are summarized in Figure 10.9. Note how they relate to the timescale of the IJV. The order of their occurrence is also important, in many respects IJV transfer pricing is one of the more predictable features of IJV management. The four main stages are:

1. at-cost transfers;
2. cost-plus transfers;
3. preferential commercial transfers;
4. fully commercial transfers.

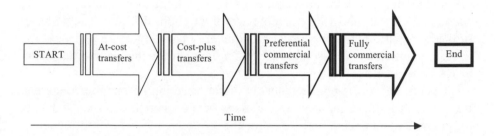

Figure 10.9 The transfer price life cycle

At-cost transfers

This apparently simple system is usually chosen as the first attempt to implement a method of transfer pricing for goods or services. The notion is that the goods or service are transferred within the IJV in return for only the costs incurred in their origination, ie without any allowance for profit. The idea is undoubtedly a sound one – the IJV at corporate level benefiting from the financial efficiency of the transfer, with the avoidance of double margins and intra-IJV negotiation.

The reality is different. Even the simplest goods or services cannot be manufactured or originated without incurring company overheads. The task of apportioning overheads to particular products or projects is a hot political issue inside most business, made more difficult by the intangibility of many of the overhead costs. Every department or cost centre will act so as to limit the company overheads apportioned to them in an attempt to try to show that they are making the maximum profit. IJVs suffer mixed fortunes at the hands of this approach. The discrete financial structure at the start of the IJV life cycle gives an easily identifiable overhead structure but this changes as the venture matures and develops organically into one which is more complicated, with a resultant increase in difficulty in apportioning overheads in a way which is seen by all parties as fair. The change is accompanied by a general maturing of the partners' approach to the idea of a joint venture business. This early stage of 'at-cost' transfers doesn't normally last long – 20 per cent of the total IJV life cycle is about average.

Cost-plus transfers

When the idealism of 'at cost' transfer pricing has lost its novelty, along comes its relation, 'cost-plus' transfer pricing. Here the idea is to transfer goods or service at slightly above cost price, the objective being to present the originating party with the opportunity to recover some of its overheads in an accountable way. This method is more useful for goods than services, because of the tangibility of the overhead costs that are incurred – fixed and variable costs of manufacture or assembly are easier to apportion than intangibles such as R&D or expertise.

The concept of cost-plus transfers has been used in, for example, transfers between government departments for many years, where it was seen as a way to 'be more commercial' without reducing economies of scale or introducing the negative sides of market pressures into otherwise close intra-business relationships. In the IJV context it fulfils a similar role, accepting the realities (and difficulties) of obtaining good overhead recovery while maintaining some illusion of co-operation between the venture partners. Despite these attempts to introduce a more rational financial approach to overhead recovery, however, the issue rarely rests quietly. Intra-parent tension about the way that overheads are apportioned are likely to continue – with the result that the cost-plus approach ultimately solves very few of the problems that it was introduced to prevent. The reality is that the phase of cost-plus transfers is, again, transitional – it is destined to change, almost from the moment it is introduced.

Preferential commercial transfers

This third stage of the transfer life cycle is seen by some managers as the first signs of financial disagreement between the constituent parts of the IJV. The point that differentiates it from the previous stage is, again, the problem of accounting for the individual partners' overheads in a way which is seen as being acceptable to all concerned. The problem is more acute in ventures that have poor financial performance in their early life which puts pressure on both partners to justify their financial performance (to each other) in the best way they can. The result is that each attempts to recoup more of its own overheads, without much concern about the organizational effect of their actions. Financial parochialism prevails.

In many joint organizations that have reached this stage, there is little that is 'preferential' left in the transfer price agreements that are reached. The agreements occupy large amounts of management time and effort, none of which actually assists in improving the bottom-line performance of the business. This is the most inefficient transfer pricing arrangement of them all – the length and *un*productiveness of the negotiations being increased by the need to continue the pretence that the activity still has some 'jointness' about it. As if to make things worse, some IJVs languish in this state for the majority of their life cycle, with little management emphasis on improving the situation.

Fully commercial transfers

As the life cycle of an IJV matures, the internal pressures towards fully commercial transfers increase. Internal transfers between the parents and their separate IJV business take place at the full market price of the goods or services concerned. To all intents the resulting transaction is no different from those which the IJV would conduct with an external commercial party, being preceded by the same type of pre-contract regulations over product, quality and price. Notwithstanding the commercial atmosphere of this type of arrangement, both contracting parties normally feel some dissatisfaction at working in this way. A mutually agreed price for the transfer rarely results in the organizational harmony that you might expect – the parties merely default to arguing about quality, timescales, documentation or similar. By this stage, there are always fertile grounds for inter-partner tensions based on the three stages of transfer pricing that went before, with all sides being heard proclaiming loudly, 'We always knew it would end up like this.'

IJV transfer pricing: is it all bad news?

Yes and no. While most IJVs have problems at some time or other with their transfer pricing policies (it has killed off some completely), the effect of many of these can be offset by a clear understanding of the chronological order in which they occur. The content of Figure 10.9 is surprisingly well proven – it is only the length of each stage that is hard to predict. The main danger with the transfer pricing cycle is the management tension that is caused between the partners in the IJV. These tensions are at risk of being interpreted as divisiveness or lack of co-operation or, even worse, mistrust. In an organization that may be suffering other management problems the transfer pricing issue is always available to make any situation worse – if you let it. On the positive side, the four-stages life cycle *is* predictable, so it shouldn't come as a surprise.

SUMMARY

Formal agreements between IJV partners are essential to hold the joint organization together. The agreements themselves can be complex and may be interpreted differently by different cultures.

The scope of agreements

Agreements need to cover all aspects of the IJV's operation including:

- ownership (initial share structure and options);
- finance (financial structure, CAPEX/OPEX, profit distribution, targets and budgets);
- quality (supply, sales-side and customer service);
- staffing (directors, managers and operational staff);
- transfer price (its life cycle consists of four stages).

Opportunities

At the beginning of an IJV, directors and managers have the opportunity to construct the agreements the way that they want. This is part of the task of *designing* the IJV organization – it will not design itself. Your lawyers will not design it either – they will only put into the agreements what you tell them.

Threats

IJVs that try to operate with incomplete or 'weak consensus' agreements run the risk of poor business direction, lack of strategic focus and expensive internal disputes.

Chapter 11

Disputes

Not all books on management like to discuss disputes. For many, the concept of dispute is difficult and distasteful – something to be pushed to one side to make room for the more positive aspects of management advice. Some go further, inferring that disputes are an admission of defeat, or incompetent management, or even that they do not exist at all.

None of this is true. Inter-parent disputes are commonplace in IJV business – they are almost part of their characters. Such disputes are not unique to any particular form of IJV – they are a by-product of the existence of a joint business operation which extends across geographical and cultural boundaries. From all the IJV businesses in operation at any moment, at least half will be involved in one or more business-threatening inter-parent disputes, while most of the others will have ongoing lower-key disagreements, any of which can escalate quickly. This is a challenging picture.

IJV DISPUTES: THE RATIONALE

There are varying views about the root causes of disputes between IJV parents. Are they caused by misunderstandings (cultural or communication) between otherwise well-intentioned parties or are they the results of basic business incompatibility, perhaps overlooked in the enthusiasm of commissioning an

IJV to exploit exciting new markets? The answer is simpler: *IT IS THE IJV FORM THAT IS RESPONSIBLE FOR DISPUTES.*

This neatly takes the emphasis away from the competence or integrity of the parents – it is the fact that they are combined in the IJV *organizational form* that is responsible for the existence of disputes, not the nature of the parents themselves. In short, all IJVs have disputes; some more than others.

WHAT ARE THE DISPUTES ABOUT?

Intra-IJV disputes (as research tells us) can arise over just about anything. Generically they divide into those with their origins in the various parts of the IJV life cycle (Figure 11.1). Take comfort from this figure that disputes do not occur except in the later 'exit' stages of the IJV life cycle.

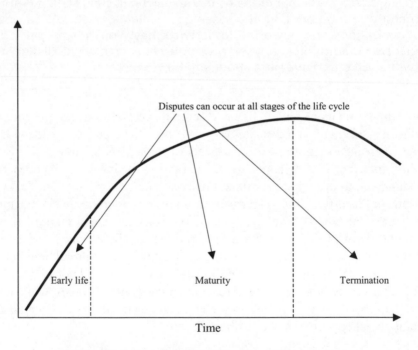

Figure 11.1 The IJV life cycle: when disputes occur

The roots of disputes can be summarized into categories shown in Figure 11.2. You can think of these as the lowest common denominators of IJV disputes – existing singly, or in combination behind the internal arguments. They are surprisingly consistent across the business sectors in which IJVs operate.

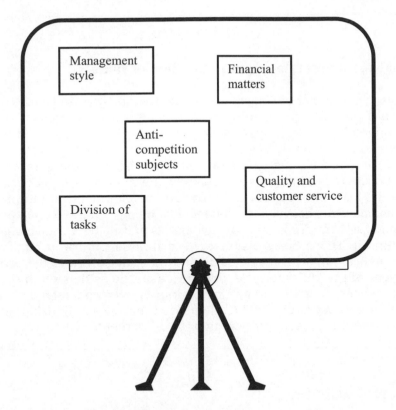

Figure 11.2 Roots of intra-IJV disputes

Management style disputes

Disputes about management styles are often a smoke screen for disagreements about other things that lie beneath. IJVs, by definition, are a synthesis of the differing management styles of the A- and B-parents – issues which are brought into focus by the geographical separation of the two organizations. The characteristics of management style disputes are:

- They occur at two levels of 'resolution' – early disagreements while both partners are becoming familiar with each other, and deeper more divisive ones later.
- They affect logical, technologically-orientated A-parents more than their developing country B-parent IJV partners. This is because the A-parent generally thinks it knows best.
- In reality, they are generally founded in cultural differences rather than deep ideological divisions about management style.
- Good managers can solve them.

CASE STUDY 11.1

Management style disputes: builders or raiders?

IJVs join together businesses from mature industrialized countries (the A-parent) and developing countries (the B-parent). Early ventures in the consumer electronics sector in the 1960s did not always run smoothly. The Japanese A-parent technology licensors argued that their overseas manufacturing B-parent partners were not builders of a business and only saw the chance for a quick profit on the back of Japanese technological development. In turn, the manufacturers accused the Japanese of being raiders – concerned simply with the domination of their market and all the manufacturers within it. These early disputes were founded more in cultural differences than business reality and most dissolved in the early stages of the IJV's life cycle. In many cases the settlement of such differences, by each partner increasing its own understanding of the other's ways of working, cemented the IJV relationship and reducing the effect of further minor disagreements.

Financial disputes

Financial disputes are normally about the more esoteric areas of management finance rather than straight disagreement over who owns what. One reason is that many of the financial provisions of the joint business organization are clearly set out in the IJV agreement (or should be). A positive aspect of financial disputes is that they carry with them their own method of solution, ie by negotiation between the parties to reach a settlement mid-way between the position of the parties. This is much better than other types of dispute where there may not be a half-way solution available, leading both parties to fight strongly to avoid defeat. The disputes usually fall into three categories:

1. funding disputes;
2. cost disputes;
3. pricing disputes (normally transfer pricing).

Funding disputes

The worst funding disputes occur in the later stages of an IJV's life cycle. At this stage, the original, robust funding agreements applicable to the start-up and early stages of the IJV start to lose their relevance – they are simply outlived by the IJV's circumstances. Because of the different financial investment criteria of the A- and B-parents in an IJV (see Chapter 8), new funding decisions to be taken in the later stages of the life cycle often prove difficult. In extreme cases, the parent organizations can have diametrically opposing views of the CAPEX and OPEX funding routes that the IJV should take. This can lead to more fundamental concerns and disagreement over financial parameters such as payback, return on parents' investment and financial exit routes.

There is no simple answer to the problem of funding-disputes. Each one has to be taken on its merits and negotiated to a settlement. As a principle, the quickest route to a solution is by using an understanding of the generic financial objectives of the A- and B-parents discussed in Chapter 8. Remember that there always is a settlement waiting to be reached – all you have to do is find it.

Cost disputes

Cost disputes are found anywhere in the IJV life cycle. They are a dynamic phenomena in that they arise quickly, caused by changes in the outside business environment. The majority of cost disputes happen under the jurisdiction of the B-parent, because they deal in the more volatile supplier markets of their developing country. In contrast, the technology-supplying A-parent trades in a more mature, stable market for the components of its technology and so is less exposed to unstable cost fluctuations.

Cost disputes can be settled, given a little time and enthusiasm. It is sometimes advisable to suspend the jurisdiction of the A-parent contingent of the IJV board and allow the B-parent to sort out the problem using local market knowledge and negotiating skills. Overly enthusiastic (albeit well-intentioned) interference by a culturally remote A-parent can make the situation worse. For peace of mind, a good IJV agreement will place the onus on the B-parent to control local costs and provide for the necessary incentives and disincentives to make sure it is done properly. This helps avoid disputes.

Pricing disputes

Most of these are about transfer pricing within the IJV structure. Disputes about the sale price of the IJV's goods or services are less common, mainly because these costs are exposed to the moderating effect of their market, and so are partially predetermined. Transfer prices are part of the commercial reality of joint venture businesses– there are few IJVs that do not have to address the problem of intra-IJV price transfers in most stages of their life cycle. The nature of the transfer pricing (as we saw in Chapter 10) follows a well-defined pattern progressing from 'at-cost', through to 'fully commercial' transfers as the business matures. It is this changing nature of the transfer pricing situation that causes the disputes.

There is a latent inevitability about the way that transfer pricing disputes manifest themselves. Early stages are characterized by one or other of the IJV partners repeatedly raising the issue at senior management meetings. This changes to an air of resignation and stoicism while 'trying to make the best of it'. The next step is normally the political phase, with lobbying of IJV board members. This initiates the discussions, or dispute, that pushes the transfer pricing structure into the next stage of its sequence. It all causes tension.

The efficiency with which transfer pricing disputes are settled is a good barometer of the operating management style of the IJV at high level. If the intra-partner understanding and communication are good, then the management system will settle the problem before it has a chance to rebound down the IJV organization into the operational units, where it can cause problems. Service-based IJVs such as communication and finance businesses are good at this. Here the structure of transfer prices forms the mainstay of their business operation, so its characteristics are well understood by both sets of IJV partners. Manufacturing and older 'process' technology-based businesses fare worse – they have greater potential for disputes, encouraged by a business culture which sees concession on transfer price to an IJV partner as a sign of business weakness.

Anti-competition disputes

These are disputes about whether any of the parties in an IJV are acting as competition to the others. One of the inherent risks of the IJV business structure is that of creating your own competitors. Many of the earlier IJVs in developing countries did little more than create low-cost competition for the technology licensor A-parent organization. Both low and high-technology sectors can experience these problems. To prevent the creation of unfair competition, anti-competition clauses are normally built in to the IJV components. While, in theory, legally binding, these clauses are open to interpretation and difficult to police. Problems arise as IJV partners attempt to lobby the managers of these agreement clauses to circumvent the restriction on anti-competitive behaviour. Not surprisingly this causes disputes, which can be subdivided into three main types:

- technical diversification;
- competitive bidding;
- third party sales.

Technical diversification

This shows itself in technology-transfer-based IJVs, in particular those in which the transfer of technology into the developing country is successful. The most common form is when the technology provided to the IJV is developed by the developing country B-parent acting alone, ie not in conjunction with the IJV. The technology is then changed or diversified in some way to circumvent any patent or licence restriction imposed by the A-parent technology owner. The result is that the B-parent gains technological assistance from the IJV which it then uses for its own benefit. Chemical and pharmaceutical processes are often diversified in this way.

The original technology owners/licensors are rarely impressed by such chains of events. They see it as technology acquisition by stealth and unfair exploitation of the technology transfer opportunity. It often ends up in rhetorical dispute between the IJV partners about what constitutes genuine technology development and what does not. The worst arguments occur in high-technology sectors where technology advances are clearly linked to business advantage. Older mature technology fields suffer less because technological information is likely patent-expired and more freely available.

Competitive bidding

Even in businesses used to the free-market economy, competitive bidding between an IJV and its parent organization(s) causes problems. The ability of an IJV to bid for business in competition with its own parent organizations is common – a well-constructed IJV will have been brought to a technical level which is equivalent to that of its parents and we saw in Chapter 5 how any technology gap closes quickly as the competence of the IJV builds. For this reason, IJV legal agreements contain anti-competition clauses, normally structured around regional exclusions or particular areas of business or customers. The weak point in the arrangement arises because of the entrepreneurial character of staff seconded to IJV organizations. As the life cycle of the IJV progresses, financial targets loom, and IJV management feel the need to meet revenue or profitability budgets. In soft or receding markets this can sometimes only be achieved at the expense of business currently held by the IJV's parent organizations.

Third party sales

The disputes here centre around on-selling of the IJV's products or services to a third party, who may in turn re-sell them to others. The most common scenario is where on-sales occur across international boundaries, and in doing so break the conditions of the agreement between the IJV partners.

High-level disputes can result if, for instance, IJV goods are re-exported back into the A-parent's country where they enter the market in competition with the A-parent themselves. Some parts of the automotive industry have been forced to live with this, because of the way that the vehicle assembly and sub-components business operates. The situation does not extend, however, to other sectors of business, particularly services, in which competition follows more traditional lines.

Paradoxically, third party selling disputes do not always result in disputes at IJV level. The effect may instead be felt at higher level in the parent organizations, or even at political level where issues such as freedom of trade and national protection are felt to be important.

CASE STUDY 11.2

Creation of competitors in the US automotive industry

A study was made of Japanese–US IJVs in the automotive components sector that had become involved in serious intra-IJV disputes. Of the 12 examples studied, 11 of the IJVs were bought out by the Japanese parents and became wholly-owned subsidiaries. This resulted in the creation of new competitors to existing businesses. US companies that sold their IJV interest admitted that they had not recognized the implications of creating competitors until the IJV relationship had deteriorated beyond help.

As one US manager put it, 'I'm not sure we ever had any common goals – they wanted a foothold in the US, we gave it to them, and they had no further use for us.'

Division-of-tasks disputes

The division of work tasks is an area of sensitivity in any organization. In a new organization split across international boundaries it is almost inevitable that there are going to be disagreements about the way that tasks are apportioned between the partners. IJVs that lack clear objectives or strategic direction often have weakly defined structures. This can cause deep-rooted uncertainty about how management roles are apportioned between the A- and

B-partners. The result is that while the business operations of the IJV will continue, they will do so in an atmosphere of tension, oscillating and vying with each other for legitimacy within the structure. Eventually, the problems rebound back up the hierarchy (if there is one) compounding as they go. It is not unusual for them to expand to involve financial or business strategy issues. The only certainty is that division-of-tasks problems at this level produce disputes which are complex and expensive.

Quality/customer service disputes

Improvements in quality and/or customer service are often one of the stated objectives of setting up an IJV. It involves transplanting the quality and customer service (QCS) abilities of the A-parent into the business operation of the developing-country B-parent. This opportunity normally arises because the QCS capabilities of enthusiastic and growing B-parent businesses are perceived as being capable of improvement. Step changes in QCS may be required, with two types of potential problem areas:

- *pre-sales disputes*: minor QCS problems identified by the IJV's own internal management systems;
- *post-sales disputes*: normally the result of a barrage of customer complaints. These are indicative of widespread 'systems' faults in the joint business's QCS reform.

There is no absolute reason why QCS problems have to grow into QCS disputes. There are many forms of businesses where the identification of QCS problems is seen as a positive step – evidence that the business has a working feedback system, to enable it to improve itself.

Unfortunately, IJVs have an uncomfortable relationship with QCS problems. The B-parent often assumes a defensive role when issues of quality or customer service are raised – they may feel the implication that they are at fault. Once again, the geographical and cultural differences between the partners serve to aggravate the situation, causing internal tensions, followed by dispute. The worst aspect of these disputes is their intangibility: arguments about quality and customer service are full of subjectivity with few tangible facts upon which the partners can agree.

Thankfully, you can expect QCS disputes to *fade* – most likely by the parties reaching an agreement not to argue, rather than them actually solving the QCS problems. In this part of IJV business, the term 'settlement' does not mean the same as *solution*.

CASE STUDY 11.3

International Technology Partners IJV: avoiding disputes

After an initial warming up period, ITP had developed their ability at not letting disputes grow out of control. Once the 'misdirection' had been placed to one side it became clear that the real problem was to do with response time to big customer orders, not quality or design, or the type of packaging.

The problem

Large retail outlets needed delivery within 10 days for their batch-ordered (500+) units from ITP. When they didn't get this they complained and kept threatening to change their supplier.

The reason

It was found that the batch-order documentation had been lying on the sales department's desk in the B-parent manufacturing site in China waiting for a response from the overseas A-parent in the United States. The A-parent was supposed to be notified of batch-orders so it could send the works a revised production schedule. This was a protection against the works doing their 'own thing' and possibly jeopardizing the standing orders of goods re-exported every month to the A-parent for resale in high-value US markets.

Solving the problem

The following steps were taken by the IJV board:

They did	They didn't
Decide that the B-parent manufacturer could act on their own initiative (as long as they met their contracted orders).	Try to transfer control to the remote A-parent.
Allow the manufacturers to manage their own production schedules.	Attempt to manage the problem at 'arm's length'.
Re-deploy one local B-parent manager who had been revelling in the delays as supposed evidence of his lack of autonomy.	Undermine the autonomy of local managers by making them refer constantly to the IJV board for simple decisions.
Continue to copy batch-orders to the A-parent but for information only.	Introduce any more paperwork chains.

The result? Better response time for batch-orders and *NO DISPUTES*.

From the previous examples of dispute categories you can see just how wide, and deep, intra-IJV disputes can be. Successful organizations do not always find it easy to work in harmony with others, even when the co-operation is self-imposed. Disputes have to be settled if an IJV's business is to be competitive. Settlement can be achieved by skilful managers (it is part of their role), but it has a downside in that it often leaves a legacy of bad feeling between the IJV partners. The nature of IJV management doesn't help – culturally-different managers will assess the settlement in different ways so that many IJVs, by the time they have reached their mature stages, are working under a constant internal shadow of previous 'settled' disputes. The result is organizational tensions.

The other way to solve the problem of disputes is to make sure that they do not happen. The avoidance of disputes is a softer but more effective way of limiting the damaging potential of dispute situations. The following two sections of this chapter compare the practical aspects of settlement vs avoidance.

SOLVING IJV DISPUTES

RETHINK: SOLVING DISPUTES

'Same as solving any other dispute, a few gentle changes (call it incrementalism if you like) – manage the people – let it roll and the strategy will recover itself, ease it all back on track. Simple as that really ... finished ... closed.'

'Sorry to disagree but the IJV life cycle clock is always ticking, undermining the incrementalism as it forms. The best bet is to just rip away the problem as soon as you see it, before it has a chance to ricochet around the interface between the IJV partners, causing all kinds of trouble.

The optimum way of solving any intra-organization dispute is by using a method that leaves everyone feeling happy and fulfilled. Happiness and fulfilment, we are told, are two of the tenets of organizational harmony and there is no reason why IJVs should be an exception. The difficulty is that these feelings are harder to achieve in an organization which straddles geographical and cultural boundaries. It is as if the diversity of the joint organization acts as a barrier to achieving a win–win resolution of internal disputes.

Starting point: solution time-pressure

Time pressure makes implementing optimum solutions to IJV disputes difficult. The best type of well-crafted incremental solutions can take too long and so are often unsuited to the transient nature of IJVs. Even those IJVs that manage to attain longer term market stability are characterized by high levels of internal change. Figure 11.3 shows a simplified view of the situation – the finite life cycle of the venture pushing against the practice of robust but extended solutions. The time pressure does not make ideal solutions impossible, but it does moderate their effect. In short, by the time a robust incremental solution to a dispute has been implemented, the organization – and the nature of the original dispute – will probably have changed.

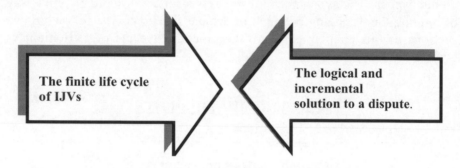

Figure 11.3 Time pressures on solving IJV disputes

The next step: addressing the phases of disputes

The phases of an intra-IJV dispute are shown in Figure 11.4. Note three important points in this figure:

- the constraining effect of the IJV life cycle;
- the practical time during which the dispute is *felt* within the IJV organization, and how it is shorter than its 'theoretical' period if the time constraints were removed. The reason is that awareness of disagreements is heightened by the existence of business time pressures;
- the practical short time available to solve a dispute (compared to the theoretical time available).

The pattern of the phases of dispute is important when trying to find solutions. Almost half of the time available is taken up by the 'feeling' of the dispute with less then 25 per cent available for its solution. The key to solving disputes is to organize their solution *around* these phases, picking and choosing the

THE THEORY

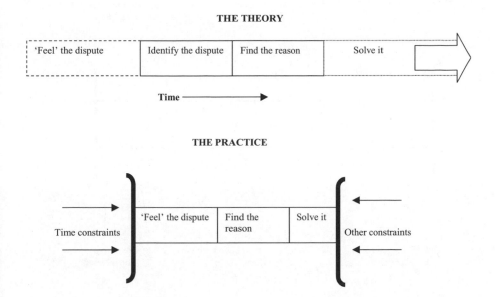

Figure 11.4 Time phases of an intra-IJV dispute

necessary bits of management technique to suit. The techniques themselves divide neatly between the three phases. Figure 11.5 shows the method:

- the early 'feeling' phase needs the application of the people-related skills from a manager's portfolio;
- the next phase, where the real reason for the dispute is identified, benefits from a mixture of logical analysis and discipline skills coupled with those actions needed to obtain organizational agreement from other managers on both sides of the IJV;
- the final short solution phase needs the proactive, often stark, skills from the management repertoire. It needs the firm actions of organizational control, but applied in an indirect way, as we saw in Chapter 7.

The endgame: making the solution stick

Given the finite time constraints on implementing solutions to IJV disputes there is little room for half-baked or incomplete solutions. The solutions to IJV disputes have to be carefully constructed, checked for completeness, and then driven into place before the vagaries of the IJV organizational form have a chance to break them up.

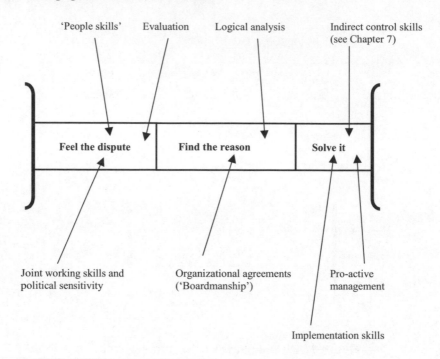

Figure 11.5 Solving the dispute

PREVENTING IJV DISPUTES

The idea of preventing internal disputes or dissolving them before they happen, is hardly a new management idea. The best-performing organizations are often those that manage to attain a high level of internal harmony, a feeling of staff togetherness and an all-pervading sense of balance about what is important and what is not. Sadly, such organizations rarely become well known for their self-management skills – they are more likely to be praised for their strong marketing, or the high quality of their product. This external performance, however, relies on the number of serious internal disputes being kept to a minimum so that the power of the organization can be applied to its relationship with its external market. Internal disputes always result in a loss of profitability, never an increase.

This means that organizations (and managers) that are skilled at avoiding disputes rarely get any credit. Perversely, the opposite can be true – there may be organizational kudos to be gained by 'winning' internal disputes, or in taking a firm parochial stance over some trifling matter of principle. Such activities cause disputes and sap the power of an organization, then everybody loses.

Because disputes cost money, reduce the strength of the business and are generally undesirable, it is better to prevent them rather than settle them. It is worth repeating this: *it is better to prevent IJV disputes than to settle them. How?* By building three key mechanisms into the IJV at its design stage. Don't confuse these with placebo measures or 'instant management solutions' to be applied when disputes start to arise. They have to be crafted into the structure and culture of the joint organization from the stages of the early partner agreements (see Figure 4.5) if they are to have any effect. The mechanisms themselves are not in conflict with any aspects that would be considered 'good IJV management' but they have to be seen in the context of their quality of dispute prevention (rather than their general usefulness as management principles). This is the key to their use. Figure 11.6 shows the three dispute-avoiding mechanisms in their order of grouping, rather than strictly their order of priority, which will vary in each individual case.

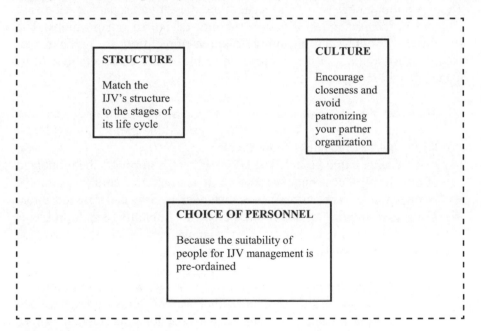

Figure 11.6 Three ways to minimize IJV disputes

Structure

When designed correctly, the structure of an organization acts as a mechanism for preventing internal disputes rather than causing them. The idea of the structure of an organization as a 'system' – with the property of viability – was looked at in Chapter 6 under the general concept of systems thinking.

We conceived the structure of an IJV as being almost independent of the personalities of the people that comprise it, with strengths and weakness, and a character of its own. This means that a structure can be designed with the specific purpose of preventing disputes between the IJV partners. The elements of structural design that can do this are based on two properties, completeness and logic:

- An IJV structure has to be *complete* (no bits missing or 'still under discussion') if it is to be able to dampen and prevent disputes.
- Only a *logical* structure can prevent disputes. Structures containing rules and procedures based mainly on obscure intra-partner politics are guaranteed amplifiers of dispute situations. Organizational inconsistencies or fallacies have the same effect.

There is nothing new, or even special, about these two properties – they are inherent in the principles of good structural design of organizations. The structural attributes that encourage dispute-prevention are perhaps best identified by looking at their opposites, ie those that cause diputes. Most managers will recognize these:

- *Matrix management structure*: This is a classical IJV dispute-generator. It divides management control, often between the partners, providing a fertile source of disputes about everything.
- *Arm's-length management*: The IJV A-parent is normally the proponent of this. It introduces huge weakness into a structure's ability to dissolve its own problems because it causes misunderstanding and misconception.
- *Unbridled hierarchy*: This has the effect of funnelling small problems upwards to the higher levels of IJV management where they thrive on the smallest inter-parent divisions and tensions.

In contrast, a good dispute-preventing structure is one which avoids as many as possible of the above attributes, in all their varied forms. A structure that is logical *and* complete will cut out those negative actions and communications that influence disputes while recirculating those that help prevent them. In this way the organization develops the property of self-healing. In parallel, a true structural approach to IJV management will design the organization so that it can act in its required way (as a dispute-preventer) independent of the individuals who inhabit it. In this way changes in managers and staff will not compromise the stability of the business. This is not an overly impersonal view of management (which would be wrong), but a way of building a mental picture of an organizational system separate to that of the people within it. For you, as a manager, this can remove confusion from the situation.

Culture

We have already seen how cultural differences between parties are an integral part of IJV organization. Culture has a role to play in dispute-avoidance as well as in its more popular context of making things happen in an organization. It is also one of the areas that has to be treated carefully if it is not to have negative effects.

Cultural contacts occur when different parts of the IJV organization interact as part of its everyday business life. The fast pace of most IJV businesses means that their interaction can be more intimate and forced than in, for instance, a business that is undergoing international expansion by organic growth or acquisition. If culture-based disputes are to be avoided, it is necessary to *manage* the form of these cultural interactions (it is impossible to avoid them) rather than let them happen by chance. The main way to do this is by designing the IJV to work in an atmosphere of cultural *closeness*.

Closeness

Closeness means that the IJV partners work together in close proximity – in an organizational as well as a physical sense. Even small gaps are undesirable as they reduce the power of the bonding between the parties. Closeness manifests itself in two ways:

1. The form of organizational roles and responsibilities. As a principle, it is better to organize these in a way which anticipates inter-partner *agreement* rather than disagreement. Rigid rule-based systems can produce an atmosphere of confrontation even if this is not the intention. People of all cultural backgrounds are (often unconsciously) sensitive to inferences hidden within their organization's rules and procedures – they are easy to misinterpret when there are people of different cultural backgrounds acting together. The assumption of co-operation does not have to mean a loose approach to IJV management, merely one which does not *value* disputes.
2. Communication mechanisms. Communication mechanisms can be a way to either facilitate or limit cross-cultural contacts. Communication which is too sparse or 'systematized' will cause a situation where everyone appears to be constantly arguing with each other. Such communication-based disputes generally start with serious management issues but descend quickly into trivia, followed by partisan rhetoric – neither of which encourage closeness.

Both the medium of communication (fax, e-mail, etc) and the rules for its content govern the way in which it can promote or prevent disputes. There are no hard rules on this but Figure 11.7 shows some typical guidelines. The general message of this Figure is that it is the *closeness* of the communication regime that helps dissolve intra-IJV disputes at their source. This is different from the more commonly held management view that more is achieved by increasing the volume of communication, in the hope that it will somehow lead to improved cross-cultural understanding and hence fewer disputes.

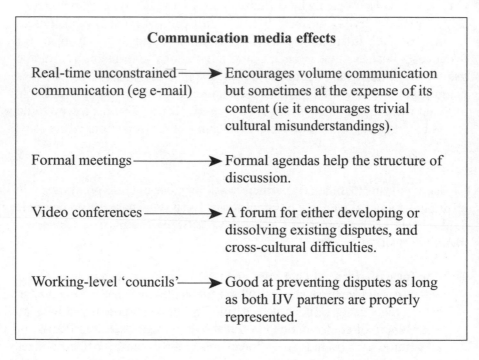

Figure 11.7 Some effects of intra-IJV communication

The increasing use of e-mail communication is an example of the application of modern technology to the management of complex organizations. While useful in providing day-to-day communication for project-based activities, its effectiveness is more limited for purer forms of organizational management information. Here, the lack of predetermined content of the information transfers can lead to the e-mail networks becoming a vehicle for management *in*decision. The practical results are twofold:

1. It becomes too easy to defer decision-making to someone else (the other IJV partner).
2. Indecision thrives on the cultural differences between the IJV partners. Sometimes more communication makes things worse.

There is also a sound theoretical basis to the problems caused by too-easy access to on-line communications. From a systems-thinking viewpoint, the viability of an organizational system relies on communication between its elements (IJV parts in this case). This does not, however, mean *unrestricted* communication – it needs to be kept in balance if the organizational system is to work effectively. This balance is one of the prerequisites for a system to be able to maintain its viability (look back at Chapter 6) in a complex business environment. Communication which is absolutely uncontrolled poses a *threat to viability*, particularly when the organization is complex, and crosses international boundaries. Be careful.

Choice of personnel

Figure 11.6 makes a controversial point. It suggests that the suitability of personnel for working within an IJV organization is preordained. This infers that people will not fundamentally change their views on the principle of a joint organization and its internal differences – only modify them. The modifying influence is the set of characteristics of the IJV (structure, culture, etc) of which they form a part. This appears an almost fallacious view – that IJV managers are incapable of changing the structure and culture of a joint organization which they themselves created. Management theorists could no doubt find numerous reasons and evidence to disprove it.

Part of the explanation why it is not a fallacy lies with what happens when two organizations decide to form an IJV. The finite life cycle of the venture drives the partners to finalize their method of joint-working abnormally quickly, causing hurried ideas, plans and procedures. The search is on for the ever-elusive synergy that will drive the venture forward. It is in these early stages of the joint organization that its structure and culture form more by metamorphosis than logical development. The result is that factors which will act to constrain the ability of managers to make fundamental changes are 'frozen in' to the IJV *at its conception*, producing an organization which has the ability to shape its managers, but an inherent resistance to being shaped itself. It acts like a viable system, not a collection of individuals. Does this change your early views on Chapter 6?

Some managers can work well under these systemic constraints while others will feel oppressed and disappointed by it. In IJV practice, the problems are distributed fairly evenly between developed country A-parent and developing country B-parent managers – both sides feel the resulting organization pressures. This pressure can push the two sides into internal disputes – the situation being heightened by the involvement of managers who are not suited to the form that the joint organization has taken.

For every management theorist that disagrees with the logic of the above arguments there are several failed IJVs that are testimony to its truth. IJVs survive or fall on the ability of their managers to dissolve the profit-burning internal bickering that is waiting to happen. Managers from established line or matrix-management positions deep within either parent organization may not be suitable. Good IJV managers need to have cultural understanding, knowledge of the systemic realities of intra-organization disputes and be used to life on the edge of organizational stability. This leaves you two options. Either *choose the managers for their specific competences in the IJV task or expect disputes*.

CASE STUDY 11.4

Avoiding disputes: bamboo networks

Japan and Korea are two members of the Asian business community who have been successful in commissioning IJVs in distant parts of the world. Many of these have been unusual in that the overseas host country has already been in an advanced state of industrial development (Europe and the United States). The Japanese and Korean IJV formula is based on a joint organization which remains pleasingly free of damaging internal disputes, leaving the business to concentrate on competitiveness.

The formula

One of the attributes believed to contribute to the structural harmony of Japanese and Korean-inspired IJVs is their business culture of dominance by 'interlocking groups' of companies. This has its roots in purely cultural aspects capped with a strong sense of economic nationalism and produces a business atmosphere that is easily extended to IJVs.

Japan

Japanese business is dominated by two types of these groups:

1. *Keiretsu*: industrial groupings containing strong supplier/sub-supplier vertical links.
2. *Zaibutsu*: conglomerate groups, many with their own banking arm (eg Mitsubishi, Sumitomo etc).

The stability of these groupings has enabled Japan to follow a policy of *Kokusaika* (internationalization from Japan), incorporating many

---

successful and long-term IJVs. This is an example of how structural factors can influence IJV success. The merit of this formula has been sufficient to overcome most of the cultural and language difficulties that isolated Japanese business from the post-war Western world.

Korea

Korea has an export-orientated culture which values market share above quick profit. It has a similar system of industrial groupings or *Chaebal* which act together with a state-sponsored banking system to produce a 'bamboo' network of horizontally and vertically integrated groups. These form a sound and stable A-parent base from which Korea has formed successful IJVs in the electronics and communication-related industries. Many of these are technology based, the lack of inter-parent disputes providing a stable platform from which to meet the inevitable reduction in complementarity that has caused problems for European parents in these fields.

SUMMARY

Research shows that IJV parents are powerful organizations who will, given the chance, disagree on just about anything.

Sources of dispute

Common sources of internal dispute are:

- management style;
- money;
- anti-competition agreements (or lack of them);
- division of tasks;
- quality and customer service.

Timescale

IJV disputes follow a well-proven timescale. It can help to anticipate this.

Solving IJV disputes

There is always time pressure to settle disputes. Even settled disputes generally leave a legacy of inter-parent tensions and disrespect.

Preventing IJV disputes

It is better to prevent or dissolve disputes rather than trying to settle them after they have occurred. The three key preventative mechanisms are:

1. IJV structure (match it to the venture's life cycle);
2. cultural understanding;
3. choosing staff with preordained suitability.

Chapter 12

Regional experiences

INTRODUCTION

Over the past 20 years the number of IJVs between developed and developing countries has progressed steadily, the impetus being increased by post-1990 developments such as the downfall of communism and the opening up of Far Eastern markets to Western influence and business cultures. Although spread world-wide, the majority of the IJVs of commercial significance have been centred on four main geographical areas:

1. China;
2. Eastern Europe and near-Asia;
3. South America;
4. Pacific Rim countries.

A study of IJV history and practices in these areas gives a useful picture of the management problems that exist in IJVs and the effect that they have on the performance and longevity of the ventures.

In this chapter we look mainly at the examples of China and Turkey to provide a flavour of operating IJVs in overseas countries. The summaries do not give exhaustive coverage, but are intended to be closely representative of situations that face IJV management. All are based on the IJV structure favoured by Northern European A-parent organizations rather than the contrasting US-style practice. Figure 12.1 shows the layout of the chapter, concentrating on IJVs in China

IJVs IN CHINA

Economic conditions

Despite rapid growth in recent years, China's current economic growth shows all the signs of a slowdown. GDP in 1997 was 8.8 per cent, matched by a

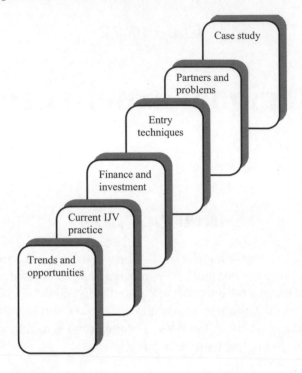

Figure 12.1 Regional summaries: IJVs in China

slow growth in industrial output. There are clear differences in economic conditions relating to state-owned and collective enterprises, with state owned enterprises (SOEs) occupying a privileged position for access to finance. The growth of retail sales in China is surprisingly slow and some other published economic indicators such as disposable income can be difficult to reconcile with other figures. China's exports are increasing by approximately 20 per cent per year, contrasting with its almost static level of capital goods imports. Inflation is near-zero with the economy being subject to the control of a rolling programme of five-year economic plans.

TRENDS AND OPPORTUNITIES

Initial conclusions about the market inside China can be misleading. The market is difficult to understand because of its mixture of command and market economies. Despite the increasing state acceptance of 'capitalist' market activity, the state still retains a firm grip on central planning priorities, designating key industrial and business sectors as having priority for development. The current sectors (1996–2000 plan) are:

- aerospace;
- power generation;
- chemical production;
- airports;
- automotive products;
- telecommunications;
- financial services;
- environment;
- food and food processing.

The breadth of these business sectors is sufficient to suggest that IJV opportunities exist in almost all areas of business although, in practice, larger 'infrastructure-size' ventures take priority. The trend for large-company IJVs is therefore biased towards larger project-based businesses. These are often accompanied by associated smaller IJVs for the provision of specialist products or services.

The history of IJVs in China

Political differences apart, China has a history of trading activity with the United Kingdom and continental Europe. It is estimated that there are more than 150,000 IJVs now operating in China, approximately 80 per cent of these having appeared in the past 10 years. No formal records are kept but there is colloquial evidence to suggest that the number of IJVs is still increasing.

A certain amount of corporate optimism and marketing gloss surrounds the experiences of European companies who have been involved in IJVs in China. Many have failed in the first few years of their life with the developed country A-parent writing off their initial investment and making a strategic withdrawal. Reasons for the failures have been attributed to:

- problems with quality;
- poor co-operation and internal conflict between the IJV partners;
- escalating costs.

All of these share the common presence of some degree of poor cultural understanding between the parties. Despite good intentions on both sides it is difficult to keep an atmosphere of cultural understanding between European and Chinese businesses. Most of the IJVs that have failed cite this as a root cause of the eventual slide to failure – although the final demise is often cloaked in long explanations about 'the state of the market' or 'quality problems'. Some specific problems experienced by large corporation IJVs are:

- *Difficulty in adapting ISO 9000-based quality management systems* to established Chinese manufacturing practices. This has caused problems in lower technology consumer goods industries.
- *Adherence to high-technology specifications*: problems have occurred with regression to lower specifications, except where tight (expensive) management controls have been maintained. Chemical processes and product manufacturing industries have suffered from this.
- *Technology mismatch*: IJVs based on complementary technological skills do not have a good record in China. Any technology gaps between the IJV parent organization have been found to close quickly, reducing the complementarity driving force so essential for the long-term existence of an IJV (see Chapter 3). In some cases the learning process has taken only a few weeks, leaving the venture facing an organizational learning 'vacuum'. Over 90 per cent of IJVs report that the Chinese B-parent learnt the essentials of the A-parent's technology more quickly than had been anticipated.
- *Bureaucracy and 'red tape' procedures* are a reported problem for most IJV businesses. Many sectors of Chinese business show the effects of long years of central planning and still exhibit the characteristics of the command economy. The main problem is with time delays – project-based IJVs frequently have problems with meeting deadlines.

The message is that IJVs in China present a formidable business challenge, but one which many corporations appear to relish. The Chinese indigenous market is large and exciting but difficult to grasp and few single-product IJVs have succeeded outside the food or telecommunications sectors. Culturally, differences remain between the practices and norms of Chinese business and those of Western European countries – differences which must be addressed seriously if an IJV is to have a chance of success.

CURRENT IJV PRACTICE

IJVs that have been set up in China follow the well-defined structures shown in Figure 12.2.

Equity Joint Ventures (EJVs)

The EJV structure is the nearest to the free-market joint business venture common to other business cultures. Equity is shared between the Chinese and 'foreign' parties following the models given in Chapters 4 and 5 but the equity distribution is calculated in pure monetary terms. There are two important restrictions; first, the foreign partner has to meet a minimum stake

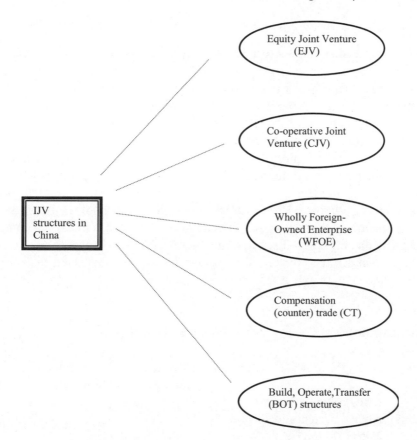

Figure 12.2 Business structures in China

requirement (currently 25 per cent but subject to government revision). Second, both partners must make a predetermined proportion of their equity investment in the form of cash. Capital contributions are not allowed to be secured on the assets of the EJV. Exit routes from the IJV are currently left unrestricted, with apportionment being agreed between the partners on the basis of the equity distribution. There are, however, restrictions on the timing of the exit routes from the IJV and a foreign partner may be unable to withdraw from the venture, or obtain early realization of its investment before the formal end of the IJV timescale. This can cause difficulties – many smaller IJVs have folded long before they have reached their contractual timescale and have lost some or all of the residual value of their investment still in the IJV.

An EJV has the status of a separate legal entity with limited liability. The choice of directors and management is left to the partners to agree and is covered, in the normal way, in the IJV's Memoranda and Articles of Association.

Co-operative Joint Ventures (CJVs)

CJVs are a rather unevenly regulated form of IJV between Chinese and foreign-based companies. They are usually found in ventures which are both technology-based and have a substantial requirement for fixed assets; infrastructure and volume manufacturing are good examples. Unlike EJVs, CJVs do not have to physically reside in China. Various levels of government regulation and control apply to this form of IJV, some with apparent business logic and some not. Figure 12.3 shows a summary. The main rationale behind CJVs is the provision of non-liquid assets by the Chinese partners while the foreign partner provides technology or key equipment – almost a classic model of a technology-transfer IJV. Practically, this inherent technology-based nature of the relationship brings with it the danger of the rapid 'fall-off' in complementarity driving force discussed in Chapter 3. The saviour of the situation is that the exit routes for the foreign investor are less restricted than for an EJV, so the venture can at least be terminated more neatly.

Constraints	Areas of freedom
● Formal IJV contracts required covering: – terms of co-operation; – apportionment of revenue and profit.	● Physical location – not necessarily within China.
● Fixed and non-liquid assets are provided by the Chinese partner.	● Investors can exit before the end of the formal IJV contract term.
	● The partners' equity ratio is not restricted to pure monetary value.

Figure 12.3 Regulation of Chinese/foreign IJVs

Wholly Foreign Owned Enterprises (WFOEs)

WFOEs are a low-co-operation form of IJV in use since 1986. The idea is that a foreign parent company wholly funds an 'implant' business enterprise in China, bringing with it some essential technology or product which will prove useful to Chinese economic development. Sometimes there is a Chinese partner involved but their role is not as participative as in the EJV or CJV structures. WFOEs are limited liability companies and are subject to not only normal Chinese law, but also to official approval as to the stability of their business activity. The principle of obtaining this approval is to demonstrate that the business fulfils one or more of the various criteria. The main ones are:

- it produces products either for export from China or as a direct substitute for existing imports *into* China;
- it introduces new technology, essential to the development of Chinese industry or general business.

There are important restrictions on the scope of WFOE activity. Chinese law does not allow WFOEs to operate in news or broadcasting media sectors or some areas of telecommunications. The situation is changing but still reflects the impact of long years of communist rule.

Compensation (counter) trade (CT)

This is also commonly referred to as Counter Trade (CT). Although qualifying under the basic definition of an IJV (see Chapter 4) CT ventures are less structured than any of the other types. They are more of a dealing mechanism than a viable organization from. The standard CT involves a split in the provision of assets – buildings and labour from the Chinese partner (or the state) with technology and management from the foreign investor. The investor obtains payment in the form of goods produced, or occasionally in combination of goods, cash and other benefits in kind. Two particular routes are available to raise capital for CT deals:

1. The foreign investor raises the capital externally and the Chinese partner makes capital and interest payments.
2. The Chinese partner raises capital via export loans from overseas banks, organizing the repayments itself from foreign exchange earned from sales revenue.

The life cycle of CT deals is, at best, uncertain and the character of CT as a deal-mechanism rather than an organizational form means that it has a short life. There are a few CT structures which have worked successfully over 10 years or so, but these operate mainly in commodity markets and bear little relation to the formal status or investment profile of an IJV.

Build, Operate, Transfer (BOT) structures

BOT is a method of investment intended for large infrastructure projects such as roads, railways, airports, power generation and telecommunications. They are subject to a raft of Chinese government-controlled BOT regulations which are in the process of being developed. This development is proving to be an iterative process with a number of pilot projects currently in place in the power generation sector. These have been financed mainly by overseas partners' export credit guarantees and by Chinese provincial governments, rather than by formal state guarantee. Project timescales range from 10 to 20 years. In principle, China appears supportive of the BOT scheme structure but in practice, things are moving slowly, waiting to see the results of the pilot schemes.

FINANCE AND INVESTMENT

Laws covering foreign investment in China have been in a continuing state of evolution since the late 1970s. While large steps are being made to bring financial and investment practices in China in line with internationally adopted standards it is still undeniably a 'frontier' market. Unlike the developed economies of the Western world China does not yet represent a totally free market investment vehicle. There are restrictions – some well understood and fixed but also some which are less tangible and subject to government policy or fashion.

Foreign exchange

China has a single currency, the Remnimbi (RMB) which is conditionally convertible and supported by the government's state intervention to make it fully convertible by the year 2000. RMB can be converted to foreign exchange in various ways:

- by selling through designated Chinese banks;
- through Foreign Exchange Adjustment (Swap) centres. This is a transitional financial facility. It is actually an artificial market and subject to regular state intervention.

Repatriation of profits

The facilities for repatriation of profits to the overseas partner form a major part of IJV government regulations in China. Dividends can usually be repatriated ex-withholding tax by using one of the foreign exchange mechanisms. A similar system can be used for royalty payments from technology licences but with different tax implications. Theoretically, there should be no scarcity of the availability of foreign exchange with which to do this. It is necessary, however, to make sure that administration requirements such as company resolutions about profit distribution have been properly organized to ensure that the repatriation runs smoothly. The IJV investment model given in Figure 8.2 in Chapter 8 shows a typical structure.

Payment protection

The majority of IJV business in China is conducted using letters of credit (l/c) payment mechanisms. The main players are the first tier 'big four' Chinese banks who have sufficient ceiling to handle most l/c transactions. Some IJVs have had difficulties when attempting l/c transactions through second tier or regional Chinese banks, although the Chinese banking system is taking positive steps to become aligned with international payment standards. Open payment terms are not common and it is, frankly, difficult to judge the creditworthiness of local Chinese companies.

Taxation

The taxation of IJVs in China is tied up in special legislation governing what are known as Foreign Invested Enterprises (FIEs). Tax holidays are available for ventures with a contracted timescale of longer than 10 years. Profits are not taxed initially but then a sliding scale tax rate is applied up to the third year of business. The tax system in China is simple compared to European and US systems and operates on a calendar year basis. There is a unified system of tax laws in China but these are still in an early stage of development – they manage to be both complicated and sophisticated, at the same time. Many IJVs are located in one of the five Special Economic Zones (SEZ) which have additional regional rules and exemptions.

ENTRY TECHNIQUES

There are characteristics in international markets that makes them suitable for particular entry techniques. The general characteristics of developing-country markets are a large size combined with more than a touch of instability. There is also the guaranteed problem of geographical location – developing countries are long distances from the commercially mature Western countries. These practical points cause difficulties in organizing market entry techniques for an IJV.

Difficulties

The prime misconception with the Chinese market is that it is single and unified, with a large population under-supplied with desirable consumer products. There are legendary, apocryphal tales of IJV managers whose market strategy was simple – to sell a single product worth a few pence or cents to each of the two billion or so Chinese population. All of these projects have so far failed, their credibility undermined by the practicalities of marketing, distribution and financing of such a venture.

Market size apart, the two main difficulties of IJV entry into the Chinese market are:

- *Unfamiliar rules and regulations*: For political reasons, Chinese business structures and practices have been at arm's length to the rest of the world. This leads to unfamiliarity. It is not that the Chinese systems are necessarily more confusing or less logical than Western systems – they just *seem* that way.
- *Language and cultural barriers*: These cause difficulties in the practical and 'housekeeping' activities needed to achieve success in any business. The difficulties are, of course, temporary – the world-wide success of Japanese corporations is testimony to the fact that such problems can be overcome.

It is the cumulative effect of these two difficulties that causes the problems of IJV entry into China. The generic solution is as shown in Figure 12.4. Note how this is a tripartite solution – all the three solution elements are needed together to be able to have an effect – they are unlikely to be effective applied separately.

Market strategy

The main issue is the geographical characteristics of the IJV market because the regions and provinces of China are so large and remote from each other. Most IJVs are located in the Eastern coastal provinces of China which have preferential government trade and investment policies. Comprehensive desk research is essential if an IJV is to have any chance of success.

The key aspect of market strategy in Chinese IJVs is the time horizon. The structure of the IJV market is organized to accept projects and ventures which have a long timescale (> 10 years for EJVs and CJVs) and contains disincentives for early withdrawal by the foreign IJV partner. This produces an interesting dilemma for IJV managers – formulating a strategy for the long term, in the full knowledge (from Chapter 4) that IJVs are a transitional form

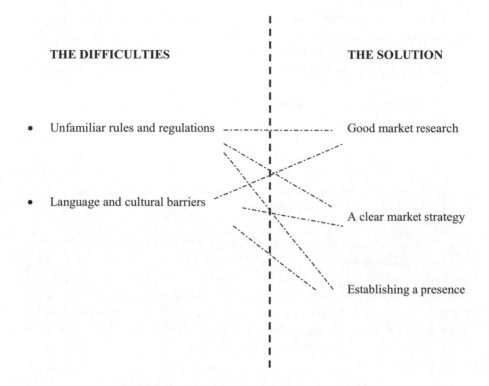

Figure 12.4 Chinese IJVs: entry techniques

of organization, destined for change. The problem is compounded by the generic character of IJVs in China, many of which are orientated totally around the opportunities of technology transfer into China from mature industrialized countries. Such IJVs are known to be in constant danger of losing their technological 'complementarity' – an effective way of shortening the life cycle. This means that to be successful, an IJV's market strategy in China must be flexible enough to resist the destructive pressures of this dilemma. The strategy needs almost to be *built around* this dilemma, rather than pretending that it doesn't exist. IJVs have failed owing to lack of attention to this tricky point.

Establishing a presence

It is next to impossible to commission a successful IJV by dealing with the Chinese part of the venture 'at arm's length'. The only effective way to gain market entry is to obtain a presence in one of the larger Chinese cities. The two common ways to do this are:

1. *Open a representative office.* Under Chinese practice, representative offices do not become involved in IJV contract deals but are allowed to act as a base for local market research, setting up technical exchanges etc. In practice, these definitions can become blurred and the office plays a part in at least the formative stages of the IJV. The costs of commissioning a representative office have to be seen as part of the financial pricing of a foreign partner's IJV strategy.
2. *Use a launchpad service.* Smaller companies unwilling to finance a representative office often use the services of agencies in Chinese cities who provide a launchpad service for prospective foreign investors. This provides most of the facilities of a representative office but is more impersonal, and therefore cheaper.

There are no hard-and-fast rules about the length of time needed to research and commission a successful IJV in China. It is rare to find one which has got to the contract stage with a suitable Chinese partner business in less than two years – so it is necessary to plan for business opportunities well ahead. Perhaps the greatest danger is trying to rush into a hastily conceived IJV in order to try to take advantage of some fleeting market opportunity – most of these IJVs fail and disappear just as quickly.

PARTNERS AND PROBLEMS

The choice of the correct Chinese partner for an IJV is difficult. The mechanics of the task are straightforward enough – it is the criteria of choice that presents the challenge. Of the European/Chinese IJVs that have become notable public failures, incompatibility of the partners has been cited as one of the underlying causes of failure. A quick look under the surface of these cases would show that the issue of poor control was paramount. We saw in Chapter 7 how the effectiveness of the control interactions between the partners is one of the key stabilizers of the IJV organizational form. Compatibility, in all its forms, is the most important issue when choosing the Chinese IJV partner.

Some of the characteristics of Chinese IJV agreements are as follows:

- the 'early partner agreements' (Figure 4.5) are easy to put in place;
- the period of organizational learning (Figures 5.10 and 5.11) is *short* – the Chinese learn quickly;
- the later stages of the IJV's life cycle are characterized by the creation of local competitors who feed off the improved technology.

It is these three characteristics of the partner agreements that can act together to make control of the IJV difficult. IJVs in China also suffer from the inherent characteristics of Chinese organizations. Some commonly reported observations are:

1. They have a history of state control with roots firmly founded in the command economy model.
2. Their potential for organizational development is constrained by their past history.
3. Organizational decision-making is complex and often unpredictable. It is based on a high degree of socialist 'consensus' thinking.
4. They are large, over-manned, and full of system inertia.
5. Their inherent understanding of concepts such as quality and profitability is totally self-consistent with thinking within China but these concepts do not necessarily mean the same as they do in other countries.

All of these are fertile sources of partner problems in the stressful environment of starting and operating a new IJV. There is therefore a strong need to choose an IJV partner carefully, to try to reduce the chances of conflicts later in the IJV's life. This is a crucial point – nearly all active IJVs experience problems so it is important that there is as much natural compatibility as possible between the partners to stop these growing out of control. As a rule, those Chinese organizations located within the Special Economic Zones (SEZs) prove more outward-looking and compatible with IJV practices than do those in inland regions. Companies in the far Northern and Eastern provinces can be expected to be more parochial and insular, with a purer 'collectivism' work ethic.

The final rule in avoiding partner problems in China is simple – be patient, don't expect to merge cultural values and business practices overnight.

CASE STUDY 12.1

Chinese motor industry IJVs

Background

Since the early 1980s the Chinese motor industry has moved from producing mainly trucks and buses to a full range of passenger and commercial vehicles. Production increased fourfold between 1989 and 1995 to more than 1.5 million units per year. Existing Soviet-based technology of 'Jiefang' and 'Dong Feng' trucks now sits alongside modern technology installed by IJVs involving overseas manufacturers such as:

- Shanghai Volkswagen – 'Santana';
- Dong Feng/Citroen –'ZX Volcane';
- Tianjin/Daihatsu – 'Charade';
- Beijing Jeep Corp – 'Cherokee'.

There are approximately 15 other motor-industry IJVs producing buses, engines and small auto parts and a further 30–40 businesses manufacturing components under straightforward licensing agreements.

Policy effects

Chinese government requirements that foreign motor manufacturers contribute to the development of the indigenous motor industry required many vehicle assembly IJVs to be preceded by smaller IJV enterprises manufacturing component parts. There is also government pressure to limit the number of assembly plants, and consolidate some of the smaller ones.

The market

Surprisingly, sales of passenger vehicles have not risen as quickly as predicted. There are serious doubts as to whether market demand can keep up with production from all the IJVs. Despite this, official figures still predict a 300 per cent increase in vehicle production by 2020.

IJV structures

Most motor industry IJVs have been based on technological 'complementarity' and large capital investments by the foreign partner. Volvo's IJV with Shanghai Automotive Corporation (producing buses) has a 50:50 equity structure – a model which is followed by similar ventures in the commercial vehicle sectors. The equity valuations of technology transfers differ significantly between the various IJVs.

Problems

There have been problems of quality and productivity at several IJV assembly plants, reflecting problems experienced in European and US plants in the 1970s and 1980s. Tensions have been heightened by oversupply in the market, leading to price wars and unfamiliar pressures on manufacturing personnel. It has been argued that there are so many motor vehicle IJVs in China that the profit margins are actually less than in other world markets.

IJVs IN TURKEY

Introduction

Turkey provides an example of the use of IJVs as part of an economic development strategy at national level. It also occupies the unusual position of playing both A-parent and B-parent roles in different industries. Turkey is a country which is in the phase of developing its longer-term IJV strategy.

Turkey: the business environment

Turkey occupies the uneasy ground between being a developed country and a developing country. An annual growth rate of around 10 per cent is coupled with a recent inflation history of 70–80 per cent per annum, firmly identifying it as a developing country. Conversely, it has some well-developed techno-logical industries, an expanding middle-class population, and is seeking to join the European Union. It has also developed a stable base of some $11–15 billion of foreign capital investment in a rapidly improving infrastructure giving it many of the characteristics of a developed (A-parent) economy.

Following the lead of European countries, Turkey started its privatization programme in 1984 and has plans for further large-scale privatization of state sector organizations. It still has a restricted banking network of about 60 banks, many of which are small or under state control. It is making progress in the financial sector with the assistance of the World Bank (structural adjustments) and IMF (macroeconomic level) support.

The IJV situation in Turkey

Turkey's cellular communication sector is expanding rapidly via IJVs with European companies (the Turkish partner acting as the B-parent in this case). The largest network, 'Turkcell' is majority owned by the Turkish Culcurova group but has ventures with Telecom Finland and Ericsson (Sweden). The rival company, 'Telsim' has an established IJV with Motorola (USA) who have invested in new telecommunications network infrastructure.

Domestic goods and vehicles are made by the KOC group, Turkey's biggest conglomerate with approximately 70 subsidiaries. KOC has recently made 10 per cent of its share capital available to foreign investors, encouraging the formation of IJVs with overseas companies.

The A-parent role

Although technically a developing country with under-utilized local markets, some Turkish businesses possess an A-parent capability in sectors such as construction and low-technology manufactured goods. In 1998 it was reported that Turkish construction companies had over $US 20 billion of investments outside the country. Typical ventures include shopping developments and hotel complexes in Russia and other Turkic CIS republics such as Azerbaijan and Kazakhstan. Structured loosely as IJVs, these projects tend to be labour-intensive, with financing being provided by a third party. Some of the newer Turkish A-parent IJVs are starting to link banking and financial facilities with their construction projects but this is in its early stages.

Characteristics of Turkish IJVs

Turkish IJVs have the following characteristics:

Structure

In common with many developing countries the structure of Turkish IJVs form quickly, rather than by a process of organic development from divisionalized or holding-company structures. Equity structures tend to follow a common majority : minority apportionment (see Figure 4.3 (b)).

Culture

The cultural form of Turkish IJVs reflects the pivotal position of Turkey between the European and pure Turkic cultures. Turkish business has restricted the cultural distance between itself and its IJV partners so its A-parent role tends to be restricted to IJVs with countries with strong Turkic cultural connections. This is a classic model of a strategy for avoidance of inter-partner disputes as discussed in Chapter 11. In their B-parent role, most Turkish IJVs are with European businesses. Here also, the cultural differences are manageable but pilot ventures with US and Japanese businesses have experienced problems with cultural integration.

Strategy

One of the main strategic influences on Turkish IJVs has been the expansion of their domestic markets, stimulated by the rise of an affluent middle-class population. This has encouraged IJVs in the domestic goods markets and had a knock-on effect on A-parent capability in the building construction sector. IJV management style has proved to be flexible without the constraining effect of an overly ethnocentric approach. The result has been a cautious IJV strategy without extremes of risk or over-extension of management capabilities.

Chapter 13

Looking forward: the future of IJV management

In this book we have looked at the tools and techniques of IJV management; some empirical and others with more robust theoretical backing. One of the few certainties of business management, however, is that everything is subject to *change* – the environment of business, the structure of the markets and the nature of an organization's products and services all change as time progresses. There is not always an obvious logic to some of the changes – there may be progression and regression at the same time as businesses try to adapt to an uncertain future.

IJV management changes more quickly and with greater unpredictability than that related to single organization businesses. We saw in earlier chapters that IJVs are characterized by instability, fuelled by the uncertainty caused by a finite life cycle. A basic assumption of IJV management therefore is that it is necessary to accept the inevitability of change in all areas. Despite the entrepreneurial spirit of the IJV management breed, the sheer rate of change can prove difficult to handle, with the result that forward-thinking, responsive IJV individuals (and organizations) can still be caught by surprise.

While some of the trends in IJV management will always be unpredictable, there are some that do have an air of inevitability about them. There are also useful lessons and insights to be gained from the way that the subject has developed to date. All this can help reduce the number of surprises and make the task of IJV management a little bit easier. We will look at each area in turn.

THE EFFECT OF TRENDS

We saw back in Chapter 1 how one of the driving forces behind the popularity of IJVs is the current position on the cyclic path of independence and interdependence between businesses. The big question is: what is the shape and length of the future of this cycle? This cycle is probably a long one – long cycles were identified in the early 1900s by the researcher Kondratiev. Kondratiev cycles can last as long as 40 years and reflect major economic and geopolitical changes that take place in the world. The cycle of business independence vs interdependence has all the necessary characteristics – the slow but inevitable incremental swings that override temporary variances caused by short-term business or management fashion.

From its start in perhaps the late 1970s we are now approximately 20 years into the independence vs interdependence life cycle. A 40-year Kondratiev assumption therefore places the current business world somewhere near the middle of the cycle. This suggests that there is a significant period still to run in which global business *inter*dependence will continue to increase, providing the impetus for the formation of IJVs. During this period IJVs will remain one of the mechanisms of business globalization, with products and services becoming increasingly homogenized across the countries of the world. General opinion is that the greatest changes will be made in the ex-communist bloc countries and the Far East, including China as it struggles to reconcile its capitalist ambitions with its communist history.

It is open to debate as to whether the end of the interdependence part of the cycle will be triggered by political or economic issues. Economically, the growth of technology and skills transfer to developing countries could probably last for a further hundred years before running out of impetus– but this is too long, even for the longer-term projections of Kondratiev's cycles. It seems more likely that the end of the business interdependence trend will be caused politically, as increasing wealth in developing countries brings higher standards of living, and a desire to play a greater independent part in the international political scene. This can bring not only harmony but also divisions and disagreement. It is feasible that the pattern of alliances between countries that has existed since the 1940s could change, causing some countries to regress into isolation, destroying the current structure of globalization – maybe to be replaced by the embryo of a different one.

The message is that for the near future at least, the conditions that encourage the formation and operation of IJVs will continue. It is unlikely that these will disappear overnight but ultimately the cycle will swing back to favour business *independence*, probably for geopolitical reasons rather than those of pure economics.

DEVELOPMENTS IN BUSINESS STRUCTURE

Business structures are developing all the time. Recent step changes caused by the downfall of full state control in ex-communist countries blend with the new organic world-wide trend towards globalization, organizational autonomy and a reduction in the role of central planning as a business model. This increased freedom continues to provide the conditions that encourage large-scale corporate mergers and strategic alliances causing businesses such as oil products, pharmaceuticals and airlines to grow larger day by day. Some are already tending towards oligopoly.

Every sign is that these business structures based on co-operation will *continue* to grow. It is feasible that the differences in structure between strategic alliances and formal IJVs will become blurred, superseded by a more unitary model of co-operation. Business sectors will then become a battle-ground between multinational strategic alliances, each with its own structural model of co-operation – the airline sector is already heading towards this. In smaller businesses, IJVs will become an accepted part of a company's portfolio, almost like having an export activity, so more and more exporting will be done by using IJVs as a vehicle for the transaction, rather than the traditional commercial buy–sell export deal.

Increasing experience of IJVs will lead to a lowering of the perceived risk involved for the parent organizations. It is possible that the structural form of the IJV organization that gives it its transient, unstable state will change, perhaps towards a more formal model based on integration of companies together across their product range, rather than only part of it. There will still be IJVs which are little more than a marriage of convenience (particularly between smaller and low-technology companies) and they will no doubt continue to experience the types of problems identified in this book. More IJVs will mean increased competition between them so the challenge to IJV managers will be, increasingly, to find ways to make their IJV operate more smoothly than their competitors. This means there will be more emphasis on eliminating the energy-sapping disputes between IJV partners because in a highly competitive environment prolonged intra-IJV disputes will amount to commercial suicide. The same developments may stimulate changes in the profile of IJV managers – IJV management could become a separate discipline with participants specially trained in international skills such as language, cultures and politics. Whatever the exact nature of developments, such improvement in the vocational skills of international management can only help.

PREDICTIONS ON MANAGEMENT STYLE

The conceptual basis of managing across international boundaries will not change because managers will still have to face the problems of finding and manufacturing a strategic direction for their business and achieving that direction through people. There is no other way. It is also unlikely that the basic organizational design problems of an IJV will change much, there will always be the dilemma of how much freedom to allow the various parts of the organization and the difficulty of exercising horizontal control within the structure of the IJV (as we saw in Figure 7.1). Two developments, however, are already in progress and so give a clue to the future:

1. *Levels of autonomy will increase*: because improvement in the stability or longevity of IJVs will lead to directors and managers feeling they can give greater autonomy to the operating parts of the IJV, without the risk of chaos. Longer time-horizons (for everybody) gives an organization time to balance itself, so short-term direct control actions are not so necessary.
2. *Cultural integration will improve*: because cultural differences throughout the world are already under pressure from the influences of worldwide communication media and easy air travel. Even the traditional 'cultural enclaves' of the world are getting smaller owing to political stability and fewer cultures are now isolated from the rest of the world than at any time in recent history. The situation is mirrored in the business world, in which communication media are growing exponentially. All this leads to cultural integration, irrespective of whether the participants like it or not, and eventual homogenization of management styles across international boundaries.

So does matrix management have a future?

Matrix management will remain because it is too well established not to. In a future business environment of strongly competing IJVs, however, it will probably be recognized for the poor model of organizational democracy that it is. The benefits of matrix management techniques in controlling single-company activities have not proved successful when transferred to IJVs with their mix of cultural differences and physical separation. Basically, it *causes* problems and disputes rather than solves them. The main enemy of the matrix management system in IJVs will be the drive for greater autonomy of the operating 'producers' of the business in their locations around the world. It will simply not be possible to be responsive if every operating decision has to be fed through a matrix structure – the result will be poor competitiveness and the inevitable slow slide out of business.

FINANCIAL EXPECTATIONS

Currently, the financial performance of IJVs rarely meets expectations. Particularly in smaller company IJVs, initial investments have been made with the hope that the first profitable year's trading is just around the next corner. To justify their participation in IJVs, companies find convenient ways to conceal poor performance by using consolidated accounts or elaborate accounting mechanisms. Over time, things should improve, with mature IJVs starting to realize healthy returns for both partner organizations. In the environment of strongly competing IJVs, those that remain will only do so by virtue of their proven ability to make profit, with less financially sound ones destined for a short life and failure.

Investment terms for IJVs are already well established. In many respects today's investment criteria reflect expectations which are ahead of the current position of IJVs – they infer a level of stability and business maturity that most IJVs have not yet achieved. There are good examples of this in Eastern European markets, in which the apparent legitimacy of a stable share price for an organization belies the real state of its finances. Poorly developed accounting practices also help confuse the situation, as we saw in Chapter 8.

The general prediction for financial expectations of IJVs is one of rationalization rather than a step change in expected returns. IJV profitability will be calculated using more widely accepted and uniform methods and conventions. This in turn will increase the credibility of IJV results, allowing external investors to make rational and informed decisions on their investment potential. Management will need to adjust their focus to deal with the increasing transparency of their IJV's performance – it will become more difficult to twist the figures to try and show that an IJV is profitable when it isn't. The result will be greater precision in financial reporting and a thinning-out of those ventures that have deep-rooted financial problems.

POSTSCRIPT: LEARNING FROM THE PAST

It is a general rule of business management that people find it difficult to learn from the experiences of the past, unless these experiences were related in some way to themselves. Even then, it is not so easy. Many of the insights and experiences that can help managers avoid the common problems of IJV management have already been experienced and documented in other fields of management – there is little that is absolutely new about the techniques of managing IJVs, it is more a case of understanding how the bits of guidance, tools and techniques are bolted together. Techniques such as 'systems thinking', avoiding disputes, corporate culture and the principles of financial structuring of risky ventures are all well documented if you go and look. The final figure (Figure 13.1) in this book is an attempt to put these other areas of management literature into some sort of order as to their usefulness to *you*, the IJV manager. This perspective is all-important if you are not to waste your time becoming too involved in the management experiences of the past – and of course you don't have the time to read everything. The subjects near the centre of the map have the most relevance to helping you become a better manager in an IJV while those nearer the outside will be of more peripheral interest. Use this figure as a guide – it is your learning machine.

Those areas of management literature nearest the centre of the circle are of the most relevance to the task of managing IJVs.

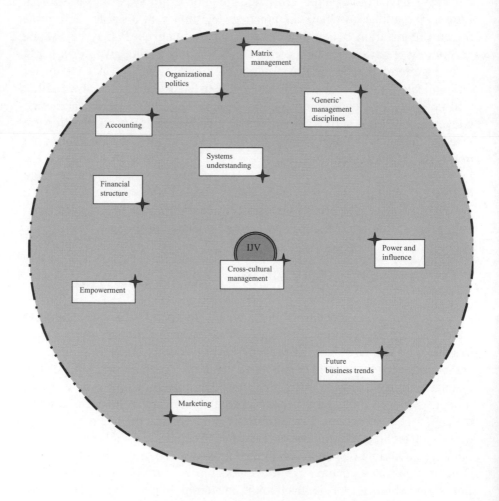

Figure 13.1 Managing IJVs: the relevance of other literature

References

Handy, C B (1987) *Understanding Organisations*, Penguin, London

Johnson, G and Scholes, K (1984) *Exploring Corporate Strategy,* Prentice-Hall International, London

Killing, J P (1982) How to make a joint venture work, *Harvard Business Review* (3), pp 120–27

Further reading

Beer, S (1979) *The Heart of Enterprise,* John Wiley and Sons, Chichester
Binney, G and Williams, C (1997) *Leaning into the Future,* Nicholas Brearley, London
Deering, A and Murphy, A (1998) *The Difference Engine*, Gower, Aldershot
Inkpen, A (1995)*The Management of International Joint Ventures: An organisational learning approach*, Routledge, London
Lewis, RD (1996) *When Cultures Collide,* Nicholas Brearley, London
Lorange, P and Roos, J (1992) *Strategic Alliances and Inter-Firm Knowledge,* Blackwell, Cambridge, MA

Index

VISIT KOGAN PAGE
ON-LINE

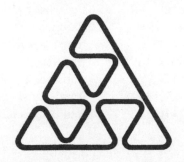

http://www.kogan-page.co.uk

For comprehensive information
on Kogan Page titles, visit our website.

Features include

- complete catalogue listings, including
  book reviews and descriptions

- special monthly promotions

- information on NEW titles and
  BESTSELLING titles

- a secure shopping basket facility for
  on-line ordering

**PLUS everything you need to know about
KOGAN PAGE**